THE BEACH BENEATH THE STREET

THE BEACH BENEATH THE STREET

THE EVERDAY LIFE AND GLORIOUS TIMES
OF THE SITUATIONIST INTERNATIONAL

♦

M^CKENZIE WARK

VERSO
London • New York

This edition first published by Verso 2011
© McKenzie Wark 2011

The moral rights of the author have been asserted

1 3 5 7 9 10 8 6 4 2

Verso
UK: 6 Meard Street, London W1F 0EG
US: 20 Jay Street, Suite 1010, Brooklyn, NY 11201
www.versobooks.com

Verso is the imprint of New Left Books

ISBN-13: 978-1-84467-720-7

British Library Cataloguing in Publication Data
A catalogue record for this book is available from the British Library

Library of Congress Cataloging-in-Publication Data
A catalog record for this book is available from the Library of Congress

Typeset in Cochin by MJ Gavan, Truro, Cornwall
Printed in the US by Maple Vail

Contents

In memory of:
Andrew Charker
Shelly Cox
Stephen Cummins
John Deeble
Colin Hood
Helen Mu Sung
in girum imus nocte et consumimur igni

Acknowledgments

My only qualification for writing this book is some time spent in a certain militant organization, then in a bohemian periphery, and subsequently in avant-garde formations that met at the nexus of media, theory and action. This was all long ago and far away, but nevertheless my main obligation is to salute some comrades from all three worlds who taught me invaluable things.

This book is for certain friends from those worlds within worlds who, for various reasons, fell before their time. Some of their names are acknowledged in the dedication, others will be known to those who need to know.

Thanks to Joan Ockman and Mark Wigley for the invitation to give the Buell Lecture at Columbia University in 2007, from which this book eventually evolved. Thanks also to my hosts for conversations at NYU, MIT, UCLA, UC Irvine, Dartmouth, Princeton, Brown, Parsons School of Design, the New School for Social Research, Laboral, Stedelijk Museum Amsterdam, Cabinet, and 16 Beaver. Thanks to my Lang College students, past and present.

Earlier versions of some material appeared in *Multitudes*, *Angelaki*, as an introduction to Guy Debord, *Correspondence* (Semiotext(e)) and in my booklet *50 Years of Recuperation of the Situationist International* (Princeton Architectural Press). Thanks to readers for useful comments, which led to substantial modifications.

Special thanks to Kevin C. Pyle for collaborating on *Totality for Kids*, part of which appears here as the cover. The Situationists détourned comics by inserting their own texts into the speech bubbles. Kevin and I reverse the process. The words I have mostly détourned from Situationist classics. Kevin's art is the new element.

Thanks for research assistance to Whitney Krahn and in particular

Julia P. Carrillo. Also to librarians at Bobst, Brown, Columbia and MoMA, and to innumerable Lang colleagues for their advice, whether I followed it correctly or not. Thanks to The New School for a faculty research grant, and to Warhol Foundation | Creative Capital for an art writer's grant.

When I gave Tino Sehgal a copy of *50 Years of Recuperation of the Situationist International* one day in Central Park, he exclaimed at once: "May there be fifty years more!" My thanks to Tino for the invitation to interpret his work *This Situation* at the Marian Goodman Gallery, and to all of the other interpreters and visitors for many hours of underpaid but stimulating conversation about "the situation."

I would also like to offer a special thanks to those who, in the true spirit of potlatch, translate and archive Situationist writings and make them freely available: The Bureau of Public Secrets, Infopool, Not Bored, The Situationist International Online Archive, Unpopular Books and others.

Lastly, a shout out to Brooklyn Rod and Gun Club and the Lakehouse Commune, and most of all: love to Christen, Felix and Vera.

Leaving the Twenty-First Century

A giant inflatable dog turd broke loose from its moorings outside the Paul Klee Center in Switzerland and brought down power lines before coming to a halt in the grounds of a children's home. The Paul McCarthy sculpture, the size of a house, reached a maximum altitude of 200 meters. Other civilizations had their chosen forms: from the Obelisk of Luxor to Michelangelo's *David*. The futurist poet Marinetti found his crashed motor car more beautiful than the *Winged Victory of Samothrace*, but he might have balked at flying dog shit.[1] In the twenty-first century, the insomnia of reason does not breed monsters, but pets. No wonder there are no longer any gods, when what is expected of them is that they descend from Mount Olympus with plastic baggies and clean up.

We are bored with this planet. It has seen better centuries, and the promise of better times to come eludes us. The possibilities of this world, in these times, seem dismal and dull. All it offers at best is spectacles of disintegration. Capitalism or barbarism, those are the choices. This is an epoch governed by this blackmail: either more and more of the same, or the end times. Or so they say. We don't buy it. It's time to start scheming on how to leave the twenty-first century. The pessimists are right. Things can't go on as they are. The optimists are also right. Another world is possible. The means are at our disposal. Our *species-being* is as a builder of worlds.[2]

Sometimes, to go forward, one has to go back. Back to the scene of the crime. Back to the moment when the situation seemed open, before the gun went off, before the race of champions started. This is a story about a small band of artists and writers whose habits were bohemian at best, delinquent at worst, who set off with no formal training and equipped with little besides their wits, to change the world. As Guy

Debord later wrote: "It is known that initially the Situationists wanted at the very least to build cities, the environment suitable to the unlimited deployment of new passions. But of course this was not easy and so we found ourselves forced to do much more."[3]

Where does one find this kind of ambition now? These days artists are happy to settle for a little notoriety, a good dealer, and a retrospective. Art has renounced the desire to give form to the world. Having ceased to be modern, and finding it too passé to be postmodern, art is now merely *contemporary*, which seems to mean nothing more than yesterday's art at today's prices.[4] If anything, theory has turned out even worse. It found its utopia, and it is the academy. A colonnade adorned with the busts of famous fathers: Jacques Lacan the bourgeois-magus, Louis Althusser the throttler-of-concepts, Jacques Derrida the dandy-of-difference, Michel Foucault the one-eyed-powerhouse, Gilles Deleuze the taker-from-behind. Acolytes and epigones pace furiously up and down, prostrating themselves before one master — Ah! Betrayed! — and then another. The production of new dead masters to imitate can barely keep up with consumer demand, prompting some to chisel statues of new demigods while they still live: Alain Badiou the Maoist-of-the-matheme, Giorgio Agamben the pensive-pedant, Slavoj Žižek the neuro-Hegelian-joker.[5]

In the United States the academy spread its investments, placing a few bets on women and people of color. The best of those — Susan Buck-Morss, Judith Butler, Paul Gilroy, Donna Haraway — at least appreciate the double bind of speaking for difference within the heart of the empire of indifference. At best theory, like art, turns in on itself, living on through commentary, investing in its own death on credit. At worst it rattles the chains of old ghosts, as if a conference on "the idea of communism" could still shock the bourgeois. As if there were still a bourgeois literate enough to shock. As if it were ever the idea that shocked them, rather than the practice.[6]

Beneath the pavement, the beach. It's a now well-worn slogan from the May–June events in Paris, 1968, at the moment when two kinds of critique seemed to come together. One was communist, and demanded equality. The other was bohemian, and demanded difference. The former gets erased from historical memory, as if one of the world's great general strikes never happened. The latter is rendered in a language that makes it seem benign, banal even. As if all that was demanded were *customer service*. Luc Boltanski: "Whole sections of the artistic critique of capitalism were integrated into management rheto-ric."[7] What is lost is the combined power of a critique of both wage labor and of everyday life, expressed in acts. What has escaped the institutionalization of high theory is the possibility of *low theory*, of a critical thought indifferent to the institutional forms of the academy or the art world. A low theory dedicated to the practice that is critique and the critique that is practice.

And so: two steps back, that they might enable three steps forward. Back to the 1950s and '60s, when another twenty-first century seemed possible. Back to the few, the happy few, who thought they had discov-ered how to leave the twentieth century for sunnier climes, though not quite as warming as ours. We do not lack for accounts of the Letterist International (1952–57) and the Situationist International (1957–72) that succeeded it. *The Beach Beneath the Street* claims no originality whatsoever. Rather, it's a question of retrieving a past specific to the demands of this present. An account that resists the sorting and select-ing which parcels out a movement into bite-size morsels, each to be swallowed by a specific discipline: art history, media studies, archi-tecture, philosophy or literature. The Situationist project implied the overcoming of separate and specialized knowledge, and has to be recalled in that spirit.

It is also easy prey for biographers, who spotlight this or that pro-tagonist, creating little subjective narratives like the plot of a novel, or (dare we hope to sell the rights) a movie. The Letterist International and the Situationist International were collective and collabora-tive projects. Sure, some figures stand out (first among equals, Guy Debord); but to reduce a movement to a biography or two is to cut a piece away from what made it of interest in the first place: the game of tactics and ruses, moves and cheats, by which each played with and against the other.[8]

Even when the Situationists are treated as a movement, the suppos-edly minor figures often drop out of the story, or become mere props to the *great men* among them. Alternatively, in order to make a coherent narrative and write the biography of a movement as if it were a subject, the differences among its members are suppressed, or turned into the stakes of a mere drama of personalities.[9] Here, instead, is a large cast of disparate characters, some more celebrated than others, where Guy

3

Debord and Asger Jorn rub shoulders with Patrick Straram, Michèle Bernstein, Ralph Rumney, Pinot Gallizio, Jacqueline de Jong, Abdelhafid Khatib, Alexander Trocchi and René Viénet. Where they come together, where they create something, is a *situation*. But situations are temporary, singular unities of space and time. They call for a different kind of remembering.

Some artifacts produced by the Situationist International are perhaps too well remembered. Do we really need another commentary on Guy Debord's *Society of the Spectacle*? Is not the one he wrote himself enough?[10] Perhaps today one could only do it justice by refusing to paraphrase it. *The Beach Beneath the Street* will bypass more than one such landmark on its route through the Situationist International, but it will also draw attention to some less well-known moments. The criterion for inclusion is not historical importance but contemporary resonance. Mention will also be made in passing to certain prominent landmarks of high theory: Jacques Lacan, Michel Foucault and so forth. But only in passing. *The Beach Beneath the Street* will not engage them on their own terrain. Rather, it opens towards another terrain.

In this version of the glorious times and notorious lives of the Situationist International, the phenomenon emerges out of the practice of everyday life, and the attempt to think it begun in Paris in the 1950s by the Letterist International. It creates a space for itself by taking its distance from certain precursors. Some are familiar: Jean-Paul Sartre, Georges Bataille, Henri Lefebvre, Le Corbusier. Some less so: Paul Nougé, Maurice Saillet. The Letterist International find common cause with Asger Jorn, who developed his own distinctive practice and a distinctive set of theories. Jorn brings into the picture Constant Nieuwenhuys (known as Constant) and Pinot Gallizio. Our attention then turns to the collective existence of the Situationist International, which unites some of the Letterists with Jorn's associates in 1957.

Along the way we shall look at a number of artists, writers and activists who entered the orbit of the Situationist International but drifted off to create their own works, each of which develops some aspect of the shared project, if often in contradictory directions. They include Michèle Bernstein's writings on love and play, Jacqueline de Jong's journal the *Situationist Times*, Alexander Trocchi's project sigma, and Constant's New Babylon. It is not as if these are fragments awaiting some sort of synthesis, however. Rather, each appropriates some elements from the Situationists as common property, and adds to it in its own way. This account of the post-Situationist legacy of borrowing and correcting is intended to encourage more such takings and leave-takings. The well has not yet run dry. The chapter on Henri Lefebvre shows what the Situationists took from him, as well as what he took from them. *The Beach Beneath the Street* concludes with the Situationists' own account of the revolutions of the late 1960s—those in Paris, but also the Watts rebellion in Los Angeles. In contrast to those groups which made a profession of turning failed revolutions into literary or philosophical success, the Situationists chose with the ebb tide of the early 1970s to disband.

Guy Debord spent a lot of time working on how to remember situations, how to document them and keep them in a way that could ignite future possibilities. For the most part, he created legends. "When legend becomes fact, print the legend," as the newspaperman says at the end of *The Man Who Shot Liberty Valance* (1962). Much of the literature on the Situationists seems designed to be disabling, to prevent any real creative use of this body of work for critical practices in the twenty-first century. The authorities on this period delight in drawing attention to the follies then committed, as if their own complacency of thought was in some sense a higher achievement. For them, all is safely consigned to the archive, enclosed in a time one can visit like a tourist before returning home to the workaday world. *The Beach Beneath the Street* makes more than occasional reference to the events of a more recent past, in which the cogency of Situationist thought and action still registers. Leaving the twentieth century was the aim the Situationist International once ascribed to itself. Leaving the twenty-first century might not be a bad ambition. On paper, at least, we have longer to achieve it.

Monsters of all lands unite!
—Michèle Bernstein

1 Street Ethnography

It is a few years after the end of the Second World War. Europe is in ruins. Out in its colonies, the will and the means come together to start throwing off the yoke. The Russians and the Americans brandish bombs at each other. Meanwhile in Paris, the City of Light, curfews and rationing slowly come to an end. The lights are lit again. The black market fades to gray. It's a time to shoot movies rather than collaborators. Formerly banned pleasures still have a special quality: American jazz, gangster movies and crime novels seem to promise unknown thrills, a sort of cultural correlate of the Marshall Plan for European reconstruction. There is a world to build out of books and mortar.

Existentialism is all the rage. All the papers say so, even if they don't approve. A doctrine that puts such a premium on freedom seems somehow both frightening and delicious. The philosophers credited with creating it—Jean-Paul Sartre, Simone de Beauvoir, Maurice Merleau-Ponty—refuse the label while selectively exploiting the attention. Self-styled existentialists turn up in their Paris neighborhood of Saint-Germain-des-Prés. They hang out in the famous cafés, hoping to rub shoulders with intellectual celebrities. After the cafés shut, it's on to the cellar clubs. The wire-service journalists started this fad. Working odd hours, in need of a drink when all else closes, they end up in the cellars, and so the cellars end up in the news.

The most famous was Le Tabou. As Simone de Beauvoir wrote: "People drank and danced and also brawled a great deal, both inside and out front. The neighborhood declared war ... at night, people threw buckets of water on the customers and even on people just passing by."[1] De Beauvoir claimed never to have been there. She did not like the way its front people, Anne-Marie Cazalis and Juliette Gréco, traded on the existentialist fashion. But she was friends with

Boris Vian (1920–59), who played the trumpet in the band. Vian was a man of parts. Besides his passion for jazz, he wrote a fake American crime novel to cash in on that craze, and he wrote the *Manual of Saint-Germain-des-Prés* (1949).[2]

The *Manual* is a mock ethnography of the quarter. Saint-Germain has its natives, those who ply respectable trades, pouring cold water on the bohemian effusions they consider beneath them. It has its incursionists, new-money people who doubtless got rich off the black market and came looking for ways to spend it. It has permanent invaders, American and Scandinavian and the occasional English.[3] And it has its *troglodytes*, the nocturnal residents of the cellar clubs. Boris Vian regarded himself and his friends as none of the above. The real Saint-Germain was to him a small coterie of creative individuals.

Here are some of them, with their dates, since time is key to this story: the poet Tristan Tzara (1896–1963), the composer Georges Auric (1899–1983), the writer Jean Cocteau (1889–1963), the writer Jacques Prévert (1900–77), the artist Alberto Giacometti (1901–66), the writer Raymond Queneau (1903–76), the writer Jean-Paul Sartre (1905–80), the writer Simone de Beauvoir (1908–86), the philosopher Maurice Merleau-Ponty (1908–61), the writer Jean Genet (1910–86), the saxophonist Don Byas (1912–72), the actress Simone Signoret (1921–85), and the singer Juliette Gréco (b. 1927). None will feature much in our story—with one exception: the poet Gabriel Pomerand (1925–72).

In her memoir, Simone Signoret describes her initiation into Saint-Germain in 1941. She quit her job on a collaborationist paper and came to hang out at the Café de Flore, hoping to get into the film business. Of the people she met there—"some of them Jewish, many of them Communists or Trotskyites, Italian anti-fascists, Spanish Republicans, bums, jokers, penniless poets, sharers of food ration tickets, ambulatory guitarists, genial jacks of all trades, temporary no-goods"—some would not survive the war.[4] Of those who did, a few would become celebrated figures of a new postwar culture, with Saint-Germain as their symbolic home. Saint-Germain was where the forces for the postwar restoration of the spectacle gathered.

American pop mixed with youthful irreverence was not to everyone's taste. In his *Manual*, Vian takes great exception to the portrayal of Saint-Germain in both the conservative and communist press.

Gullible cellar-dwelling troglodytes, he suspects, can be cajoled into saying pretty much anything for the price of a drink. They give the place a bad name. The legend the press starts is that Sartre is the Magus and jazz the Pied Piper of an evil cult. Worse, Simone de Beauvoir's *Second Sex* (1949) ruins the morals of impressionable girls. Vian quotes some choice bits of journalese: "Beginning of the legend: an amateur existentialism of destruction. The whole story: blood, sensuality, death." Poor troglodyte existentialists, mere teenagers, living in cheap hotels they can't afford. They are "unwholesome" and "violent," "intoxicated" by American crime novels (or perhaps by Vian's copies of them). In the clubs they can be found "screaming like banshees." The press has fabulated a *folk devil* here, about which to whip up a *moral panic*.[5]

"These zealots recognize each other through thousands of little items of clothing: cowboy shirts flapping in the breeze, red, yellow and green, plaid shirts that hang open down to the belly button." The troglodyte existentialist belongs to a *subculture*.[6] "The women of the tribe are fond of smocks that come in maybe two or three colors: their hairstyles give them the look of a drowning victim ... they are none too fond of soap or hairbrushes, but they dance one hell of a boogie-woogie." The press can't decide if they have too much sex or not enough, but either way their desire is out of line, a threat to bourgeois enjoyment.[7] They gather in Saint-Germain, in the shadows cast by its luminaries, to reinvent themselves, by means both fair and shady. Bohemia's other face is delinquency.

She loved to dance: Vali Myers (1930–2003) left home at fourteen and moved to seamy St Kilda, a waterside neighborhood in Melbourne, Australia. She worked in a hair salon for a while, and as an artist's model, but preferred factory jobs. What money she made went towards study with the Melbourne Modern Ballet. In 1950 she left Australia, aged nineteen, determined to dance in Paris. She found a ruined city, cold in winter; poor all the year round. The war had shattered one way of life, and another had not yet risen from the ashes. Myers dropped ballet and went dancing in the cellars where African drummers played. Tourists threw money at her feet. She learned very little French, but picked up the argot of the streets. This is what she wrote about those times:

The kids who survived after the war years in our quarter, Saint-Germain des Prés, can be counted on one hand. It was … a world without illusions, without dreams. It had a dark stark beauty like a short Russian story of Gorky that one doesn't forget. They were uprooted kids, old for their years, from all over Europe. Many had no home or parents, no papers (stateless), no money … We lived in the streets and cafés, like a pack of "bastard dogs" and with the strict hierarchy of such a tribe. Students and workers were "outsiders." The few tourists on the lookout for "existentialists" were "game" (for a meal or a drink), but no one sold himself. There was always cheap booze and Algerian hashish to get by on. What we had we shared, even the butt end of a cigarette.[8]

Sometimes she slept in cafés or movie houses; sometimes she slept rough. For a while she had a tiny room at the Hôtel d'Alsace-Lorraine, where the concierge was reputed to have worked for Marcel Proust in his last years. She slept by day, and danced through the night as if consumed by fire. Her whole delinquent "tribe" was nocturnal.[9] There was Kaki, the beauty of the quarter, a former Dior model, the daughter of collaborators who killed themselves after the war. Kaki joined her parents at age nineteen. There was Fred, the big blond Corsican, in and out of prison, who later became a *success*: as an artist, husband, and father. There was Robert the Mexican, said to have killed a man. There was Eliane, who had run away from both home and the reformatory. There was Ralph Rumney, dodging military service in Britain. Vali Myers lived on and off with Pierre Feuillette, who was known as the Chief. Unpredictable, with a walk like a cat, he was not the sort of character it pays to romanticize. He cut her once, in a fight. When she danced, it was he who collected the money the tourists threw. These were the scenes and characters from what she called her "opium years"—which lasted until 1958.

Gabriel Pomerand introduced Myers to opium. He was one of several men of the quarter who made her into a bohemian muse. Pomerand wrote that "she disobeys every last law of conventional beauty," and compared encountering Myers to meeting a "cheetah on a leash." The Dutch photographer Ed van der Elsken gave her the leading role in his book *Love on the Left Bank*. "She danced like a Negress," he said. George Plimpton, the expatriate American, wrote in *Paris Review*: "Her dancing is remarkable—a sinuous shuffling, bent-kneed, her shoulders and hands moving at trembling speed to the drumbeats." Plimpton quotes another admirer: "You saw in her the personalization of something torn and loose and deep-down primitive in all of us." Even the great gay Spanish writer Juan Goytisolo idolized the "solemn, hieratic girl, systematically dressed in black, with her face painted like a mask," who declared that she lived in a "damp cave with mice and called on the most daring to try her one night in a cemetery."[10]

Myers said that for her Saint-Germain was "like a little battle-field." Tired of parrying the glances of so many attentive men, she left Paris for a secluded valley in Italy. She would henceforth prefer the company of animals. The remarkable thing is that she survived her marginal Paris life. One of the press stories Vian disparages contains at least a kernel of truth: "Existentialism has ripened so quickly that it is already divided by class warfare. In fact it is necessary these days to distinguish the rich existentialists from the poor ones." Bohemia is fine for those who enter it voluntarily, and its legend is sustained by those who succeeded through it. For those who aren't rich, aren't men, aren't white, aren't straight, for those from the provinces, for those without a home to go back to, it is no picnic. People like Myers's tribe were doubly dispossessed, too young and too marginal. There was nothing for it but to stick together. As Ralph Rumney put it: "Our social exclusion made us a closed group."[11]

It has become an impertinence to say *we*. The collective pronoun is to be distrusted. Only the voice of the self is authentic. This voice declares itself from endless *status updates*, with whole spiders' nests of self-affirmation: ME! ME! ME! It's a world of free agents vainly attempting to establish themselves on the slender résumé of their own qualities. The twenty-first century is the culmination of two forms of individualism. In the first, individuals are all the same; in the second, they are all different. The first is classically bourgeois, the second distinctively bohemian. But whether different or the same, in the twenty-first century it's the same difference. Bourgeois individualism is now infused with bohemian flourishes. In the 1950s Vali Myers stood out even in Saint-Germain. In the 1970s, when she gave the singer Patti Smith her first tattoo, this might still have been a gesture with a point. Now you can get your tattoos at the mall. It's romanticism for everybody, with a little blood and pain thrown in for the price. The collapse of bourgeois and bohemian individualism into the warm embrace of the commodity is the defining style of the middle-class sensibility of today's disintegrating spectacle.[12]

There are also two kinds of collective belonging. In the first, we belong because we are the same; in the second, we belong because we are not.[13] The most insistent form of collective belonging in Paris after the war was the Communist Party, which was definitely of the first kind, a collective belonging that obliged of its members a certain unity and identity as *proletarians*. Wrapping itself in the scarlet mantle of the Resistance, the Party exerted its gravity upon artists and intellectuals even if they were not members. While directing a withering criticism at the surrealist old guard, Sartre agonized over how to align himself with the Communists, who he still took to be the representatives of the working class.

Saint-Germain offered its own alternative to the collective belonging of communism—the collective belonging of the Letterist movement, led by the charismatic Romanian poet and film-maker Isidore Isou (1925–2007). The rogue surrealist Georges Bataille once described him as a genius who lacked nothing except talent. Sartre hated the Letterists almost as much as he hated Bataille: "Letterism is a substitute product, a flat and conscientious imitation of Dadaist exuberance. One's heart is no longer in it, one feels the application and haste to succeed."[14] Yet not the least merit of the Letterists is that they were one of the few groups who managed to stay outside of both bourgeois postwar French culture and its Stalinist alternative. They managed to make something enduring, by seizing control over their own self-presentation. These were things for which Myers and her tribe lacked the wherewithal.

Romania gave the world Tristan Tzara, the poet of Dada, and it gave the world Isidore Isou, the prophet of Letterism, who first achieved fame in postwar Paris by publicly embarrassing poor old Tzara, even as he began his own avant-garde practice by appropriating the best Tzara had to offer. Notoriety led to the publication of two of Isou's books by the venerable, if somewhat compromised, house of Gallimard. Saint-Germain was at the time the center of the French publishing world, so it made sense for a provincial gate-crasher like Isou to install himself the cafés there while finding a way to both scandalize and break into one of the quarter's few industries. Its other racket was cinema, drawing the likes of Signoret. Isou would tackle that one too, in his extraordinary film *Treatise on Spit and Eternity* (1951).[15]

While most people approached the postwar years as a time of reconstruction, Isou wanted to push the destruction of culture still further. His trans-historical theory of culture took the will to create as its primary axiom. Not Marxist necessity, not Sartrean freedom, but creation was the highest form of human activity. Creation takes us from the spit of unconsciousness to the eternity of a consciously created history, for while the artist creates within history, the act of creation touches the eternal. All forms—aesthetic and social—move from a stage of *amplification* to one of *decomposition*. In the amplification stage, a form grows to incorporate whole aspects of existence. The amplified form shapes life and makes it meaningful. During the period of decomposition, forms turn on themselves and become self-referential. Forms fall from grace and from history. As the form decomposes, so does the life to which it once gave shape. Form becomes unreal, and language becomes tame: "Tarzan learns in his father's book to call tigers *cats*."[16]

Isou applied this theory to all forms, from art to cinema, but poetry had a central place, for he was interested in both the history of poetry and the poetics of history. In modern French poetry, Victor Hugo took the amplification stage as far as it could go. Its decomposition then advanced, phase by phase, through Baudelaire, Verlaine, Rimbaud, Mallarmé, and Tzara. Dada rendered all existing forms worthless. Dada was conscious decomposition. Isou's self-appointed task was to complete the reduction of the word to the letter, through a deliberate chiseling of poetry down to its bare elements. By creating a new alphabet, a new language would be possible, which would reconstruct, amplify, and retell the story of the world. Isou's mission was to gather disciples for an all-out attack on spent forms, and the creation in their place of a fresh language.

Treatise on Spit and Eternity is almost the masterpiece Isou so confidently proclaimed.[17] It has three movements. In the first, Isou wanders the streets of the quarter in his plaid jacket. "The neighborhood of Saint-Germain-des-Prés is an invention of the author, and represents nothing but the author's calvary." The voice-over recounts his (or rather his fictive double Daniel's) attempt to expound his vision of a new cinema to a hostile audience at a film club who shout him down, usually with stock leftist jibes. Cinema has become obese, he declares.

Its images have become too banal, too *artistic*. Cinema is merely "an industry organized in defense of current production." The cinema of classic unities has to be rent asunder. He proposes a *discrepant* cinema, where image and sound are severed from each other. It is time to spit out the old masterpieces. Cinema should aspire to a gangrenous beauty worthy of the Marquis de Sade. "The more the subject matter is spoiled and perverted, the more beautiful it is ... The novelty of creation alone interests the creator. That is why the ugliness of our era preoccupies him: it is new and therefore beautiful."

After wandering about Saint-Germain in the first act, Isou meets up in the second with Eve, a Norwegian beauty. Now he attempts to enact the "Manifesto of Discrepant Cinema" just expounded. Isou thwarts the spectators' expectations: "The author knows that people go to the movies to swallow their weekly Saturday night dose of tenderness. And though they don't give a damn about the story, they retell it in the hope of a deserved success. The author does not care for this type of legend, because these are questions of personal taste. Only systems where form goes beyond story are of interest to him." What he ends up with is a charmless account of his alter-ego Daniel's misogyny.

Still, the second act achieves two insights. Daniel recounts how expulsion from the Communist Party felt like a kind of annihilation: "How astonishing to find oneself alive the next day." The other is an observation voiced by another girlfriend, Denise: "How many corpses in the maze of the dictionary? ... Our vocabulary is full of real corpses, a cemetery of men who died for words." Given the brutality of the history Isou survived as a Romanian Jew, the statement carries a certain gravity. It is no accident either that across stock footage of a church service, Isou has scratched the Star of David and that stock footage of the colonial officer class routinely has the faces and bodies scratched out. For Isou, "the evolution of art has nothing to do with the revolution in society." It is a refuge from it.

All one could say in favor of the film's second act is that it manifests the latent male aggression towards women that is an undercurrent of bohemian sexual practices. "I installed myself in her," he says of Eve, before discarding her. The third act can then devote itself to Letterist poetry, with two great performances by François Dufrêne (1930–82), perhaps the most accomplished of Isou's followers where poetry was concerned. In the third act Isou promotes Letterism against all rival avant-gardes. He dismisses jazz, for instance, as "white-collar primitivism." Eisenstein's *Battleship Potemkin* is just the "*King Kong* of the revolution." Cinema in particular has failed as an art. "The God of cinema is dead," like the God of legend who died while making the universe, leaving it unfinished. Isou sets himself the task of completion. "Actually what interests you is creation, invention, discovery. That's what creation is. An unceasing destruction of surfaces to reach a subterranean pool." The film ends with Daniel's voice-over account of his abandoned girlfriend Eve, wandering Saint-Germain and succumbing to madness, until the police round her up and deport her. An indifferent Daniel, who witnesses her downfall, decides to play pinball with a friend, who wins a free game.

The unnamed friend in the film's last act could well have been Gabriel Pomerand. Like Isou a Romanian Jew, his mother was deported to Auschwitz. He spent the war in Marseilles, in the Resistance, but still found time to read the poetry of Arthur Rimbaud and the Comte de Lautréamont. He came to Paris after the war, meeting Isou in a soup kitchen for Romanian refugees. Pomerand quickly enlisted in the Letterists' shallow ranks. In the early postwar years he was a perpetual scandal in motion. He was a mainstay of the Letterist poetry readings at Le Tabou, and produced the first sustained work of *metagraphic* poetry, which synthesized image and word in a visual language. In it he presents a less flattering portrait of Saint-Germain than that drawn by Vian or even Isou. Pomerand's *Saint Ghetto of the Loans* (1950) is a *grimoire* of the quarter, a book for evoking its damned spirits.[18]

Saint-Germain is a ghetto, he says: its denizens all wear a yellow star. It is a "drowned drunk peacefully floating from one bridge to another." It is where American anarchist millionaires cross paths with swells whose wealth lies in castles built beneath the bridges. There is no Saint-Germain. "There are only spirits who survey the streets, from terrace to terrace, awaiting the occurrence of unique events," or for someone to pick up their tab. It is an "open-air temple," a "bullet-holed beauty spoiling in the sun." It is where language is pounded beyond recognition. "How sweet to subsist in a world that is falling apart." Saint-Germain is a Letterist ground zero.

Pomerand compares Saint-Germain to the imaginary city of Donogoo Tonka, from the novel by Jules Romains (1885–1972).[19] In this novel, a geographer faces professional embarrassment because a city he describes in the Brazilian jungle does not actually exist. So he enlists the help of an adventurer to create it. The adventurer finds some unscrupulous bankers, who provide the backing for the Donogoo Tonka company, which outfits an expedition to the jungle. The expedition thinks it is going to an already thriving city, when actually the men will have to build it themselves. When they arrive they find that others have already started work on building the city, drawn by the publicity campaign of the Donogoo Tonka company. In Saint-Germain as in Donogoo Tonka, the place makes a spectacle of itself. It is where the spectacle pulls itself up again by its own bootstraps.

Pomerand and Isou were younger than Vian's notables, but half a decade older than Vali Myers. She ran with a younger crowd, some of whom were attracted to the Letterists, some of whom had their own ideas. There was Henry de Béarn (1931–1995), who lived in a loft with Ivan Chtcheglov (1933–1998) near the Eiffel Tower. The lights from the tower kept them awake at night, so they planned to blow it up. There was Jean-Michel Mension (1934–2006), fortunate not to be orphaned by the war. First they came for his father, a communist militant. Then they came for his mother, both a communist and a Jew. Like many who washed up in Saint-Germain, Mension was drifting away from family, school, the law. But unlike some he had read his Sartre and his Prévert. Like Pomerand before him, Mension found his way to the poetry of Rimbaud and Lautréamont. After that self-education there was nothing for it but drink and mischief.

Mension spent his eighteenth birthday on the street, drinking and talking to Guy Debord (1931–94). Unlike Mension, Myers, and the tribe, Debord had a student allowance, so it was probably he who bought the wine (red for Mension, white for himself). As Mension recalls it, "we would set the whole world to rights while polishing off a liter or perhaps two liters."[20] Though little interested in his university classes, Debord studied Mension and others like him closely. Debord was a sort of street ethnographer, although his method was more intoxicant peregrination than participant observation. "He had a particular fascination with young people like me," Mension says. "He must have been searching in me for the kind of trigger that causes someone to snap one day and begin living without rules." Debord was researching a people who were neither bourgeois nor proletarian nor bohemian — and decidedly not middle-class.

Cursing is the work of the drinking classes. A short text Mension wrote in the early 1950s called "General Strike" declares "nothingness, perpetually sought, is simply, our life." Debord was in search, not of the organic intellectuals of the working class, but of what one might call the alcoholic intellectuals of the non-working classes. He had read his Louis-Ferdinand Céline (1894–1961), whose coruscating prose was capable of dispelling most illusions, not least about the nobility of labor: "We're workers they say. Work, they call it! That's the crummiest part of the whole business."[21] Mension's strike was not against work but against life, and while it strikes the right note of negativity, it does not quite rise to the level of a critique of delinquency—and this was the least of what Debord had in mind. There are plenty of celebrations of bohemia.[22] What is rare is to turn a critical theory of delinquency into a *delinquent critique.*

The first real statement of what would come to be a properly Situationist writing would come not from Mension but from Ivan Chtcheglov, in his celebrated "Formulary for a New Urbanism" (1953).[23] This is the text that pointed the way to the exit from the twentieth century as we know it. It's the key document of the Letterist International (1952–57), the group Debord cofounded and to which Chtcheglov belonged, forming a breakaway from the older Letterists such as Isou and Pomerand.[24] It would contribute some key ideas and practices to the movement that did not yet bear the name *Situationist.*

The Letterist International was a young people's affair. They discarded Isou's self-referential theories and personality cult, but took with them a certain practice of intellectual seduction and the ambition to chisel modern art down to nothing, to clear the ground for something else. The Letterist International dreamed big. They foresaw the end of the workhouse of modernist form. They discovered a new city via a calculated drifting (*dérive*) through the old. Theirs would be a city of play, love, adventure, made for arousing new passions, a city that might finally justify the conceit that this is a civilization worthy of its predecessors: "Although their builders are gone, a few disturbing pyramids resist the efforts of travel agencies to render them banal."[25] They were the other side to the spectacle of bohemia, its delinquent side, its marginal side. They created out of this marginality a collective being, and rendered that collective being in a low theory specific to it, and as we shall see, in a distinctive kind of practice.

2   No More Temples of the Sun

"We are bored with the city, there is no longer any Temple of the Sun," declares Chtcheglov. It is unclear whether he means the Temple of the Sun in Beijing, the Pyramid of the Sun at Teotihuacan or the Pyramids of Egypt, but he was certainly none too fond of the Obelisk of the Place de la Concorde. Besides being fascinated by pyramids (both Egyptian and pre-Columbian), Georges Bataille also had a thing about this obelisk, which had formerly graced the entrance to the Luxor Temple. Bataille called it a "petrified sunbeam."[1] For Bataille, the Place de la Concorde was the locus from which to announce the death of God, "precisely because the Obelisk is its calmest negation." The obelisk stood for the pharaoh's military power, the pyramid for his union with the eternity of the gods. The removal of the obelisk to Paris turned the Place de la Concorde into a negative sacred site. It gave the finger to what was once the eternal heavens, a gesture to the lost union of earth and sky, the point around which the mundane tumult of the city orbited.

Before the war, Bataille had wanted to create a ritual on this site, to transform its meaning. The idea was to soak a skull in brine until it softened, place it at the base of the obelisk and tell the press that the King's skull had mysteriously returned.[2] This was the place, after all, where Louis XVI had been executed—followed not long after by Danton, Robespierre, Saint-Just and not a few others. Chtcheglov had no interest in that. In any case the death of God had already been announced, and from the pulpit of Notre Dame no less, by a group of Letterists. During a quiet moment of the Easter High Mass in 1950, Michel Mourre (1928–77) ascended the pulpit dressed as a Dominican monk to read a sermon written by the Saint-Germain identity and subsequent Letterist International founding member Serge Berna

(b. 1925): "Verily I say unto you: God is dead." The organist quickly pumped out a few chords to drown out the rest. Then all hell broke loose. Mourre and two others were arrested. Pomerand slipped out undetected.[3]

All this anti-clerical stuff was old hat to Chtcheglov. "For we are in the twentieth century, even if few people are aware of it." Now was the time to leave the old avant-garde stunts behind. The failure of the earthly city to renew itself was the problem, not the vanishing heavens. "Everyone wavers between the emotionally still-alive past and the already-dead future." Chtcheglov proposed a quite different approach to the space of the city than Bataille. The problem was how to replace God's stabilizing presence with a new relation between the city and the cosmos; the solution was not to fix a place for a ritual sacrifice, but a new arrangement of movement.

Bataille's view of the city took as its starting point the sacred architecture at this center, which he made the site from which to dethrone God. Chtcheglov's view of the city took as its reference point not its ancient, sacred form, but its modern and seemingly rationalist one. His text is aimed squarely against the *radiant city* of Le Corbusier (1887–1965), which if it had its way would erase even more of the city than wartime bombing and replace it with cross-shaped tower blocks aligned along gun-barrel highways and vast open parks. For Chtcheglov, this was the wrong path along which to imagine the postwar reconstruction. He sought not the rational city but the playful city, not the city of work but the city of adventure. Not the city that conquers nature, but the city that opens towards the flux of the universe.

Le Corbusier was the *bête noire* of the whole Situationist project, but it is worth pausing to consider what the thinking of Le Corbusier and Chtcheglov had in common. Le Corbusier wrote that "architecture, which is a thing of plastic emotion, should, in its domain, also begin at the beginning, and use elements capable of striking our senses, of satisfying our visual desires, and arrange them in such a way that the sight of them clearly affects us through finesse or brutality, tumult or serenity, indifference or interest."[4] This understanding of the city as a totality of sensory and emotional affects, this at least they share. The philosopher Jacques Rancière speaks of a "distribution of the sensible," which "reveals who can have a share in what is common."[5] In these terms Le Corbusier and Chtcheglov are close, for both imagine

the whole space of the city as something everyone experiences aesthetically. Yet the Letterist International is already pushing against the
limits of Le Corbusier's program. His architecture might be for the
people, but it is decidedly not of them or by them.

New forms are needed to express a new ruling order. Le Corbusier's
architecture is addressed to the ruling class, which does not quite realize
the new kinds of forms it needs. The bourgeois at home seem "sheep-
ish and diminished, like tigers in a cage; one sensed clearly that they
were happier at the factory or their bank." The forms he offers them,
patterned after bomber planes as much as ancient temples, connect
modern technology to a spiritual order. Architecture signals the "trace
of an indefinable absolute persisting at the core of our being" and "a
unifying management in the universe."[6] If for Bataille the temple of
Luxor was a sacrifice to an absent God, to an impossible order, for Le
Corbusier the harmony of heaven and earth could be reconstituted —
but only through modern versions of Luxor's ancient geometric form,
shorn of all ornamental excrescence. Le Corbusier imposed the geometry of the temple onto the entire space of the city, and onto everyday
life in its totality.

Le Corbusier's city was not modern: it was already out of date. It was
a product of a retrograde culture, lagging behind science. The physical
world is no longer understood as an orderly geometry, but culture has
yet to catch up. The purpose of technology is not to make a city puri-
fied of complexity, a Platonic form gleaming in the sun. Life is earthy,
not heavenly; life is movement and form, spirit or idea. Chtcheglov's
sources for this way of imagining the city were twofold. One was a
certain strain of art and literature that proposed fantastic landscapes,
such as the paintings of Giorgio de Chirico, in which could be glimpsed
a new conception of space and time.[7] The literature Chtcheglov draws
on includes Thomas de Quincey, Edgar Allan Poe's "The Domain of
Arnheim," and, most interestingly, a Russian children's book by Lev
Kassil.

Chtcheglov's Ukrainian father had been exiled from Russia for his
political activities, and had been involved in a taxi drivers' strike in
Paris, but it was probably his mother who introduced him to Kassil.
Lev Kassil (1905–70) started out as an avant-garde writer in the orbit
of the great futurist poet Vladimir Mayakovsky. He survived the
brutal years of the Stalinist era, like more than a few others, by writing

children's books. In *The Black Book and Schwambrania*, two brothers find a novel way to escape from the discipline of family and school: "There was no need to run away, to search for a promised land. It was here, somewhere very close at hand. We had only to invent it." This world they call Schwambrania: "Our world was a bay jam-packed with boats. Life was an endless journey, and each given day was a new voyage. It was quite natural, therefore, that every Schwambranian was a sailor."[8]

Adventure is close at hand. It does not require Rimbaud's "derangement of the senses," but rather, an arrangement of the sensible. There is nothing exotic about it. It does not require a surrealist expedition to foreign lands. What James Clifford calls a "Surrealist ethnography" still relies on a notional other, an exoteric to contrast to the esoteric, however much it might trouble or surprise accepted notions of which is which.[9] A Situationist ethnography has its own distinct methods. It emerges out of Debord's close study of Saint-Germain delinquents. It adopts their habits, their *ethnos*, and turns it into method. The Letterist International are ethnographers of their own difference, cartographers of an attitude to life. This life did not lie outside the modern, Western one, but inside, in the fissures of its cities. It did not yearn for a *primitive* life from before history, but rather for one that was to come after it. In the life of the Saint-Germain delinquents' *tribe* could be found particles of the future, not the past, and not from some colonial Donogoo Tonka but from the very epicenter of what history had wrought: the colonization of everyday life at the heart of empire.

Chtcheglov's other source was not previous art or writing, but a certain kind of practice, what he and his friends would call the *dérive*. It's a curious word. A note in the Letterist International's journal *Potlatch* gives some of its resonances.[10] Its Latin root "derivare" means to draw off a stream, to divert a flow. Its English descendants include the word "derive" and also "river." Its whole field of meaning is aquatic, conjuring up flows, channels, eddies, currents, and also drifting, sailing or tacking against the wind. It suggests a space and time of liquid movement, sometimes predictable but sometimes turbulent. The word dérive condenses a whole attitude to life, the sort one might acquire in the backwaters of Saint-Germain-des-Prés.

"Note: a certain Saint-Germain-des-Prés, about which no one has yet written, has been the first group functioning on a historical scale within this ethic of drifting."[11] It is the dérive, writes Michèle Bernstein, "from which we expect to draw educationally conclusive results."[12] Bored with her university studies and her bourgeois background, Bernstein (b. 1932) started hanging around Saint-Germain in 1952 and found herself in the company of the Letterist International. She was the one who, on a rented machine, typed up the articles for *Potlatch*, which mixed news snippets, in-jokes, theoretical texts and notes on the dérive. As her friend Jacqueline de Jong says: "Without her there would not have been any *Potlatch*."[13]

"'Alienation'—I know it is there whenever I sing a love song or recite a poem, whenever I handle a banknote or enter a shop, whenever I glance at a poster or read a newspaper. At the very moment the human is defined as 'having possessions,' I know it is there, dispossessing the human."[14] Henri Lefebvre introduced many French readers to Marx, but to a Marx not quite containable by party orthodoxy. When Lefebvre published his *Critique of Everyday Life* (1947) he was a member of the Party, but—and one can't resist the gesture—he was increasingly alienated from it. The party was an imitation, a thing apart, not an expression of proletarian power. Lefebvre's critique of the abstract and mystified disaffections of the surrealists with everyday life nevertheless implied another critique, of the limits of official Marxist orthodoxy. What he did not yet have was a practice that could produce a knowledge of the relation between the workers' dispossession of the product of their labor during the working day, and the encounter with these same products as potential possessions during leisure hours.

Lefebvre writes of how capital makes the modern city. Capitalism divides time into work time and leisure time. It further divides work time up into equivalent units—workers are usually paid by the hour—and tries to make each unit as productive as possible. Leisure time is free from work, but tends increasingly to be used for consumption. The worker is paid to work in the factory, and pays to spend her free time consuming factory-made products. Such is the standard Marxist view of time. It corresponds to a certain experience of space. There is work space, leisure space, and resting space. The worker works in one space, spends free time in another, and schleps home to sleep in a third.

A graffiti slogan proposed in *Potlatch* for the dormitory suburbs around the factories: "Remember, you are sleeping for the boss!"[15] Unlike the surrealists, the Letterist International put little faith in the dream world. They stay awake nights. They implicitly accept the denunciation mounted from such otherwise incompatible sources as Sartre, Isou and Lefebvre of the futile gestures of surrealism. Rumney: "It was an exquisite corpse that was beginning to give off a bad smell."[16] Their chosen terrain was not the dream, but rather a lucid practice outside of and against the work and leisure diptych. Debord's attack on latterday surrealists was called "The Big Sleep and Its Clients" (1955) which neatly connects the title of a Hollywood movie, the most palpable channel of unconscious desires in postwar France, with the aging surrealist champions of radical desire.[17]

Patrick Straram (1934–88) arrived in Saint-Germain in 1950, but left for Canada in 1958 to avoid national service. In that brief time he hung out in the jazz cellars, drank with the tribe, signed texts by the Letterist International and wrote a novel about it. *The Bottle Reclines* (1953) describes dérives with characters resembling Debord and Chtcheglov in a style somewhere between the surrealists and the Beats: "The wine went to his head. Rambler well led despite himself in a labyrinth of colors and shadowy forms, incapable of assimilating them, distorted interpretation, according to a deformed optic, and however shockingly accurate."[18]

The dérive, with Straram, is a groggy and disorienting affair, continued from night to day:

It was already dirty and bluish whiteness, something lazily mechanic, the chloroformed ambiance of sprawled-out rays of a staggering, sleepy sunrise. A nearly medical beam of scraped sun on the heavy walls of unhealthy sleepwalking, perpetual surveillance of the city, clinical guards/prisoners. The battle picked up from the point where it was brutally interrupted yesterday, from the heap of bricks and fire, automatic incubator, and from the perverse perforation, certain, of light. The ultimate everyday renaissance.[19]

Straram never finished his novel. Perhaps the novel is not the ideal form for writing about the dérive. Perhaps the dérive could be a practice that leads to quite another project than literature.

While the critical theory of commodified experience of time and space that Lefebvre initiated would become a commonplace in the postwar years, Chtcheglov, Debord, Bernstein, Straram and friends were one of the few groups to imagine a *critical practice*.[20] The dérive cuts across the division of the space of the city into work, rest and leisure zones. By wandering about in the space of the city according to their own sense of time, those undertaking a dérive find other uses for space besides the functional. The time of the dérive is no longer divided between productive time and leisure time. It is a time that plays in between the useful and the gratuitous. Leisure time is often called *free time*, but it is free only in the negative, free from work. But what would it mean to construct a positive freedom within time? That is the challenge of the dérive. The breakaway Letterist International created a new practice, a new way of being in the world, out of which to derive a new kind of practice.[21]

Strikingly, both capital and labor accept the division between work time and leisure time. Capital extends or intensifies the working day; labor struggles to shorten it, and within it to resist speed-ups and other attempts by capital to extract more value from it. Perhaps it is this shared fixation on productive time that will draw both capital and labor towards the middle-class cultural norm.[22] While they are at odds as to its use, both take for granted a certain functional concept of time, and a certain acquisitive and accumulating approach to everyday life that comes with it. The Letterist International sought a quite different concept of time, resolutely based on non-work.

Debord's first major *work*, by his own later accounts, was a simple three-word graffiti that translates as "Never work!"[23] Rather than reduce the working hour, avoid it as much as possible. But if there is no work, then there is no leisure either. It is rather like Nietzsche's annunciation of the death of God which is also the death of a certain understanding of Man, since God and Man form a conceptual couple, each made in the other's image.[24] Debord's "Never work!" frees time from its binary form of work time and leisure time. The dérive then becomes the practice of lived time, time not divided and accorded a function in advance; a time inhabited by neither workers nor consumers.

Chtcheglov's text announced some forthcoming books, including one by his friend Henry de Béarn which provisionally names the people of the dérive and their passion: *The New Nomadism*. This book would never be written, or at least not by de Béarn. In the 1970s, the philosopher Gilles Deleuze (1925–95) would join with the psychiatrist and activist

Félix Guattari (1930–92) to write *Anti-Oedipus* (1972) and its sequel, *A Thousand Plateaus* (1980), which among other things would propose a *nomad thought*.[25] They start with a burlesque of psychoanalysis and expand it into a whole worldview based on the productive powers of desire. As they write: "A schizophrenic out for a walk is a better model than a neurotic lying on the analyst's couch."[26] By the time they wrote this, much of what had once been critical thought had laid its weary head on that analyst's couch—depressed, anxious, irritable, neurotic. Obsessed with old wounds. Unable to forget. Unable to get up. At its melancholy end.

Deleuze and Guattari's exemplary walkers were literary characters, but it turns out Chtcheglov was that schizophrenic out for a walk, and he already had a theory of his own nomadism. Years before Deleuze and Guattari, he already saw the dérive as a kind of analysis. "The dérive is certainly a technique, almost a therapeutic one." Unlike psychoanalysis, it did not sever language from the continuum of practices in which it is embedded. "The dérive (with its flow of acts, its gestures, its promenades, its encounters) was to the totality exactly what psychoanalysis (in the best sense) is to language," Chtcheglov writes. The Letterist International refuse the separation of urban space from urban culture, each assigned to their own specialists. They refuse the separation of the external, social space of the city from the internal, private space of subjectivity. The subjective belongs to the city and can be analyzed experimentally, much as the city is subjective and can be reconstructed to expand with our desires.

The dérive was an intervention against geography as much as against psychoanalysis. Academic geography in France arose out of the defeat of the Franco-Prussian war. If the dominant form narrowed its focus to an objective science of landscape existing outside of social practice, there was also a counter-geography, more interested in social practices of landscape-making.[27] Paul-Henry Chombart de Lauwe (1913–98) offered a synthesis of both the objectivity of the former and the attention to social process of the latter. From an aristrocratic family, Chombart was a Catholic, with progressively more leftist leanings throughout the 1940s and '50s. Before the war he studied with Marcel Mauss, from whom he took an organic conception of socialism and a commitment to social science as the study of social problems, with a view to their solution. He crossed the Sahara in 1936 on a tourist flight, as his contribution to Marcel Griaule's legendary ethnographic expeditions.[28] During the war he joined the Resistance, before becoming a fighter pilot for the Free French. His monumental study of Paris and its environs came out in 1952, and would become a critical point of reference for the Situationist theory and practice of *psychogeography*.

Chombart used a range of methods to construct an understanding of the city as both form and process, ranging from aerial surveillance to interviews with workers. Drawing on his wartime experience he became an expert in techniques of aerial surveillance, and these in turn had given Chombart a bird's-eye view of class struggle. He could clearly see in the photographs of Paris a slightly squished version of the concentric rings that the Chicago School claimed defined urban space. These concentric zones, like the rings of Saturn, orbit what the Chicago urbanists christened a *central business district*.[29] (A notion that would have horrified Bataille.) The qualities of the zones are determined by the price of land within them, which is a function of their distance from the center. Or as Chombart might say more directly: class maps onto space.

Chombart came to advocate a participatory approach to town planning, but always with something of an aerial—or what Bataille would call Icarian—view, flying over and detached from the city and its tangle of situations.[30] He represented the best of progressive postwar urban thought: leftist but not Stalinist, sympathetic and engaged with working-class struggles, but viewing these from within orthodox social science as problems to be solved rather than battles to be engaged. He recuperated social geography for the science of landscape. He was all too easily seduced by the idea of housing the working class in Corbusian mega-blocks, for their own good.[31] All this made him a conspicuous target for attack by Debord and friends. Chombart's aerial techniques in particular were to be détourned in the service of a quite different practice—psychogeography.

Psychogeography is a *practice* of the city as at once an objective and subjective space. It is not the city as mere prompt for surrealist reveries. Nor is it a thing apart, to be dissected by social science, no matter how well-meaning. The city of Debord, Chtcheglov and their friends is a complex beast, always in process, with its own rhythms and life cycle, as it is for Chombart. What Chtcheglov and Debord add to this is a certain turbulence. The city simultaneously has subjective qualities that are nevertheless interpersonal. Debord: "From a dérive point of view cities have psychogeographical contours, with constant currents, fixed points and vortexes that strongly discourage entry into or exit from certain zones." The dérive discovers these contours. The city is an aesthetic practice irreducible to the interests of state or market.

The surrealists brought psychoanalysis to the streets, but it was only a detour, on the way back to literature.[32] Chombart brought social science to the streets, but again it was a detour, back to planning from above. The Letterist International invent a new kind of knowledge, a street ethnography, whose primary method is the dérive. What the dérive discovers is psychogeography: the lineaments of intersubjective space. In place of the chance encounters of the surrealists, they create a practice of play and strategy which invents a way of being, outside of commodified time and outside of the separate disciplines of knowledge—including geography. Henceforth the city will not be a site for fieldwork but a playing field, in which to discover intimations of a space and time outside the division of labor. The goal is nothing less than to invent a new civilization which will make a mark on historical time with the grandeur of the Temple of the Sun.

The civilization of play had already existed. Even little Saint-Germain—a handful of city blocks—left a trace. The artist Constant Nieuwenhuys (1920–2005), who will feature in our story further on, had a rather different experience of the place to Vian's bohemians, Vali's tribe or Chtcheglov's renegade Letterists, because he was there with his little boy: "The Parisians are not so nice, that is why they paint abstracts, and that is also why they slam the door when, with Victor holding my hand, I ask for a room. Yes, everything is abstract here …"—even compassion. And yet writing about it later Constant could not but agree with Chtcheglov: "The atmosphere of this bourgeois quarter of Paris was so profoundly altered by a small group of intellectuals, the so-called existentialists, that it acquired international fame and even became a tourist attraction."[33]

The model, in negative, for a city of play is Las Vegas: a city in the desert, with no harbor, no river, which since 1931 was dedicated—if not consecrated—to wasting time. To Chtcheglov, the ideal setting for a new avant-garde was not the metropolis of commerce or industry, but tourism. Las Vegas would eventually sprout its own pyramid, and take on all the pretensions to immortality that to Bataille already seemed ridiculous, and are perhaps more so in the twenty-first century. In 2003 the United States government issued a warning that if nothing was done, Las Vegas would run out of water by 2025.[34] Much as it fascinated Chtcheglov, Las Vegas was not the prototype of the Situationist city.

In the jungle is a city that moves. When its inhabitants build new districts it is always to the west. Each time they cut the ribbon opening a new quarter, an old one to the east is abandoned, gradually to disappear beneath the overgrowth of tropical vegetation. This is more like it! The moving city would burst the bubble of the *sustainable* city, the fantasy that the city can become one with its environment, a pure homeostasis, outside of history.[35] It would lay bare the process by which the city transforms nature into second nature, in the process making nature appear as a resource for the city's consumption. And besides, the ruins left behind in the east would be perfect terrain for the dérive. Why can such a city not exist? The conceit of private property is that it is something fixed, eternal. Once it comes into existence it remains, passed in an unbroken chain of ownership from one title-holder to the next. Yet in the course of time whole cities really do disappear. We live among the ruins. We later cities know we are mortal. And yet in the name of property we would hold back the very sea.

The village of Siasconset sits atop a bluff on the island of Nantucket, Massachusetts, a prize location for those of means, except for one thing. Erosion, like Marx's old mole, is burrowing away underneath, threatening to topple the palaces perched above.[36] So in 1992 twenty or so owners of such mansions joined together to form a Beach Preservation Fund, which intends to spend at least $25 million of its own money on dredging 2.6 million cubic yards of sand from a site offshore and pumping it onto the beach below the cliff. "They realize that the sand will inevitably wash away, so they are prepared to do much of the work all over again, perhaps as often as every five years." There seems now more merit than ever in the proposal for a city in the jungle, a city that records its own consumption of the terrain. Chtcheglov's intuition of the opening of the city to the temporality of the cosmos was perhaps more profound than he knew. Even the great city of Teotihuacan failed to stop time. "Today much of the city is buried under five towns, one of Mexico's largest military bases, numerous farms, commercial centers and a string of highways."[37]

What the Letterist International intended was not a new kind of urban planning, but a critique of it. "We need to flood the market—even if only for the moment the intellectual market—with a mass of desires whose fulfillment is not beyond humanity's present means of action on the material world, but only beyond the capacity of the old social organization."[38] They had the old Marxist faith that the development of the forces of production, the machinery of industrial capitalism, would yield the means to free us from necessity. Yet as early as 1953 they realized that capital could not go on treating all of space and time as resources for its own quantitative expansion. They had lived through the war as children and knew, at least secondhand, of the destructive power of modern technology. Why could that power not be used to build a different kind of civilization in the ruins? In the twenty-first century we live more and more with the consequences of the failure to make just such a qualitative break.

The Letterist International used the practice of the dérive as a method for creating a kind of knowledge outside of the division of labor, and outside even of the intellectual division of labor between disciplines. They aimed it not only at rival avant-gardes, but at geography, urban studies, sociology—the legitimate knowledges of the city. It was a "subcultural knowledge,"[39] drawing on a delinquent's distrust of social scientists and their questionnaires. Psychogeography made the city subjective and at the same time drew subjectivity out of its individualistic shell. It is a therapy aimed not at the self but at the city itself. Letterists did not shrink from the aerial surveillance made possible by wartime technical advances, but did not make a fetish of it either.

It may well seem that the moving city is impractical, impossible. But is it any less impossible than holding back the sea? Is it any less impossible than building garden suburbs in the Nevada desert? The Letterist International discovered the power of a kind of *negative action*. They show what cannot be done within the limits of actually existing capitalism. As Debord writes: "The greatest difficulty in any such undertaking is to convey through these apparently extravagant proposals a sufficient degree of serious seduction."[40] As with any seduction, a kind of strategic game is in play, the key move in which is to act as if the new desire already exists. What will emerge out of the dérive, as practiced by the young Letterists, is a quite different concept of space and time, which, like the dérive, would be outside of property. It may only exist in a few interstitial moments out and about in Saint-Germain-des-Prés, but those few moments marked the exit to the twentieth century.

Having failed to take that exit, now we are trapped on an expressway that seems to keep going until the end of the world. There could be worse plans than turning back to look for the last exit, for which the Letterist International thought it saw the signs. Actually, the Letterist International scouted at least two exits. One leads to a small-scale, local and temporary situation, discovered via the dérive. The other points to a larger scale and a longer duration, perhaps to history itself, but grasped by its most tenuous emanations —language, images, the sign.

3   The Torrent of History

A scandal: historian Stephen E. Ambrose admits that he plagiarized many passages of his book *The Wild Blue*. Ambrose's books on General Custer and Richard Nixon also turned out to contain a good few sentences derived from other works. More scandal: the historian Doris Kearns Goodwin admits that she borrowed passages in her book *The Fitzgeralds and the Kennedys* from three works by other authors. Still more scandal: she then concedes that in 1987 her publisher, Simon & Schuster, paid to settle a legal claim by one of them under a confidentiality agreement. She said she confused verbatim notes with her own words.[1] Take pity on our poor authors! Not even they can tell their own words from another's. They are caught between the monotonous consistency of official historical narratives and the demand that the middle-class author have a unique *vision* that is his or her personal property. No wonder they resort to copying one another. Hypocrisy is the hush money that vice pays to virtue. Given the poverty of middle-class history, perhaps what the times require is a double reappropriation: both of the history of Debord and company, and of the mode of historical thinking to which they aspired, and which they occasionally achieved.

The Marquis de Vauvenargues once wrote that "old discoveries belong less to their original inventors than to those who put them to use." So it is with some justice that lines lifted from the soldier-aphorist should show up, with some slight but key corrections, in the *Poésies* (1870) of Isidore Ducasse, the self-styled Comte de Lautréamont (1846–90). The purpose of the *Poésies*, he wrote, was to take the most beautiful poetry and "correct it in the direction of hope." Thus Vauvenargues' maxim "One can be just, if one is human" becomes "One can be just, if one is not human." In a celebrated passage,

Lautréamont expands on his distinctive poetics: "Plagiarism is necessary. Progress implies it. It closely grasps an author's sentence, uses his expressions, deletes a false idea, replaces it with the right one. To be well made, a maxim does not call for correction. It calls for development." It's a passage often taken as saying something about poetics, less often as saying something about history. Lautréamont corrects, not back to a lost purity or some ideal form, but forward—to a new possibility.

Lautréamont's best-known work is *The Songs of Maldoror* (1869), a giddy fringe-romantic epic, which includes the murder of children and sex with a shark. A drunken God presides from a throne of gold and shit. The works of Man don't amount to much, either. The pyramids of Egypt are "those anthills reared by stupidity and slavery." It was a surrealist favorite. In a famous line, set to become a cliché, Lautréamont anticipates the surrealist aesthetic: "As beautiful as the chance meeting on a dissecting table of a sewing machine and an umbrella."[2] But there was more to Lautréamont, and the Letterist International would make off with the best of it.

In a beautiful passage, Lautréamont writes:

Flights of starlings have a way of flying which is theirs alone and seems as governed by uniform and regular tactics as a disciplined regiment would be, obeying a single leader's voice with precision. The starlings obey the voice of instinct, and their instinct leads them to bunch into the center of the squad, while the speed of their flight bears them constantly beyond it; so that this multitude of birds thus united by a common tendency towards the same magnetic point, unceasingly coming and going, circulating and crisscrossing in all directions, forms a sort of agitated whirlpool whose whole mass, without following a fixed course seems to have a general wheeling movement round itself resulting from the particular circulatory motions appropriate to each of its parts, and whose center, perpetually tending to expand but continually compressed, pushed back by the contrary stress of the surrounding lines bearing upon it, is constantly denser than any of those lines, which are themselves the denser the nearer they are to the center.

Lautréamont is here describing his own swarming poetics—only these lines are lifted straight out of the natural history writings of the Comte de Buffon.

In the early 1950s, something of a scandal ensued when it was discovered that Lautréamont had purloined some of *Maldoror*'s most thrillingly poetic passages from text books. The method announced in the *Poésies* had already been practiced in *Maldoror*. Some, like the literary critic Maurice Saillet (1914–1999), felt the need to defend Lautréamont.[3] Saillet was one of the founders of the self-styled College of Pataphysics. He was a noted scholar of the works of Alfred Jarry (1873–1907), to whose memory the College was consecrated. Started in 1948, the College was a playful, armchair version of the avant-garde impulse. Some of its instigators had day jobs. Others, like Jacques Prévert, Raymond Queneau or Boris Vian were well-known writers. While Saillet could defend Lautréamont in the spirit of linguistic play, the Letterist International credited him with the discovery of a more far-reaching method. Their name for it was *détournement*, as in to detour, to hijack, to lead astray, to appropriate. And it was no joke. The task was to systematize it and—more to the point—practice it.

If there was a precedent in avant-garde poetics for détournement, it came not from the Paris surrealists around André Breton (1896–1966) or even the dissidents around Georges Bataille (1897–1962) but from their Belgian contemporary Paul Nougé (1895–1967). It was Nougé who saw in Lautréamont not a prophet of excess but the inventor of a method. There is, he says, "a certain inclination common to a few minds which leads them to find the elements of creation as close as possible to the object to be created; to the extent that the thing to be desired would come into being by the introduction of a single comma in a page of writing; of a picture, complex in its execution, by the animation of a single stroke of black ink."[4] The texts Nougé corrected ranged from a Baudelaire poem to porn. Some were originally published in *Les Lèvres Nues* (1954–1958), a magazine edited by his friend Marcel Mariën. *Les Lèvres Nues* also published the text that gave this method its name: "A User's Guide to Détournement," by Guy Debord and Gil J. Wolman.

Gil Wolman (1929–95) was not entirely of the Saint-Germain tribe. He had a home to go to—and often brought others to crash there. He lived with his mother. His Jewish father, deported during the war, never returned. Unlike Debord he had a real gift for Letterist poetry. Where Isou chiseled it down to the letter, Wolman pushed on to a poetry of pure sounds, and on again, to a performance art of the diaphragm, of the epiglottis, of corporeality itself. He also pushed Letterist cinema past Isou's comfort zone. Isou's *Treatise on Spit and Eternity* deployed stock footage, scratched images, discrepancies between image and sound; Wolman's *L'Anticoncept* (1950) used no images at all. Unlike Isou's macho posturing, the voice-over of Wolman's film evokes in gentle and sensuous terms the experience of wandering the streets and making love where one can: "in the rain we kiss in the parks I caress you through your dress our muscles tense on the grass …"[5]

Debord and Wolman both pushed Letterism against itself. "Negation is the transitional term to a new period," as Wolman had written in the preface to *L'Anticoncept*. "Negation of the intrinsic, immutable, pre-existing concept, projects this concept outside of matter, reveals it after the fact to an extrinsic reaction, becomes mutable by as many reactions." Which could be a somewhat abstract way of formulating Isou's theory of the poetry of history and the history of poetry, a key point of reference for both Debord and Wolman. For a moment during the mid 1950s Wolman and Debord's projects flowed together, but the smallest differences would end up pulling them apart. For the moment they were comrades in a civil war against a culture intent on settling for some warmed-up leftovers, banalities such as abstract painting, Beat writing, or existential philosophy, as if these would suffice to fill the void opened up by the war itself.

In "Why Letterism?" (1955) Debord and Wolman characterize the first decade after the war as a time of generalized failure to effect change and a retreat into merely formal elaboration. "One knows, moreover, to what laborious phenomenological refinements professors devote themselves, who otherwise do not dance in cellars."[6] Art and thought appear as a dismal mess—albeit a profitable one. "On a spiritual level, the middle class are always in power." It matters little whether the work takes the form of the bourgeois novel, socialist realist art, the literature of commitment, or the (pseudo) avant-garde: each is just a tactic for restoring middle-class sensibility. "It is necessary to finish with this spirit." This is why there was nothing for it but to join the Letterists, who at least unleashed a potentially fatal *inflation* in the arts, with their reduction of all its forms to the elementary particles of the letter. But the Letterists got caught up in their own fame. Isidore

Isou and his factotum Maurice Lemaître (b. 1926) happily appear in a light entertainment called *Around the World with Orson Welles*. They don't notice Welles's sly glance to camera, that makes the viewer complicit in silent ridicule.[7]

Letterism at least pushed formalism to the limit, where it collapsed of its own accord. It was proof of the relative independence of formal development within the arts from social and economic determination. In "Why Letterism?" Debord and Wolman steer between Isou's purely formal theory of art and Marxist determinism. Art has a relative autonomy, its forms develop in their own time, only partly coinciding with a wider historical process. Isou's theory of the formal development of art is linear and autonomous. For Debord and Wolman, development might require going back in order to go forward. For instance, the Precocity movement of the seventeenth century might now reveal itself as a great precursor, a critique in advance of capital's separation of living space from work space according to function. Despite the slanders of Molière, Precocity's devotion to strolling, to conversation, its ideas about décor and architecture, are resources for the construction of a whole attitude to life.[8]

"We write so that our works—which are practically nonexistent—remain in history." This is the hint in "Why Letterism?" of the significance of détournement, which Debord and Wolman only begin to grasp one year later in "A User's Guide to Détournement" (1956). The originality of the Letterist International consists in understanding form not as literary form, in terms of genre, style, poetics and so forth, but as material form, as the book, the film, the canvas. Materiality is the key to the lag by which past culture shapes present culture. If the effects in the architectural domain seem mostly negative, there might be some hope in the lag effect of certain texts. But for past works to become resources for the present requires their use in the present in a quite particular way. It requires their appropriation as a collective inheritance, not as private property. All culture is *derivative*.

Rather than chiseling language down to its bare elements, Debord and Wolman propose something else. Not the destruction of the sign, but rather destruction of the *ownership* of the sign. "It is necessary to eliminate all remnants of the notion of personal property in this area." Détournement offers "an ease of production far surpassing in quantity, variety and quality the automatic writing that has bored us for so long." The surrealist appropriation of Lautréamont's *Poésies* took up his cry that "poetry should be made by all" and read it through *Maldoror* as a poetry that bypassed conscious individual intention in the interests of the collective imagination.[9] The Letterist International's version of a poetry made by all meant two quite other things.

One is that it should be made by and for all the senses at once. Thus dérive as method creates psychogeography as a knowledge via which to design whole new poetic ambiances — the *unitary urbanism* anticipated by Chtcheglov. The other sense of a poetry made by all is a poetry made by the communal appropriation of the past in the present. Chombart's aerial surveys of Paris, not to mention his detailed social science on its everyday life, is not to be quoted but appropriated, détourned, for not only understanding but living the city otherwise.

"Clashing head-on with all social and legal conventions," détournement "cannot fail to be a powerful cultural weapon in the service of the real class struggle. The cheapness of its products is the heavy artillery that breaks through the Chinese walls of understanding. It is the real means of proletarian artistic education, the first step towards a literary communism." The text is true to itself. Debord and Wolman took more than a few lines from Saillet's defense of Lautréamont, and corrected, or rather, developed them. Where Saillet spoke of a communism of genius, this becomes a literary communism. The term *genius* still clings a little to the romantic idea of the text as the product of an individual author's unique gift.

A more crucial détournement is from Marx and Engels's famous *Communist Manifesto* (1848):

> The bourgeoisie, by the rapid improvement of all instruments of production, by the immensely facilitated means of communication, draws all, even the most barbarian, nations into civilization. The cheap prices of its commodities are the heavy artillery with which it batters down all Chinese walls, with which it forces the barbarians' intensely obstinate hatred of foreigners to capitulate. It compels all nations, on pain of extinction, to adopt the bourgeois mode of production; it compels them to introduce what it calls civilization into their midst, i.e., to become bourgeois themselves. In one word, it creates a world after its own image.[10]

The inflation introduced by détournement, even more than that of Letterism, is the development that undermines bourgeois culture in turn.

Capital produces a culture in its own image, a culture of the work as private property, the author as sole proprietor of a soul as property. Détournement sifts through the material remnants of past and present culture for materials whose untimeliness can be utilized against bourgeois culture. But rather than further elaborate modern poetics, détournement exploits it. The aim is the destruction of all forms of middle-class cultural shopkeeping. As capital spreads outwards, making the world over in its image, at home it finds its own image turns against it.

It's easy to miss the significance of this claim, buried as it is in a text that spends quite a bit of time on the poetics of détournement. Debord and Wolman discuss a metagraphic composition by Debord—a memorial for Kaki—and the way classified ads about bars for sale contribute to the affect of a remembrance for a suicide. "A User's Guide to Détournement" could be reduced, in other words, to a somewhat limited and clinical statement about *intertextuality*. Tom McDonough: "To carry class conflict into the realm of language, to insist upon the central place that realm occupied in the collective construction of the world to be made, to announce the arrival of a 'literary communism'— these were the inseparable aims of Situationist détournement."[11] Quite, but it is all too easy to elide the significance of literary communism, which is not merely something added to modernist poetics. It is its undoing. It brings class struggle both into and out of language.

Détournement is merely a means to an end. Literary communism is a precursor to architectural communism, to the détournement of built form and the ambiences it can generate. A poetry made by all and a poetry made for all the senses unite in a proposal for the "exact reconstruction in one city of an entire neighborhood of another." An idea which, bizarrely, almost happened—although not entirely as Debord and Wolman intended. In 2008, Dubai businessman Saeed Al Ghandi signed a £350m agreement with the French city of Lyon to build a replica of it in Dubai. "He fell in love with Lyon while strolling along the river-bank," according to José Noya, a Lyon bureaucrat. "He wants to recreate Lyon's soul." The idea sprang from a plan to build a university in Dubai, in partnership with the University of Lyon, that would rival Abu Dhabi's version of the Louvre. This second Lyon would cover an area of about 700 acres, about the size of the Latin Quarter of Paris. The reproduction would not include Lyon's sub-Corbusian tower blocks.[12]

Détournement is the opposite of quotation. Like détournement, quotation brings the past into the present, but it does so entirely within a regime of the proper use of proper names. The key to détournement is its challenge to private property. Détournement attacks a kind of fetishism, where the products of collective human labor in the cultural realm can become a mere individual's property. But what is distinctive about this fetishism is that it does not rest directly on the status of the thing as a commodity. It is, rather, a fetishism of memory. It is not so much commodity fetishism as *co-memory fetishism*. In place of collective remembrance, the fetish of the proper name. The name Lyon, for instance: Al Ghandi's project is a merely a quotation, no matter how vast the scale. Détournement restores to the fragment the status of being a recognizable part of the process of the collective production of meaning in the present, through its recombination into a new meaningful ensemble.

Key to any practice of détournement is identifying the fragments upon which it might work. There is no particular size or shape. It could be a single image, a film sequence of any length, a word, a phrase, a paragraph. What matters is the identification of the superior fidelity of the element to the ensemble within which it finds itself. Détournement is in all cases a reciprocal devaluing and revaluing of the element within the development of a unifying meaning. Détournement is the fluid language of anti-ideology, but ideology has absolutely nothing to do with any particular arrangement of signs or images. It has to do with ownership.

Michel Foucault (1926–84) undermines the romantic theory of authorship by speaking of *discourse* as a distribution of author functions.[13] For Foucault, a statement is authorized by a particular form of discourse, a regime of truth, a procedure for assigning truth-value to statements. It's not hard to see why this captivated the minds of academics. It made the procedures in which academics are obsessively drilled the very form of power itself. As if that by which academics are made, the molding of their bodies to desks and texts, that about which they know the most, even more than they know their allotted fields, were the very index of power. Reading Foucault is like taking a master class on how the game of scholarship is to be played, and with the reliable alibi that this knowledge of power, of knowledge as power, is to be used in the interests of *resistance* to something or other. Détournement, on the other hand, turns the tables, upends the game.

The device of détournement restores all the subversive qualities to past critical judgments that have congealed into respectable truths. Détournement makes for a type of communication aware of its inability to enshrine any inherent and definitive certainty. This language is inaccessible in the highest degree to confirmation by any earlier or supra-critical reference point. On the contrary, its internal coherence and its adequacy in respect of the practically possible are what validate the symbolic remnants that it restores. Détournement founds its cause on nothing but its own practice as critique at work in the present. Détournement creates anti-statements. For the Situationists, the very act of *unauthorized* appropriation is the truth content of détournement.

Needless to say, the best lines in this chapter are plagiarized. Or rather, they are détourned. (It hardly counts as plagiarism if the text itself gives notice of the offense — or does it?) Moreover, many of these détourned phrases have been corrected, as Lautréamont would say. Plagiarism upholds private property in thought by trying to hide its thefts. Détournement treats all of culture as common property to begin with, and openly declares its rights. Moreover, it treats it not as a *creative commons*, not as the *wealth of networks*, not as *free culture* or *remix culture*; but as an active place of challenge, agency, strategy and conflict.[14] Détournement dissolves the rituals of knowledge in an active remembering that calls collective being into existence. If all property is theft, then all intellectual property is détournement.

Not surprisingly, official discourse has a hard time with this concept. The decline of critical theory in the postwar years is directly correlated to the refusal to confront détournement as the most consistent approach to a knowledge made by all. The meandering stream that runs from the Letterist International to the Situationist International and beyond is the course not taken, and remains a troubling memory for critical thought. The path not taken poses the difficult question: what if one challenged the organization of knowledge itself? What if, rather than knowledge as a representation of another life, it is that other life?

Meanwhile, détournement has become a social movement in all but name. Here the Situationists stand as a prophetic pointing of the way towards a struggle for the collective reappropriation and modification of cultural material. One that need only become conscious of itself to re-imagine the space of knowledge outside of private property. Every kid with a BitTorrent client is an unconscious Situationist in the making. What remains is the task of closing the gap between a critical theory gone astray, still caught up in the model of knowledge as property, and a popular movement that cannot quite develop its own conscious-ness of its own power. As Wolman wrote in his preface to *L'Anticoncept*, "there is no negation that does not affirm itself elsewhere." There might be a link between so-called plagiarism and progress after all.

At stake is the viability of history itself. Officially, history is a spir-itless chronicle of events, one damned thing after another. It is so unsatisfying that apocalyptic thinking about time has made a big come-back. To some it seems more plausible that they will shake hands with Jesus than that they could have a hand in their own destiny. But there is official history and there are other histories, including a history of the desire not to end history but to partake of it.

The very idea of history as a process of collective self-making has itself been through a few historical stages.[15] Along came Friedrich Engels (1820–95) and his mechanical time, grinding on. Then came György Lukács (1885–1971) and his expressive time, history as totality, the parts reflecting the whole. Then came Louis Althusser (1918–90) and structural time, differences meshing and permutat-ing. Then, in desperation, some brought back from the dead Walter Benjamin (1892–1940) and his messianic time, which recasts history from the perspective of its redemption.

As the twentieth century flopped from one horror movie to the next, many gave up on history, but what looked to them like defeat was to others the napalm smell of victory. Sure, the Marxists had their history, which developed through its own internal laws of motion from feu-dalism to capitalism to socialism, but for Walt Rostow (1916–2003) the latter is just a wrong turn, the industrial state gone mad. The real terminus of historical action was American liberal capitalism. Or perhaps there was another stage to come, what the sociologist Daniel Bell (1919–2011) christened the *post-industrial society*.[16] The computer will overcome all the alienating shortcomings of capital. Work itself will become playful and creative. Commodities will not be mass-produced but custom-made. Not socialism with a human face but capitalism with a smiley face.

The cold war was a clash of historical fictions, Marxist versus anti-Marxist. The outcome seemed far from certain. But with the memory of the communist role in the Resistance fading, Moscow's grand narrative seemed less and less appealing. This left fellow-traveling Western artists and intellectuals with few choices. One was to attach themselves to another promised land. For Régis Debray (b. 1940), this was Cuba. For Althusser this was China. The renewal of history would come via the third world's overthrow of imperialism. The revisionists left the destination of socialism intact, just changed its address and the route to get there. Another choice was to go back to the past in search of the turning point where the narrative of history went wrong, and to become, if not the actual, then at least the spiritual inheritor of the October revolution. This was the choice of the Trotskyites. Alternatively one could abandon historical time altogether, like Jean-François Lyotard (1924–98), and announce the postmodern as a time beyond all these choruses of the grand recital of history.[17]

The Situationists will take another tack. They will not abandon historical thought, nor chime in with one or other chorus as the representative of its destination. To them all the capitals of this world, from Washington to Moscow to Beijing, are capitals of the same spectacular society. This tiny band would set themselves against power in its totality. A futile project, perhaps, but powerful in its very futility, in casting the whole century in negative relief. Against the abandonment of historical possibility on the left, and the triumphant declaration that this is the best of all possible worlds on the right, it's time to step back into the current. The other history, the historical practice left unexplored, restores causality but renders it fluid, complex, turbulent. But not for all that arbitrary or formless. History is no machine, no structure, nor does it call for the solace of a merely figurative redemption.

By the mid 1950s Guy Debord achieved some notoriety with his film *Howls for Sade* (1952), and drew around himself the motley collection of drunks, drifters and geniuses known as the Letterist International.[18] He painted its slogan by the banks of the river Seine—"Never work!"—and did his best to live up to it. He discovered that this implied another, even harder discipline, the unwritten slogan: "Make no art!" In later life Debord would turn the milieu from which the Letterist International spawned into a legendary counterpoint to the spectacle, perhaps even more central than the legend of May '68. Yet in 1957 the Letterist world was more of a constraint on its own ambitions for upending the world. The Letterist International too had to die in the war of time. It was no longer adequate to its own discoveries.

The Letterist International passes on to the Situationist International the practice of a negative action, which lays bare the gap between everyday life in twentieth century capitalism, and what it leaves to be desired. What the Letterist International have going for them is the consistency of an everyday life lived as negation. What they do not have is either the depth of experience or the consistency of theoretical invention that might come with it. That will come from the encounter with Asger Jorn.

4   Extreme Aesthetics

Once upon a time there lived a beautiful dancer, whom some called Tintomara, but who went by many names, all derived from novels and plays. Tintomara was very striking, and both men and women could hardly help but be captivated by her. Or by him, for Tintomara had both a male and a female aspect, like one of those eight-limbed beings of Aristophanes, who met all their own desires and lacked for nothing.[1] One day Tintomara the dancer was rehearsing with the ballet master a piece based on some primitivist fantasy or other. Dressed as a Native American savage girl, he was to be pinned to the floor by four of the chief's men, only to break free and turn away from his captors.

Only he did not just break and turn. "Like a rose that does not want to come into bloom, the savage girl had indeed gone noticeably outside the turn … A movement clearly due neither to forgetfulness nor ineptitude." Was this too part of the drama? "The savage girl's movements were so exquisite, so charming, that only quite exceptional art or simple nature, whilst transgressing the whole sense of the dance, could yet excite the ballet master in so strange a fashion that he, delighted to see it, was unable to intervene and hinder her from committing so gross a breach of the pantomime's design."[2]

This fable comes from an extraordinary novel by Swedish writer Carl Jonas Love Almqvist (1793–1866). Regardless of whether Asger Jorn ever read *Tintomara*, he was fond of Almqvist and shared with him commitments to a distinctive Scandinavian cultural tradition, to a peculiar combination of mystic and materialist thought, and to a radical conception of aesthetics which could combine extremes of romanticism and realism. All are expressed in Tintomara's gesture. Neither male nor female, nature nor culture, flesh nor spirit, form nor feeling, Tintomara is Almqvist's image of an undivided being, irreducible to any form or essence. Tintomara's fate is not a happy one. In the end her lifeless body will be left to twist in the wind. But from Almqvist to Jorn there is a line of thought, of creation, of cultural action that tries to make a world fit for its Tintomaras.

Asger Jorn (1914–73) is admired as an artist. The art historian and former Situationist T. J. Clark calls him "the greatest painter of the fifties."[3] He is less well known as a theorist, and certainly not often acknowledged as a key theorist of the Situationist International. It is possible to extract from Jorn's texts a unique take on the Situationist project, one he was entitled to claim as his own more than most. Jorn the theorist is intimately connected, not just to his art, but also to his extraordinary life. In 1936 Jorn took off for Paris on a motorcycle. He joined the studio of Ferdinand Léger and worked briefly for Le Corbusier. He spent the war years in his native Denmark, secretly printing a monthly Communist journal and working with the Hell-Horse group, whose project fused leftist politics, modernist aesthetics and pan-Scandinavian culture. After the war he returned to Paris. He met Constant Nieuwenhuys at an exhibition of the Catalan surrealist Joan Miró (1893–1983). Jorn and Constant, together with Belgian surrealist poet Christian Dotremont (1922–79) would be central figures in the Cobra movement, which lasted from 1948 to 1952.[4]

Dotremont and Jorn spent much of 1951 in a Danish sanitarium, recovering from tuberculosis. It was here that Jorn found time for an extensive reading of Kierkegaard thanks to a priest at the sanitarium who had the collected works.[5] It was here that Jorn wrote *Luck and Chance*, the first of a series of strange, intense, theoretical works, blueprints of a sort both for his art and for his continued wagers on collaborative forms of action.

The Movement for an Imaginist Bauhaus was Jorn's next bid for collective acton. Started in Italy in 1954, its impetus was Jorn's antipathy to the Swiss artist and designer Max Bill (1908–94). Like Jorn a person of credible anti-fascist credentials, Bill was commissioned to create a curriculum for a design school in Ulm "following Bauhaus principles," according to Bill. He studied at the Bauhaus in Dessau for a year or so before the war, and had developed his own aesthetics and politics out of his close contact with modernist artists and designers of the interwar years. From Theo van Doesburg he took the idea of *concrete design*, which "arises out of its own means and laws, without these having to be derived or borrowed from natural phenomena."

In Bill's aesthetic, beauty both derives from function and is a function. And yet this beauty is Platonic, reductionist, a shearing away of the accidental to arrive at a certain formal purity: "The whole environment created by us, from the spoon to the city, had to be brought into harmony with social conditions, which implied shaping those conditions too." Where the Bauhaus had originally housed both artists and designers, and concerned itself with both the formal and the symbolic, with objective functions and subjective experiences, Bill completely excluded the aesthetic experimental dimension from his postwar restoration of the Bauhaus aesthetic. "We have to guard against the danger of going by appearances and instead attempt to bring all our contemporary powers into a harmonious balance—into what we'd like to call *the good form*." Yet Bill was an artist, albeit one who could claim "we have eliminated every parasite in painting" by which he meant anything figurative, or any hint of the material world at all. Nothing could be further from Jorn's understanding of the legacy and significance of Bauhaus artists such as Paul Klee (1879–1940) than Bill's declaration that "art is an order, a prototype of harmony."[6]

Jorn's antipathy for Bill's new Bauhaus prompted him to revise and elaborate his own writings on form, eventually published by the Situationist International as *For Form*.[7] Jorn is not as optimistic about postwar culture as Bill. "Culture no longer takes place in a situation, because we can only speak of a situation when there is an event, and an act only becomes an event at the moment it is able to trigger sensation." Jorn's own art, like his collective actions, are attempts to reignite sensation through experiments in emergent form. Jorn thinks of movement and matter rather like Lautréamont's starlings, where discernible form emerges out of random movements of definite proportions. "This new view of the whole leads us to the awareness of a new dynamic method in formal and artistic creation. But this also teaches us that we must throw ourselves into the confusion and act directly on the contradictions by creating new ones, if we want to fertilize development."

Aesthetics means experiment, elaboration, not purification. For Jorn, Bill's pronouncements are "doctrines that merely repeat the antipoetic perspectives of old Platonism … and more generally the whole of Hellenic idealism." It is ignorant of the complexities and organicism of other traditions of form, in Europe and elsewhere. It has not kept up with developments in the materialist worldview which rediscover these traditions. "Modern science has reached the point where it recognizes that phenomena consisting of a sufficiently large number of separate phenomena acting without causality, nevertheless strictly obey the law of causality in their ensemble." Jorn wants an aesthetics that is abreast of modern understandings of the physical world, rather than one that harks back to a classical mechanics.

The creative act cannot concern itself solely with the beautiful and the functional. "The rationalists seek an absolute symmetry between form, structure and function, while evolution occurs precisely through an increasing dissymmetry among these three elements." The evolution of form is driven by dreams, longings, imaginary aims, the desire for sensation. The ultimate purpose of a new form cannot be known in advance. "Evolution is a perpetual anomaly." Out of such anomalies — ugly, functionless — emerge new sensations, new situations, and sometimes new enduring forms. "Ugliness is no less rare than beauty." Everything else is just a middling boredom.

With the Imaginist Bauhaus Jorn wanted to revive, on a broader footing, the experimental aesthetic practice of Cobra (1948–52). He saw such collaborative aesthetic experiments as an essential component of the Bauhaus legacy. Imaginist Bauhaus would merge with the Letterist International into the Situationist International in 1957, in the process shedding Jorn's contemporary Ettore Sottsass (1917–2007), who would go on to fame as an industrial designer. Where Sottsass introduced a playfulness and openness quite foreign to Bill, and central to the formation of a *postmodern style* in design, neither Bill nor Sottsass really thought critically about the creation of form within the social and natural worlds in the manner to which Jorn aspired.[8]

Jorn was seventeen years older than Debord, who he met in 1954. His intellectual, artistic and activist formation had come earlier. His politics came from arguments on the Scandinavian left. His practical abilities emerged in the communist-aligned cultural resistance to Nazi control of Denmark. His intellectual formation is a more complicated matter. Jorn developed an original and extensive aesthetic and political theory of art, abreast of, but outside, the established avant-garde patterns of the time. If one seeks the precursors to the Situationists, they might more easily be found not at the Parisian epicenter but in the periphery, in Isou's Romania, in Nougé's Belgium, and in the Denmark of Asger Jorn.

The suns around which Jorn's thought orbits are, as for so many others, Darwin, Nietzsche and Marx, although his path was more elliptical than most. The Marxist in Jorn expects capitalism to collapse, but not through class struggle so much as *ontological* struggle. Its inability to grasp its own nature condemns it. For Jorn, "the socialist way of life is the natural way of life."[9] Everything about Jorn's thought and actions can be read through this statement, including his critique of, and eventual break with, Marxism. Class division is original sin, and the struggle on the aesthetic, political and philosophical planes alike is to restore, not a lost unity but a lost process, an open, creative, play of differences in which collective human endeavor transforms nature without imitating it, but without dominating it either. Being is just like Tintomara's dance, where the turn becomes embellished, ornamented, shaped with and by desire.

Marxist aesthetics is in thrall to the classical. Marx and Engels had not thought through the consequences of their discoveries. Their idealized view of classical—particularly Greek—form distorts the whole of Marxist thought and practice. Here Jorn turns to Nietzsche, and his distinction in *The Birth of Tragedy* (1872) between an Apollonian aesthetic of form and the Dionysian aesthetic of process. Jorn views Apollo and Dionysus as a tension between aristocratic and folk life. When the cultural representatives of the ruling classes make war against serpents, dragons, sirens, they are at war with nature, including human nature—our species-being. They are at war, more precisely, with the Dionysian aspect of our species-being that the subordinate classes embody. Jorn: "It is precisely this distaste for the freedom and richness of life, its color and variation, which one calls *good taste*."[10] Expression, like Tintomara's turn, is for Jorn the key to a Dionysian aesthetics. The Apollonian version of classical culture represses creation, process, difference, and leads to a slavish reduction of flux to static and ideal forms, to representation rather than expression. This might apply as much to Greek vase painting as to Plato's eternal forms.

It is not so much that there is a conflict between the Dionysian and the Apollonian, but that they are two different ways of understanding and practicing conflict. For Jorn there are two kinds of dialectic—dualist and monist. The dualist dialectic is an external conflict between irreconcilable differences. The monist dialectic is a more subtle kind of movement. This is key to Jorn's critique of Marxism: "The defective concept of the whole determines the defective grasp of economic wholeness."[11] The Dionysian experiences antagonism as alternation, flux, turbulence, complexity, and Marxism has not quite internalized this. While Jorn still speaks in a Marxist vein of dialectic, he reads the dialectic as flux. Creation emerges out of giving oneself over to the play of alternating and ramifying movement, out of which something new can arise organically. Strangely enough, he sees in Engels's *Anti-Dühring* (1877) a critique of metaphysical thinking that can be extended to a critique of classical conception of form—and turned against itself. Engels's dialectic is not quite as mechanical as it is often taken to be.[12]

Here a space opens up for an *artistic materialism*. Parallel to the Marxist tradition runs an aesthetic one, from Cézanne to Miró and the Bauhaus artist Paul Klee.[13] Crucial to Jorn's reworking of Marxist thought is his radical revision of the locus and significance of the aesthetic. Art belongs to the infrastructure of society, not to the superstructure. Art is a fundamental kind of social production. Marxism breaks with classical tradition by assigning priority to action rather than contemplation, but its error is to consider art only as a form of contemplation. Art is action.

Engels wrote that "the economic structure of society always furnishes the real basis, starting from which we can alone work out the ultimate explanation of the whole superstructure of juridical and political institutions as well as of the religious, philosophical and other ideas of a given historical period."[14] Jorn would agree with this, but with the proviso that aesthetic practice is part of the economic structure, not just one of the "other ideas" within the superstructure. The qualitative practice of art is as much part of the base of the capitalist social formation as its quantitative production process. The ontological failure of capital, its inability to perceive and produce its own reality, stems from the domination of the quantitative over the qualitative process.

Jorn breaks with the privileging of science that he finds particularly in Engels. Jorn distinguishes between what he calls a *worldview* and an *attitude to life*. Both, he insists, can be materialist, but they do not always go together. Even when science has a materialist worldview, it does not necessarily have a materialist attitude to life. It remains

Apollonian. It sees matter as reducible to quantitative data, which in turn measure abstract forms and yield eternal laws. In 2009 Australian scientists discovered that bees on cocaine are much more enthusiastic about sources of food they have found.[15] The cocaine for these experiments was kept locked away by the university's ethics department, which released only enough for each experiment, thus ensuring that no cocaine would be consumed by scientists to make them more enthusiastic than otherwise about their data. This surely would qualify as an instance of the materialist worldview at work — scientific procedure, falsifiable results — without the materialist attitude to life. Everything about it is to remain partitioned from the everyday, which continues in its routine form, free from any whiff of the experimental. The materialist attitude to life is precisely materialism which takes the qualitative transformation of matter into life as primary. The limit for Jorn to *scientific* socialism is that it embraces a materialist worldview, but not a materialist attitude to life. His artistic materialism proposes to fill this gap.

Aesthetic experiment is the necessary complement to scientific experiment, but it is not an imitation of science. While science extends knowledge and expands the materialist worldview, art creates a way of life by shaping material characteristics according to desire. If science concerns itself with objective truth, then art will search for subjective truth. "Rather an entangled and chaotic truth than a four-square, beautiful, symmetrical and finely-chiseled lie." But, crucially, Jorn sees subjectivity as non-individualistic. The art that matters is a subjective realism that extends beyond the individual and invokes a collective practice: "art, therefore, is not a representation, a mirror, of nature but a direct transformation of nature."[16] Art is experimental social practice which transforms nature into second nature, but without reducing nature to essence or order.

Aesthetics is prior to ethics. Aesthetics is about desires; ethics is about duty. The capacity that matters in art is that of actualizing desires. What is best in the aesthetic is not the work of art as a representation of phenomena. Rather, the aesthetic has the capacity to become a part of people's habits of life. The aesthetic is a *cultivating* factor, forming and transforming habits of life. As such, the aesthetic is prior to science, which extracts regularities from the aesthetic, but is dependent on a given stage in its development for its materials. The aesthetic is also prior to all the branches of philosophy. It is that within which philosophy is situated. It is that which philosophy begins to think.

Ruling-class art—the Apollonian—represents the world as made in its own image, and assigns a subsidiary role in that representation for that which it fears. What it fears is the alignment of popular power with the forces of nature as an open-ended process, as the capacity to overthrow form, including political form. Dionysian art is folk memory of the social capacity to merge the processes of nature and desire. This is what attracted Jorn to ritual and mysticism. Unlike Bataille, he was not looking for traces of an ineffable absolute, but rather for a form of knowledge of the capacities latent in the social apprehension of the world. Art is a particular kind of knowledge and practice of the possible: "the highest achievement in art must lie in an orchestration of all our senses together in a communal expression."[17] The dérive already struck out on a path comparable to this. Communal expression will become a core program of the Situationist International, at least in its early years.

Art is playful; play is social. Play may take nature as its object, but not as a means to an end: "play is not consciously directed to any goal but is a delight, an identification with things themselves. This is why play develops best in community."[18] To correct a line from Lautréamont, poetry should be played by all. While Jorn aligns himself with the popular against ruling-class art, he does so critically. For a famous series of works called *Modifications* (1957–62), Jorn painted on some amateur pictures he bought in the flea market, but without obscuring the figures and landscapes of the Sunday painters. While Jorn approved of the democratization of art, it fell short of its own power. "The art of naïve adults in our society represents nothing more than the clumsy attempt to master the current forms of classical art."[19] The mistake lay in the imitation of existing forms, which tended also to preserve the idea of art as something separate from life. Popular art risked losing its playful quality. Following the Dutch historian Johan Huizinga (1872–1945), Jorn thought that "if play lacks its vital purpose then ceremony fossilizes into an empty form."[20] The solution was a popular art which did not imitate isolated forms but which applied itself to the transformation of matter. Art can extend the cooperative qualities of nature into social life.

From the Russian anarchist Peter Kropotkin, Jorn takes a sense of nature as cooperation, not as Darwinian struggle. Jornian nature does not really yield an ethical model to imitate. Nature, as Spinoza says, "subjects all things to a certain indifferent will."[21] Nature has no final cause, no end determined for it. Without at this time quite realizing it Jorn is heading away from the historical determinism of his Marxist training. In some respects he anticipates the Spinozism of Gilles Deleuze. Against the conventional image of one organism competing against another of the same kind, Deleuze proposes the image of the wasp and the orchid, two dissimilar organisms which cooperate to reveal and increase each other's powers.[22]

A reading of the natural sciences still has some critical work to do, however. From it Jorn extracts an ontology of nature as flux, difference and also cooperation on the basis of which Jorn asserts that class struggle is an aberration, and that the social Darwinist model of nature as competition is false. For Jorn, "man's nature is just to cultivate and nourish his urges."[23] Our species-being is *homo aestheticus*, close to what Huizinga called *homo ludens*, the playing kind. It is not *homo economicus*, or the war of all against all. This image of nature is merely a distorted image of capitalist society: "there is nothing so unnatural for man as what the bourgeoisie calls naturalness."[24]

It is Engels who leads Jorn down the slippery slope of a dialectics of nature, and like Engels he risks a somewhat vapid generalization of certain figures from scientific literature which, while in some ways different to capitalism's ideological recourse to a self-image as natural, are no less partial. But what distinguishes Jorn from Engels is not just that his readings in scientific literature are more contemporary; they are readings of a different kind. Jorn does not aspire to a materialist worldview, as Engels did, but a materialist attitude to life. He wants not a metaphysics legitimized by science but a *pataphysics* that reads science creatively. Rather than imitate scientific writing, Jorn—like Alfred Jarry—appropriates from scientific writing according to his own desires.[25] Truth for Jorn is subjective, but subjective truth is social. His ontology is true to the collective experience he lived through, of Hell-Horse, Danish socialism, the Resistance. His version of Marx diverges from all the main currents of what would come to be known as Western Marxism.[26] Unlike Lukács he embraces Engels's dialectic of nature; unlike Althusser he distances himself from the scientific worldview.

"All that we know of life is that it is organized movement." It is chaos and complexity: Tintomara's turn. The aesthetic begins by organizing the powers of matter and elaborating them in a way that responds to their complexity. A word for this might be *ornament*, but where ornament is not an exclusively human phenomenon: "we see air currents forming ornaments across the earth." Jorn is drawn to those frilly styles that modernism generally repudiated: Gothic, Rococo, Jugendstil. But the modern moment has its uses, and here Jorn's thinking comes close to Isidore Isou: "The tremendously consistent purge of empty ornamental elements of form is in reality classicism's Pyrrhic victory. It is a *tabula rasa* for what is to come; for an art of the future." That art will return to ornament not as an addition to nature or its representation, but as a process of drawing it out and turning it towards the expansion of the possibilities for social life. At its best, ornament demonstrates a "pact with the universe."[27] Ornament in art extends and distends the line as it is discovered in the social practice of qualitative engagement with matter. Ornament is the aesthetic key to Jorn's monism, the signature of a being that is univocal, and the reminder that history has diverged from coherence in flux.

Jorn's thought is opposed to art as representation, but also to abstraction, both in Max Bill and, more fundamentally, in Le Corbusier. His problem with Le Corbusier is that while he also drew inspiration from nature, he understands nature in Apollonian terms, paring away at complexity — nature's own ornamentation of itself — to get at an eternal geometrical essence. Le Corbusier aligns the aesthetic with a materialist worldview, but not a materialist attitude to life. Perhaps it is no surprise then that Le Corbusier took a top-down approach to building new worlds. Likewise, abstract art became dominant because a new ruling class could tolerate neither the symbols of the old one nor the express desires of the people. But the problem for the development of a popular art is a split between the symbol and the community. The symbols artists can come up with now are diagrams of personal forces, not social ones. This is a problem even for radical artists. Surveying the generation before his, Jorn observes that Klee found symbols, but not popular ones; Mayakovsky became the voice of the people, but at the expense of the symbol.[28]

Jorn took his distance from both socialist realist art and from abstraction, thus dodging the aesthetic fissure of the cold war. He found a way to reconcile them in what is best described as the *diagram*. He shared with Debord an attachment to the beauty of Paris street plans and subway maps, and saw them as part of a larger aesthetic tradition. "A map of the metro is not naturalistic, but it certainly cannot be said that it is unrealistic. We know the same method of working from modern [comic] strips in color magazines as well as from Bronze Age rock-carvings, from Chinese and Egyptian murals, from the drawings of Australian aborigines as well as from the modern art of people like Klee and Miró, and all this is in glaring contrast to the whole classical tradition of composition."[29] The goal must be a pictorial process free and open to the whole of life, a diagram of forces, trajectories, possibilities, rather than a representation of an object, cut from the world as a frozen moment.

Jorn was almost but not entirely seduced by the *primitive*. Natural culture for Jorn does not date from the Paleolithic, which is rather a time of alienation: "Class society arises when an unproductive tribe of hunters, specialized in weaponry, comes to dominate a cultured people and forces them into servile labor." The historical precedent for a natural culture is Neolithic agrarian society, with its experimental transformation of nature via agriculture, and its combination of the division of labor with a rough equality. Here humans "found the key to nature's way of developing."[30] Naturalism for Jorn is not a question of imitation but of qualitative development. Jorn's is a mystical materialism, in that he sees mystery as the intuition of the unity of being, of totality. But the significance of mystery has been betrayed by the course of historical development. "Instead of the materialist's ecstatic love for matter, life, mankind and himself, religions have turned to the non-existent, which is really to be equated with death but which religion calls God."[31] The sense of the univocity of being is lost, and with it the intuition of difference and flux.

Religion emerges because of the deviation from a truly naturalistic and social human development. In class society, religion replaces an open totality with a closed and imaginary one. Most strikingly, Jorn asserts that "communism is much older than all religions."[32] By communism Jorn means both a consistency between the spiritual and the temporal, and a collaborative practice of aesthetic transformation of nature. Originary mysticism is the worship of fertility, the materialistic cult par excellence. A modern reinstatement of mystery can supply a cultural ideology to Marxism which encourages everyone towards cultural activity. Put simply: "Art is cult." Culture is our species' love affair with the earth. This was the idyllic line of thought Jorn proposed in the wake of an era of mass destruction. "We have lost our paradise on earth and what is worse, those who seek to restore this paradise are seen as idiots estranged from life or individuals who are dangerous to society."[33] It is not God that is dead; death is God.

Dualism comes from class society: ruling-class spirit pits itself against subordinate class matter. From his—eccentric—reading of Kierkegaard, Jorn derived class society's three neuroses: art, ethics, and religion. Each produces a worldview of illusory unity in isolation from social processes. Against this, Jorn asserted the vitality of a spontaneous, creative aesthetics and a series of three revolutionary forms from below: anarchist, syndicalist and communist. But Jorn's attachment to the Communist Party waned rapidly after the war. Cobra failed as a movement at least in part because it positioned itself as a communist art form, only to be rejected and vilified by party art commissars.[34] It is not hard to see in his feverish theoretical activities of the 1950s and his various organizations an attempt to create a fourth form of radical monism, one for which Debord would propose the name —Situationist.

One thing that united the two men was Jorn's explicit and Debord's implicit rejection of the dualistic philosophy of Jean-Paul Sartre, in which *situation* figured as a key if somewhat troubling concept. Sartre's wartime classic *Being and Nothingness* (1943) famously makes the category of *freedom* a central one, but in so doing it has a sly recourse also to the category of situation. That which is for-itself, consciousness, presupposes something external to it. "There can be a free for-itself only in a resisting world."[35] It is because of the intractable physicality of things that freedom arises as freedom. If it were enough to conceive of a project for it to be realized, then, like the surrealists, Sartre would be "plunged in a world like that of a dream in which the possible is no longer in any way distinguished from the real," and Sartre could no longer distinguish a fiction from a desire. Once this gap disappears, then freedom disappears too. To be free is not to have what one desires, but to determine oneself to desire. To desire is to act on that desire. To be free is, paradoxically, not a choice. We are "condemned to freedom." Even a decision not to be free presupposes freedom. Freedom exists only in the end it posits, but its existence is not given in that end. "Thus the empirical and practical concept of freedom is wholly negative; it issues from the consideration of a situation and establishes that this situation leaves me free to pursue this or that end."

What then is this situation that leaves Sartre free to pursue this or that end? Writing during wartime, Sartre's example of a situation is telling: "Remove the prohibition to circulate in the streets after curfew, and what meaning can there be for me to have the freedom ... to take a walk at night?" Sartre goes out for a walk in the city at night during curfew. The street might look beautiful to him, or it might not, but this is just the street as an object of contemplation. As a situation it is something else. The situation is the common product of its own unknowable facticity and of Sartre's freedom. The situation is an ambiguous phenomenon in which consciousness cannot distinguish in advance the contribution of freedom and the contribution of the in-itself.

The street Sartre wants to walk is the object of his freedom. His freedom selects it. But what his freedom cannot determine is whether it can be walked safely without running into the police. This is part of the brute existence of the street. But the street only reveals its hazards to his walking it when he makes it the object of his desire to walk. He integrates it into the project of walking. He cannot determine in advance what comes from freedom (the for-itself) and what from the in-itself of the street. Sartre: "it is only in and through the free upsurge of a freedom that the world develops and reveals the resistance which can render the projected end realizable." There is no obstacle in an absolute sense. It is Sartre who determines what is a constraint on freedom by positing freedom in the first place. Thus while the curfew appears as a limit to his action, it is his freedom which constitutes the method and the ends of action in relation to which the curfew appears then as a limit.

What meaning can there be in the freedom to walk at night, through the Paris of the mid 1950s, the curfew of the occupation lifted and the curfew of the Algerian war not yet descended? The dérive appears almost as if it is a direct answer to this question. The dérive is the experimental mapping of a situation, the trace of the probabilities of realizing a desire. There is still the police to contend with, and delinquent Letterists and their friends would occasionally end up in jail for the night. But the dérive is more than the no-man's-land between

consciousness and facticity, for-itself and in-itself, freedom and constraint. It is rather the flux, the monist dialectic, which produces as one
of its effects the experience of the gap between in-itself and for-itself
in the first place.

Practices like dérive, détournement and potlatch, which will become
the defining practices of the Situationist International, produce among
other things the possibility of new concepts outside of Sartrean
dualism. The interest is not in consciousness and its freedom, but in the
production of new situations as an end in themselves. In the Letterist
International, Jorn saw fellow travelers engaged in the critical practice
of producing an autonomous space for new practices.

Jorn's amateur Marxist theories from the 1940s and early '50s went
largely unpublished at the time and received scant attention. The most
influential appropriation of Marxist thought would not be Sartre's but
that of Jorn's contemporary, Louis Althusser. They could hardly be more
different.[36] Althusser spent the war in a POW camp, not the Resistance.
Althusser's thought was in Jorn's terms clearly that of a materialist
worldview. It took science rather than aesthetic practice as its model.
Althusser stayed within the Communist Party (with Maoist sympa-
thies) rather than break with it. He made Marxism respectable within
the space of the academy, rather than attempting to found a new nexus
between theory and practice outside of it. Althusser was much more
interested in history as objective process than as subjective practice.
Where Althusser became a respected academic philosopher, Jorn's
academic advisor gently suggested that his thesis was not really the
sort of thing that could even be submitted. Like Walter Benjamin's,
Jorn's doctoral work is of interest because of its failure of good
academic form.

And these are precisely the reasons why Jorn now merits attention,
and why his thought deserves development. Jorn points towards the
question of practice, outside of, and now after the eclipse of, both the
Communist and bourgeois versions of history. If Althusser cements a
place within the academy for developing Marxism as a critical postwar
discourse, he does so at the expense of aligning it with high theory.
Marx is absorbed into the conventions of academic thought, into its
spaces of authority, its codes of discipline, its temporality of semesters
and sabbaticals. Jorn offers something in addition to all that. His is a
development of Marx as a critical postwar discourse that creates its

own games, makes its own rules, answers to a quite different time, and belongs to a more marginal but more interesting space, the space not of an institution but of a provisional micro-society, within which the practice of thought might be otherwise.

5   A Provisional Micro-Society

The Situationist International was founded at a meeting of three women and six men in July 1957. All that remains of this fabled event are a series of stirring documents and some photographs, casual but made with an artist's eye, by founding member Ralph Rumney.[1] The Situationist International dissolved itself in 1972. In its fifteen years of existence, only seventy-two people were ever members. It was born out of the fusion of two and a half existing groups, the Movement for an Imaginist Bauhaus, the Letterist International and the London Psycho-geographical Society (the last represented by its one and only member, Rumney). Its founding conference took place in Cosio di Arroscia a little Ligurian town where founding member Piero Simondo's family had a small hotel. Or at least that's the official story. Debord writes in a letter to Jorn: "I think it is necessary for us to present the 'Conference at Cosio' as a point of departure for our distinct organized activity."[2] From the beginning, Debord has a fine hand for the tactics of appearances.

Debord the tactician saw the Letterist International as something of a dead end. The dérive could only be taken so far. After he was institutionalized, Chtcheglov would write Debord and Bernstein from the sanatorium explaining that the dérive has its limits, and cannot be practiced continually. "It's a miracle it didn't kill us. Iron infected our blood."[3] To even propose a new architecture for a new way of life took more resources than they possessed. The complete renunciation of what one might now call middle-class life cut them off from vital resources. "To reach this superior cultural creation—that which we call the Situationist game—we now think it necessary to be an active force in the actual terrain of this era's culture (and not on the fringes of it, as we cheerfully were ...)." Hence the change of policy from the "pure (inactive) extremism" of the Letterist International.[4] Going forward called for taking a few steps back. The project would — temporarily — require some resources to advance its aims. The Situationist game must proceed "by all means, even artistic ones."[5]

Debord skillfully positioned himself as the secretary for a new movement, the Situationist International. Of all the roles Debord chose for himself, not to mention those assigned to him by posterity, the one that receives the least attention is that of secretary. Late in life he was to say: "I have been a good professional — but in what?"[6] While the question was meant to be rhetorical, one not entirely implausible answer would be — as a secretary. Not the least interesting thing about him might be the tactics with which he ran the Situationist International, and the best way to approach them is via his *Correspondence*. Prepared by his widow Alice Becker-Ho (b. 1941) and published posthumously, the *Correspondence* presents a carefully vetted and selected account of Debord the secretary.

The secretary's task, as Debord conceives it, involves the organizing of exhibitions, provocations, occasional publications and, above all, the journal *Internationale Situationniste*. It is, Debord writes, "our 'official organ,' the ideological coherence of which was made my responsibility." Debord will act as secretary with remarkable tenacity and industry. *Internationale Situationniste* would not be a duplicated flyer like the Letterist International's *Potlatch*, but a beautifully edited, illustrated, designed and bound affair. By 1960 the author of "Never work!" would be complaining: "I am overwhelmed with work." Here he is discussing the use of a material called Lumaline for the cover, in a way that will bring a smile to anyone who has ever labored over manufacturing something beautiful: "The effect is obviously superb. But the price is terribly high: 100,000 for the cover (for only 1,600 copies of the journal), but especially 60,000 for supplementary expenses to the printer, representing a lot of work in folding and sewing, entirely by hand — the machines break the Lumaline, which soon tears. And then we will have nearly lost the stock at that stage of assembly (in this process, one loses at least 10 percent due to badly sewn copies)."[7]

Debord labored in the service of producing *Internationale Situationniste* as a collective expression, a document of a provisional micro-society whose practice is to treat all of culture as collective property. "Our editorial committee has a heavy hand (and, as you may imagine, no respect for literary propriety)." Détournement was both a signature Situationist practice and a theory of how culture as a totality works. Debord writes to Straram in Canada: "All the material published by the Situationist International is, in principle, usable by everyone, even without acknowledgment, without the preoccupations of literary property. You can make all the détournements that appear useful to you."[8]

One makes a movement with what one has. The practice of the *exclusion* of members from the Situationist International begins very soon after its founding. As a good secretary, Debord has little tolerance for opportunism or ineptitude. He writes to Walter Olmo, a founding member: "I reproach you for having accepted, in particular circumstances, several ideas that are stupid." Olmo will not last long. Ralph Rumney lasts almost a year. Debord writes to him in March 1958: "you still haven't done any real work with us."[9] To compound Debord's annoyance, Rumney boasts of his Situationist connections to art-world acquaintances.

Rumney's official offense was to submit his psychogeographical report on Venice too late for inclusion in the journal. Between harassment by his mother-in-law, Peggy Guggenheim, and the birth of his son, Rumney had his hands full.[10] Since he was the one at Cosio who advocated zero tolerance towards anyone not fully committed to the cause, his expulsion was fair enough. Rumney's "The Leaning Tower of Venice" went unpublished at the time, but it is not without interest. It took the form of a détournement of the photo-romance strips then particularly popular in Italy, and is an early example of Situationist détournement of narrative graphic art.

Rumney took photographs of the Beat writer Alan Ansen and arranged them as a narrative with captions. "It is our thesis that cities should embody a built-in play factor," reads one. "We are studying here a play-environment relationship." Rumney's photographs follow Ansen on a "trajectory through the zones of psycho-geographic interest." Its subject is specifically play, as "play and game are not synonymous." Ansen's gambols are not constrained by formal rules. There is no boundary marking of the space of a game from the space outside it. Play has no conditions for winning or losing, and no end condition determined in advance. Play simply comes to an end when Runmey spots Lawrence Alloway, the English art critic, and in this case spoil-sport.[11]

Becoming a Situationist required a certain rigor. Debord: "I am still with the Situationist International and, as long as I am in it, I will keep a minimum of discipline that excludes all collaboration with uncontrollable elements."[12] To today's middle-class sensibility, submission to a discipline for reasons other than getting paid seems like some kind of perversion, and for that reason membership in the Situationist International seems as unintelligible a sacrifice as the mysteries of religion. A more common model for what remains of the artist in today's disintegrating spectacle is that of the small business proprietor. Take as an example Jeff Koons (b. 1955), who "staked his budding penchant for expensively fabricated art by working as a commodities broker on Wall Street for six years ... Today he has a factory in Chelsea with ninety regular assistants."[13] To be an artist, it seems, has become just another kind of middle-class ambition, the dream of a franchise with your name on it.

The exclusion of members is sometimes taken to reveal some sinister side to Debord's character, so it is interesting to read in the *Correspondence* that "Jorn was the first partisan of the measure of exclusion." Jorn was one of the few Situationists who had ever been a member of an orthodox Communist party. But while the Situationist International is often compared to such a party, the parallel is usually made by people who have never belonged to one. Certainly, to an ear trained by the cold war to protect its precious individualism, the Situationists can sound like invasive body snatchers, as for example in this telegram to an excluded member: "The I without we falls back into the prefabricated mass."[14] What the Situationists were struggling to achieve was a new kind of collective being, unlike both the Communists and previous avant-gardes such as the Letterists.

Situationists were expected to know what was expected of them, and without being told. Debord's policy as secretary was "to place a priori confidence, in all cases, and only until the first proof to the contrary, in a certain number of recognized comrades, based upon objective criteria." The reason for most exclusions is not mysterious. It was a failure to live up to expectations. Members are what they do: "No problem in our collective action can be resolved by goodwill." A certain unsentimental understanding of how friendships form and dissolve, of how character becomes different to itself as it struggles in and against time, underlies the distinctive quality of Situationist subjectivity in which "neither freedom nor intelligence are given once and for all."[15]

Bataille had thought that what binds community together is the experience of death.[16] Under the guidance of the surrealist turned Stalinist Louis Aragon (1897–1982), postwar communist culture created a real cult out of its dead Resistance fighters. The red flag shrouds its martyred dead, whose blood dyes its every fold. The Situationists borrowed at least this much from the communists—that the exclusion of living members meant social death. Given that communist culture really did comprise an entire social world, to be excluded from the party really did mean excommunication. The Situationists had no such power. But they wrestled with the problem of how to make collective belonging meaningful, as something requiring some sacrifice. The possibility of exclusion made participation in the Situationist game meaningful.

Not the least difference between the Situationists and the Communist Party is that the former rarely recruited. "I have no need of fabricating false disciples." Nor was adherence to doctrinal orthodoxy required. "Quite surely, never any doctrine: perspectives. A solidarity around these perspectives." Indeed, doctrinaire postures could be grounds for exclusion. Debord writes to Simondo: "situationism, as a body of doctrine, does not exist and must not exist. What exists is a Situationist experimental attitude"—something like the Jornian materialist attitude to life. This is the paradox of the doctrine of no doctrine. To Pinot Gallizio, who Jorn had recruited for the Imaginist Bauhaus, and who was the key figure among the Italian founders of the Situationist International, Debord writes: "We have always been sure that you are strongly opposed to the metaphysics of which Simondo currently reveals the dogmas."[17] The exclusion of Gallizio would take a while longer than Simondo.

In his letters, Debord often mentions "propaganda" and even "internal propaganda." Both for external and internal purposes, statements were to be formed and made tactically. The Situationist International formed itself in part out of the material of the art world, but anticipated the overcoming of art as a separate practice. Hard to grasp for the middle-class sensibility of what Debord will call "bourgeois civilization" is that there really might have been a threat to the organization—in the form of the opportunistic exploitation of the potential cachet of the

Situationist International, particularly by its artist members. The Situationists were never an *artistic* avant-garde. Debord: "we already have amongst us too many artistically old men who have missed out on their own nineteenth century."[18] Artists were only accepted as members if they appeared ready to move beyond art, in a "brutal evolution"—as Debord said of the ill-fated German artists of the Spur group.

Situationists create new collaborative play-forms out of the old materials of the separate creative practices, of which art was just one. The moments of inclusion and exclusion within the Situationist International are best explored in relation to this strategy, rather than attempting to decode them as banal dramas of personality. "The most urgent problem, tactically, is to firstly balance, then as quickly as possible surpass the number of painters in the Situationist International with the largest possible number of architects, urbanists, sociologists and others." This ambition came with its own dangers. "We can hardly have confidence in 'specialized collaborators' who do not share Situationist experimental positions. If not, we will discover bitterly that the architects, sociologists, urbanists, etc. are as limited as the painters in their defense of the particular prejudices of their separate sectors."[19] The Situationist International was not a collaboration between specialists, but the overcoming of specialization in the name of a new kind of collective activity.

As secretary Debord tacks this way and that, trying to keep the International together. Debord's problems are compounded by the presence of several powerful personalities, all of them his senior. Around the time the Situationist International was founded, Debord was twenty-five, Constant was thirty-seven, Jorn was forty-three, and Gallizio fifty-five. These discrepancies should be borne in mind when reading his letters to each of them. Given his relative youth, the self-confidence of the letters is extraordinary. The tone of Debord's writing fluctuates considerably in his attempts to engage with each of these outsize personalities, even if he does not lack confidence in calling all of them to account. As one of Debord's favorite writers, the Cardinal de Retz, says: "The talent of insinuation is of more service than that of persuasion, because one can insinuate to a hundred where one can barely persuade five."[20]

Giuseppe Gallizio (1902–64), Pinot to his friends, was, by his own account, an "archaeologist, botanist, chemist, parfumer, partisan, king of the gypsies."[21] To which one might add: chancer, amateur, dandy, dilettante. It was he, together with Asger Jorn, who convened the Congress of Free Artists in 1956 in Gallizio's hometown of Alba. This was the event that laid the groundwork for the formation of the Situationist International the following year in Cosio, where he would become a founding member. Gallizio's approach was consistently experimental, and he saw the materials and practices of an experimental comportment as available to everyone: "the masses have understood and already the breathlessness of a new poetic moment is anxiously beating at the doors of people bored by the tired ideals fabricated by the self-righteous incomprehension of the mysterious powerful of the earth."[22] Gallizio called his method *ensemble painting*. His goal was what he called an *anti-patent* process for the sharing and modification of life.

Gallizio's ensembles did not just produce rare and singular works, like other artists. They produced *industrial painting*. These were only very minimally the product of actual machines. The idea was more that painting could be made using mechanisms of repetition and variation to undermine the unique gesture. The result would bring together the creative and singular with the serial and repeated. He invented, in short, a synthesis of the two opposed strands of the avant-garde: surrealism and constructivism, in what Michèle Bernstein called "a shrewd mixture of chance and mechanics." As art historian Mirella Bandini put it, his project was to "unleash inflation everywhere."[23]

Debord pours considerable energy into arranging Gallizio's debut in the French and German art worlds. At first all goes well: "The tumult over your glory grows great, despite the discretion we maintain." But art-world success is Gallizio's downfall within the Situationist International. This is less the fault of the exhibition itself than of the way it is used tactically: "The most serious deficiency was that Pinot, in his practical attitude toward the Parisian public, more or less consciously accepted the role of a very ordinary artist recognized by his peers (by contrast, the exhibition of détourned paintings by Jorn [the *Modifications*] was, I believe, a very rough break with this milieu ...)." The upshot was the exclusion of Gallizio and his son Giors Melanotte for "sickening arrivisme." As Debord would comment much later: "the Situationist International knew how to fight its own glory."[24]

While Debord could recognize, even in retrospect, Gallizio's "virtuosity," he was nevertheless the *right wing* of the Situationist International.[25]

Its *left wing* was Constant Nieuwenhuys. He had been a member of the Cobra group with Jorn, but had moved away from painting towards experiments in new kinds of potential urban form. In the "Amsterdam Declaration" of 1958, Debord and Constant called for "the development of complete environments, which must extend to a unitary urbanism" which they saw as "the complex, ongoing activity that consciously recreates man's environment according to the most advanced conceptions in every domain," as the "result of a new type of collective creativity."[26] A poetry played by all; an *all* played by poetry.

It was Gallizio who set Constant on the path to his famous New Babylon project of *unitary urbanism* when the two of them were together in Alba. Gallizio, who was on the local town council, solved the problem of the town's antipathy to visiting Romani, or Gypsies, by making some land he owned available for their camp. It was an idea not without precedent. As Alice Becker-Ho writes, quoting from a 1569 text: "Their sojourns in particular villages are always sanctioned by the local squires or dignitaries."[27] Gallizio commissioned Constant to design a new kind of mobile architecture that might house them. Constant's model was never built, but it set Constant on a new path. He would come to reject art in general, and painting in particular, and like Gallizio posit the machine as the central fact of contemporary creativity, writing: "A free art of the future is an art that would master and use all the new conditioning techniques."[28]

Yet Constant and Gallizio were in many respects quite incompatible figures, and not just as personalities. For Constant, art had come to an end. A unitary urbanism of constructed situations supersedes all of the separate arts. "The artists' task is to invent new techniques and to utilize light, sound, movement and any invention whatsoever which might influence ambience. Without this, the integration of art in the construction of human habitat remains as chimerical as the proposals of [Ivan Chtcheglov]."[29] In principle, Debord agrees. "No painting is defensible from a Situationist point of view." But where Constant insists on the principle, the secretary does not want to get too far ahead of the memberships's level of consciousness. "Yes, any spirit of the 'pictorial' must be hounded and this, though obvious, isn't easy to get everyone to acknowledge."[30]

Debord looks to Constant as a tactical ally, but tries strenuously to keep him from pushing the organization too far too fast. He wants

Constant to work on the editorial line for the journal with this in mind: "This will certainly help the really experimental faction in the Situationist International." But Debord is initially reluctant to break with Gallizio or Jorn, both of whom are earning Constant's stern disapproval as *artists*. "I don't have the right—and I do not have the least desire—to try to impose directives on the painters (for instance) in the name of a real movement that is no more advanced than their work."[31] A shrewd move, since for Debord to attempt to direct the painters would only draw him—and the Situationists—deeper into the obsessions of the art world.

The unraveling of Debord's relationship with Constant is the great moment in the early life of the Situationist International, and shapes the whole space of what will be possible for it. Debord is caught between the left and right wings of the movement. And though the artists are excluded one by one, Constant is not appeased and resigns anyway, and the movement, so to speak, moves on. But this is the moment, like the opening scene in a novel or film, where circumstances are fluid, where many things are possible. One discovers in the first three years of the Situationist International many potential versions of it, besides the ones of legend or even historical record. This is perhaps why so many keep returning to them, and to these early years in particular, as the scene of a moment in still-living movement, or in other words, a situation.

Debord's judgments in the *Correspondence*, whether one agrees with them or not, are not purely capricious. Against Constant and the Dutch section, Debord makes two charges, both in many respects perspicacious. The first is that there is a strand in Constant which, despite his denials, is close to the utopian legacy of Saint-Simon and Auguste Comte, particularly in the way it privileges an intellectual class as the only agents for bringing about a new world: "when you only find progressive forces in the 'intellectuals who revolt against cultural poverty,' you yourselves are utopians. What can intellectuals do without liaison with an enterprise that brings global change to social relations?"[32] Liaison, in short, with the proletariat. While Jorn was starting to rethink class in interesting ways, the Situationist International was at something of an impasse, caught in the old dilemma between romantic revolt and class struggle.

The second issue concerns the status of unitary urbanism. Where Constant is focused on the way unitary urbanism realizes and overcomes the more limited achievements of the separate arts, Debord is already looking ahead to realizing and overcoming unitary urbanism: "Our necessary activity is dominated by the question of the totality. Take note of it. Unitary urbanism is not a conception of the totality, must not become one. It is an operational instrument to construct an extended detour."[33] While Debord and Constant are allies in their embrace of technicity (against the rather technophobic Jorn), Debord does not think it enough any more to just break down the arts and combine them in the construction of new ambiences, new terrains of play. Unitary urbanism is much less a positive, constructive modeling and more a negative and critical tactic for opposing the kind of tower-block mentality that characterized postwar reconstruction. The chimerical quality of Chtcheglov's version of unitary urbanism still has a tactical value.

Legend has it that when Debord broke with people he simply cut them dead and moved on. With Constant this was not the case, and for once the correspondence continues on, to the stage of a love gone wrong. "Passion leads you astray," writes Debord to Constant, sounding for all the world like Madame de Merteuil in *Dangerous Liaisons* (1782). Playing Valmont, Constant retorts by telegram: "If passion misleads me, indecision causes you to be lost." Debord resorts to threats: "it is up to you to choose the terrain."[34]

"Staying friends with Constant was quite difficult. He liked to fight," says Jacqueline de Jong. At stake are 200 copies of Constant's book, which Debord feels are owed to him. It may sound like just a pretext, but one of the essential components of the Situationist International was the internal exchange of documents and their *donation* to external parties. As this incident highlights, the group was held together by the gift. The gift enters via the writings of the socialist anthropologist Marcel Mauss (1872–1950), which were taken up and expanded into a theory of the general economy by Georges Bataille. Both drew on anthropological work by Franz Boas (1858–1942) and others working among Native Americans of the Pacific Northwest, and their concept of *potlatch*. This version of the gift linked it closely to reputation. The gift is not selfless charity, nor is it a Christmas present.[35] Rather, it is a very special kind of donation, in which the donor gives away valuable time, matter and energy in order to acquire reputation. The journal of the Letterist International was called

Potlatch, and despite the meager resources of the group it was given away for free.

The Situationists sold their journal in bookshops, but many were given away and for the same reasons: to exchange time, energy and materials for reputation. The Situationist International was a provisional micro-society founded on its own quite particular economy of donation and reputation. While some of its activities might be supported by selling art to collectors or other banal forms of compensated labor, there is a sense in which the Situationist International was a grand potlatch, consigning to the flames the thought and work of a whole little community, daring the world to match its extravagant consumption of its own time. Hence the donation of copies was no mere pretext in Debord's quarrel with Constant, for if Constant refused to donate them it would constitute a real break in the economy—if that is what it was—of this micro-society. It was a quite paradoxical economy.

The philosopher Jacques Derrida (1930–2004) was Debord's contemporary, although beyond that they had little in common except perhaps rather nuanced notions of the gift. Derrida: "The gift is the gift of giving itself and nothing else."[36] Marcel Mauss had thought of a gift economy as driven by an underlying generosity, the very *mana* of socialism. Debord and in particular Jorn practiced it in much the same spirit, and even saw it as the basis for a break beyond socialist thought and action. But Claude Lévi-Strauss (1908–2009) took thinking about the gift away from the "shop girl's philosophy" of everyday life, and in the direction instead of a structural logic of exchange.[37] This line of thought would flourish in the hands of Roland Barthes (1915–80) and Louis Althusser, where gift exchange reappears as the structural logic of symbolic exchange, and becomes the technique by which the superstructures of capitalist society can be decoded. They wanted a parallel competence to the *marxisant* political economy still thought to explain the workings of the base. Derrida proposes instead that the gift must interrupt the economy. The gift is not supposed to be returned. It is outside circulation and circular time. Giving suspends all calculation. The gift is canceled by any reciprocation, return, debt, countergift or exchange. Derrida departs from anthropology by thinking the gift in its singularity, outside of exchange, to reveal just how troubling it is to any such structural logic.

If the recipient of a gift recognizes it as a gift, then it ceases to be one.

"If it presents itself then it no longer presents itself." For Derrida this opens up an intriguing realm of paradox and a way to get payback on his structuralist precursors. For the Situationsts, the very impossibility of the pure gift calls into being a whole terrain of possibility for an art and politics of the impurity of the gift. Every impure donation forces both giver and receiver into the invention of an attitude to life that can accept the donation, but not exchange it. The invention of everyday life could be nothing but the inventive accommodation to donation, to the subtle art of not returning the donation, of giving again in a way that is not circular, that does not simply pass on the debt.

Exchange affirms the identities of givers and receivers, and the value of the thing exchanged. Exchange arises as a way to contain the disturbing capacities of the gift. "The subject and the object are arrested effects of the gift." This might be the last nobility left to life: to give and not receive, receive and not gift, to invent *unreturnable acts* (another name for which might be situations). Not only does Derrida construct a theory of the gift, his writing inserts itself into just such an unreturnable practice, or tries to. The Situationist International composed a whole micro-society on the premise of potlatch, that is, the art and politics of the donation. Potlatch is not really sustainable. It's a game, a challenge. It isn't a circular exchange. The early years of the Situationist International are a game of potlatch, of the donation time, in which the players, in the end, run out of moves. For Debord in particular, the challenge of the gift of time went, in his terms, unmet. It was time to forget and move on.

In the end, the gifted but impetuous left of the movement is no better for Debord's purposes than the *sprezzatura* of the easygoing right. Here, in a couple of sentences addressed to Constant, Debord speaks all at once of a crisis of friendship, of tactics and thought at a crossroads: "I am sure that, here, we have arrived at the point where the Situationist International must immediately choose (or must be abandoned). Because you know well that I have always thought that 'there are moments at which it is necessary to know how to choose'; that you haven't needed to teach this to me; and that, if there has been a certain opportunism in the Situationist International, I have been among those (you, too) who have counter-balanced it."[38] The collapse of the Situationist International into the art world that Debord feared did not happen, at least not yet. The vigorous application of the principle of exclusion—that generously ungenerous act—took care of that.

The Situationist International exercises a continued fascination because its members made a gift of their time that was not returned. They did not really take their place in the exchanges of views between the journals and groups of their time. Their beautiful, expensive journal—with Lumaline covers or not—did not so much circulate as spiral off into the void. Until May '68 appeared, and appeared to many as the return of the gift in spades. But still, something remains of an uncanceled gift.

The early years of the Situationist International are ones in which it may develop itself, elaborate itself, ornament itself—in many possible directions. The movement exercises a lasting fascination on art historians for this reason. All of the major figures of the early years have their favorites, who excise them from the game and hoist them up as their champions. What is perhaps more interesting is to keep these figures in play, to view what passes between them as what matters. And perhaps also what passes unnoticed, undetected in this flux of passions between temperamental men. When Michèle Bernstein writes in her two novels of exactly this remarkable time in which the Situationist International was born, the squabbles that animate the men barely rate a mention. It is just something a character not unlike Debord takes a train to Amsterdam to attend to, before hurrying back to a quite different kind of game. A game in which women not only figure, but which they may even win.

6 Permanent Play

On the subject of love, bourgeois novels are variations on two themes. The first is the couple in love getting together despite all obstacles; the second is how unhappily they live ever after. "Marriage seems to have been invented to reward perversity," the utopian socialist writer Charles Fourier once said.[1] Marriage, says the bourgeois novel, is the worst of institutions for a woman, except for all the others. In the novel, a woman can refuse marriage. She may be drawn towards sexual ecstasy, but that way lies poverty, misery and social exclusion. Proper love is of the sacred domesticated kind, placed in the service of reproducing the heterosexual family and passing on property. Socialist writers, from Fourier to Engels to Alexandra Kollontai had long opposed marriage as a relation which makes women into property, and pointed to the hypocrisy of the bourgeois gentleman who polices the sexual fidelity of his wife yet goes adventuring in bohemia for a bit on the side.

And yet in postwar France, the figure of the monogamous, heterosexual couple became ever more widespread. Kristin Ross: "the construction of the new French couple is not only a class necessity but a national necessity as well, linked to the state-led modernization effort. Called upon to lead France into the future, these couples are the class whose very way of life is based on the wish to make the world futureless and at that price buy security."[2] The couple was a modern alternative to both the more reactionary order of the wartime collaborationist Vichy regime, and the autonomous female sexuality embodied by Saint-Germain figures like Juliette Gréco or Françoise Sagan, and promulgated as a theory in Simone de Beauvoir's *The Second Sex*. The couple refuses both the patriarchal past of Vichy and the feminist future of *The Second Sex*, and secures a private space where the good life of the spectacle can be brought home and domesticated.

In the third issue of *Internationale Situationniste* is a reproduction of the "Map of Tenderness" by the Precocity movement writer Madeleine de Scudéry (1607–1701). This famous drawing was included in her popular multivolume novel *Clélie*. The map charts three possible journeys from the town of New Friendship at the bottom. Friendship could take the paths of Inclination, Esteem or Gratitude to one of three destinations in the center of the map. It could wander off course, and end up in dismal places such as the Lake of Indifference. Or the journey could go too far, into uncharted territory. For de Scudéry, love requires skill and tact if it is not to lurch towards great ecstasy, which also brings great pain.

The goal was not marriage. De Scudéry was more interested in erotic friendship between women. Hers was a Sapphic alternative to Platonic relationships between men, a tenderness that can be sustained, developed, transformed and ornamented, without rupture. De Scudéry initiates a counter-tradition, skeptical of the sacred quality of ecstasy, indifferent to questions of property and outside the heterosexual norm.[3] While acknowledging the power of feeling, it can nevertheless be crafted and directed. It can become the material of play and strategy.

How is a modern woman who lives in a so-called *open relationship* with a man supposed to retain her hold on him, if he starts an affair that has a little more intensity than usual? Affairs are allowed. They are within the rules, but they are not supposed to break with a fundamental agreement between the man and the woman. And if this man is coming too close to breaching that agreement, what stratagems can the woman employ to see that he returns to it? This scenario can be found in what Debord calls Michèle Bernstein's "fake novel" *All the King's Horses*, and its sequel *The Night*.[4] These books, which both describe the same events, concern the lives of three characters who are not unlike Michèle Bernstein, her husband Guy Debord, and his lover Michèle Mochot. Bernstein borrows from socialist, bohemian and aristocratic writings to create an alternative to the middle-class ideal of the married couple. "The personal is political," as feminists would say later in the 1960s, but for Bernstein, writing in the early '60s, the political is very, very personal.[5]

Both novels cover the same events in the lives of Gilles and Geneviève, but from different perspectives and in different styles: *King's*

Horses adopts the style of Françoise Sagan (1935–2004); *The Night,* that of Alain Robbe-Grillet (1922–2008). Saint-Germain identity Sagan's racy novels coincided with the arrival of mass paperback publishing in France in the 1950s. Those of Robbe-Grillet were a high-modernist analogue of the new consumerist and technocratic France of those years. Lefebvre called them "pure spectacle." As Maurice Blanchot pointed out at the time, what was once a cultural rhythm to the diffusion of writing had with the arrival of the paperback been replaced by a technical one. The technical purported to solve all problems. "There is no need for political upheaval, and even less for changes in the social structure. It suffices to reproduce works."[6] Even radical works started appearing in paperback. Literature discreetly integrated itself into the spectacle.

Bernstein's strategy was a détournement of the spectacle of the novel, first in its popular form, then its literary form. "There is not much future in the détournement of complete novels," declared Debord and Wolman, "but during the transitional phase there might be a certain number of undertakings of this sort." Elsewhere, Debord sets out the tenets of a Situationist approach to literature in the transitional phase: "In the novel, the fundamental question of time resided more in the liberty of beginning and ending the story at significant points, rather than in the choice of including certain moments and excluding others … I believe it is this form of sovereignty (used derisorily in the novel) that everyday life aims at appropriating."[7] In the absence of the means to construct situations, the détourned novel might at least gesture towards the liberty of beginnings.

Debord met cabaret singer Michèle Mochot in 1955, at a Paris opening for the Belgian surrealist painter Jane Graverol.[8] Bernstein's fictional Gilles meets Carole a few years later, also at an opening of a surrealist painter, only Bernstein's painter is male and Carole is his stepdaughter. In *The Night* we learn of the sexual tension between them. The painter covets his stepdaughter. "Though by her spite she showed that she wanted no part of it, still she encouraged it a little, admitted it was there."[9] With a little prompting from Carole's mother, Gilles and Geneviève whisk Carole away from the old man. Gilles takes her wandering around the streets of Paris, and in the morning finally makes love to her.

In *Horses*, we only hear in general terms about Gilles and his art of wandering. Geneviève goes home to sleep and the story picks up again the next day. *The Night* is structured around the dérive itself.

> They pass beside a column, a streetlight rather, on which is fixed, above their heads, a blue and white sign indicating by an arrow: Cluny Museum. On the same column, another signal, luminous and blinking, is the only one that attracts the glance of the passersby. At regular intervals, for the pedestrians, the permission to go or the order to wait flashes. Gilles and Carole pass near the column without seeing it. Gilles waits, before crossing, for the cars to stop. Carole follows Gilles, who holds her by the nape of the neck. They take the direction indicated by the sign Cluny Museum, and skirt the railings of the garden of the museum.

The dérive is Carole's initiation into the knotted streets of the sleeping city. "I'd like to be in a labyrinth with you," says Carole. "We already are," says Gilles.[10]

A Galton machine is a grid of equally spaced pins, arranged vertically, above which is a single slot that releases balls, and below which is a series of slots that catch them. If the top slot is positioned in the middle and balls are released into the grid of pins, the chances are that most balls will deviate a bit when they hit the pins but will fall in one of the center slots below. A few of the balls will end up bouncing farther off the center line, but overall the device will show a *Gaussian distribution*. It's essentially pinball without the fun. Pinball arrived in Saint-Germain bars such as the Mabillon and the Old Navy after the war, and became a favorite way for quarter people to waste time. Arthur Adamov wrote an absurdist play about it called *Ping-Pong* (1955).[11]

In pinball, the ball is always going to end up passing through the middle between the flippers, but some balls—through luck or skill—will take longer to do so. The Galton machine, or pinball, is Jorn's image of a *situology*, both ludic and analytic, "as a game device, this machine that tilts, can be found in most Paris bistros, and is the possibility of calculated variability."[12] Time and space are not smooth or even. There are tilts, there are eddies, there are zones that attract the balls and zones that repel them. Debord and Wolman had already proposed a détournement of pinball, in which the "play of the lights and the more or less predictable trajectories of the balls would form a metagraphic-spatial composition entitled *Thermal Sensations and Desires of People Passing by the Gates of Cluny Museum Around an Hour After Sunset in November.*[13] They abandoned this idea, for Paris was already a pinball machine. All that remained was to bounce around it like a shiny silver ball, and find its psychogeographic centers of gravity.

The grid at the Galton machine is like a street layout or a telephone network, a flat and even field, a distributed network.[14] A ball could land anywhere; a call could connect any two points. There are infinitesimal eddies and fissures shaping the ball's trajectory, or the call's circuit, or the swerve of someone on a dérive who takes this street rather than that. Actually, some passages are more likely than others, but only by playing the game does this become clear. The city, unlike the Galton machine, may have several vortices of gravity. *The Night* is structured around the passage of Gilles and Carole through the streets of Paris, bouncing from one trajectory to the next. *The Night* subordinates the narrative of the affair to the description of the dérive. *Horses* is rather more conventional, and the dérive there is just a moment. It reverses the relationship between situation and story.

Gilles' affair with Carole causes at least two rifts in the libidinal universe. Carole's girlfriend Béatrice is jealous and possessive. Geneviève's feelings are perhaps more complicated. It is not the first time Gilles has had other lovers, but Geneviève is a little worried about this one. *The Night* can be read as an account of the disturbance the affair causes Geneviève. Her character is in the habit, on waking, of putting the events of the previous day in order, but in *The Night* events refuse to fall into place. The novel jumps from one fragment of time—charged with affect—to another. It is a beginning that doesn't end.

Horses presents a rather more straightforward version of Geneviève's strategies for holding on to Gilles. One tactic is to become Carole's intimate friend, establishing a relationship independent of Gilles between the two women. It is an emotional intimacy—Sapphic, in de Scudéry's sense—that is perhaps greater than the sexual one between Carole and Gilles, if rather one-sided. Carole confides in Geneviève, but not vice versa. It's a tactic on Geneviève's part, to be sure, but not quite as coldly manipulative as the similar move in *Dangerous Liaisons*, a book from which Bernstein freely borrows.[15] Another tactic is to take the same liberties as her husband. Whereas Gilles found Carole at a party hosted by passé old surrealists, Geneviève finds her love interest at the rather more advanced soirée hosted by Ole, an artist perhaps modeled on Asger Jorn (Ole is the name of Jorn's son). There she hooks up with a young man called Bertrand, fucks him in a hotel, throws him out next morning, then telephones Gilles to tell him about it. This tactic doesn't work: it doesn't make Gilles feel as jealous as she feels. Bertrand is handsome enough, but, if anything, bringing him into the picture only gives Gilles more license to love Carole.

Both Carole and Bertrand make bad art. Carole dabbles at painting, merely repeating the clichés current in the art world. Bertrand's poetry is worse, in thrall to experiments that have long since lost their charge. As Debord once wrote to his old Letterist comrade Patrick Straram, "poetry, yes, but in life. No return possible to surrealist or preceding poetical writing."[16] What neither Carole nor Bertrand quite realizes is that they already embody the aesthetic. Neither knows that they are in play in a game of everyday life. Of the two, Carole comes closer, at least when she sings. She has a small repertoire of old French songs. When she sings for Gilles she appropriates their words as her own, détourns them, and reveals a capacity that leads Geneviève to suspect that here might be a rival.

The four of them, Gilles and Carole, Geneviève and Bertrand, go off on vacation. They meet Bertrand's friend Hélène, a slightly older and very sophisticated woman from the literary scene. On returning to Paris, Geneviève discards Bertrand and takes up with Hélène. This gets Gilles' attention. Gilles drops Carole. The trio of Geneviève, Hélène, and Gilles hang out together for a while, but it doesn't last. In the end it is just Geneviève and Gilles again—for now. But the game has changed. *Horses* ends with letters from Carole and Hélène in which it is clear that Carole, although still young, is beginning to appreciate a new way of thinking about life, while Hélène, encrusted with habit, is left to her fate.

In her letter to Bertrand, Hélène dismisses Gilles and Geneviève as "damaged people," but she does not really understand them.[17] Neither Gilles nor Geneviève are really heartless libertines. They appreciate beauty but not just as an object, a thing apart. Their romantic strategies are not about conquest or possession. Gilles really does fall in love, and often. Geneviève's strategies are aimed mainly at sustaining Gilles' love for her, because she cannot help loving him. This love is hardly romantic. Their feelings are genuine, but feelings can be shaped aesthetically, in pursuit of adventures, in the creation of situations, in the river of time.

Love is temporal, an event. There is nothing eternal in it. Timeless Love, like God, like Art, is dead. Eternal love is death itself, the metaphysical principle that plagues romance, that would make the lover one's private property for all time. All that remains is the possibility of constructing situations. Odile Passot: "In Bernstein's universe, there is no transcendence, divine or diabolic; humans are subject to their own negativity, which they cultivate to destabilize their century's received truths."[18] Like the devils in Marcel Carné and Jacques Prévert's film *The Devil's Envoys* (1942), Geneviève and Gilles trouble the sheets of the bourgeois bedchamber by disregarding property and propriety in the name of a quite different ethic of love.[19] For all its *genderfuck* charm, *The Devil's Envoys* still affirms in the end that love is eternal; in Bernstein's world it is not.

As Geneviève says of Gilles: "When I met Gilles three years ago, I realized quickly that he was far from the cool libertine most people took him for. His desires always contain as much passion as he can put into them, and it's this same state that he always pursued in various love stories that you'd be crazy to call unserious. The climate he created everywhere is one of honest feelings and a heightened consciousness of the tragically fleeting aspect of anything to do with love. And the intensity of the adventure was always an inverse function of its duration. Trouble and breakups happened with Gilles before any valid reason appeared: afterward, it was too late. I had been the exception, I was immune."[20] Strategy, as Debord says, "tends to impose at each instant considerations of contradictory necessities."[21] Geneviève's strategies aim at the very least to preserve her immunity, but perhaps she has other ambitions as well. She might surpass her master at his own game.

Geneviève trumps Gilles' desire for Carole when she presents him with her affair with Hélène. While Gilles is intrigued by Carole's now lost love of Béatrice, he is much more attracted to Geneviève's for the elegant Hélène. The reconciliation between Gilles and Geneviève entails not so much a renunciation of their desire for others, but rather a gift of the renunciation of that desire to each other. But while this ending has the appearance of equity, it is really Geneviève who wins the game. She secures her alliance with Gilles and puts her rival in her place, without invoking proprietary rights—but while taking her pleasures with Bertrand and Hélène. She does not insist that Gilles be hers, or that she is his.

Horses highlights the story of Geneviève's triumph. *The Night* puts the story back into the situation of multiple and parallel encounters. While Carole or Bertrand are part of Geneviève's story, she is also part of theirs. The reader glimpses a whole playing field, a veritable arcade of pinball machines. Jorn would later co-author an elaborate mock ethnography of Paris bohemia, which would do for structuralist theories of myth what James Joyce did for the myth of Ulysses. The elaborate kinship diagrams of his imaginary tribes seem baffling at first, until the reader decodes the forest of symbols and realizes that anyone can fuck anyone. It could be a mock-theoretical diagram of the world of *The Night*.[22]

The soundtrack to the lives of these characters, besides the American jazz popularized by Vian, was a distinctively French version of the folk-music revival. The title *All the King's Horses* refers to an old song, "Aux marches du palais." Carole sings it on the night when she and Gilles and Geneviève fall into one another's lives. It is a song about a queen and her lover. One evening, the knight steals into the king's castle and lies with the queen in her bed. Together they make a river that all the king's horses cannot cross. Greil Marcus: "It is as deep and singular an image of revolution as there has ever been, but in *All the King's Horses* so distant an element is barely an image at all."[23] When one is bored with the desire for mere things, there is only the desire for another's desire. Gilles desires Geneviève's desire for Hélène. But what if one could create a desire so strong that it put a river between it and its other? A desire that, like a river, has to keep moving, has always to change, a desire that can play out in time and play in the end into the sea. This then might be what the novel is still good for: that the situation of desire might not pass away all at once, but pass rather into another time.

7   Tin Can Philosophy

Abdelhafid Khatib, a comrade of Debord's from the Letterist International days, wrote a detailed psychogeography of the Les Halles district of Paris, noting with care how its ambiences morph from one place to another, from one time to another. Here the dérive starts to yield definitive results. Particularly appealing to Khatib is the way the carts of the vegetable vendors make temporary barricades in the streets at delivery time, forming a changeable maze. Shifting from psychogeography to the prospect of the construction of situations, Khatib declares that "any solution aimed at creating a new society requires that this space at the center of Paris be preserved for the manifestations of a liberated collective life."[1] It is a model for "perpetually changing labyrinths" constructed consciously for drifting. It hints at a space and time free of necessity, in which a liberated life could be free to create its own necessities, its own games.

Khatib's text came at a time when other necessities imposed themselves. Since it began in 1954, the Algerian war of independence had been met with increasing French repression. Colonial war destabilized the French state, and brought Charles de Gaulle to power in 1958. But rather than strengthen French power in Algeria as some of his supporters wished, de Gaulle began searching for an alternative policy. This led in turn to assassination and coup attempts against de Gaulle. As the war reached its peak, Paris became the scene of bombings and reprisals. A curfew was declared. It would not be healthy for an Arab man like Khatib to be wandering the streets at night, jotting things down in a notebook.

Opposition to the war among French intellectuals generally took one of four positions. One was Catholic, and appealed to conscience. One was republican, and appealed to the rights of man. Another was third-worldist, and put the anti-colonial struggle in place of class struggle as the motor of history. The last was revolutionary, and scripted the line the Communist Party ought to take if it really was the representative of the international proletariat.[2] Situationist thought and action always conceived of itself outside of the conscience-talk of public intellectuals, and was never romantic about underdevelopment. Debord's *Correspondence* of the late 1950s shows instead a skeptical engagement with the would-be Bolsheviks and non-party Marxists of the French left.

The anti-colonial struggle, the crisis of the French state, and the theoretical debates of the time converged to force a more profound articulation of Situationist theory. Initially skeptical of the Socialism or Barbarism group, Debord would gradually warm to their consistent critique not only of capitalism and colonialism, but also of the socialist states. They saw in the wildcat strikes and periodic eruptions of revolt in both Eastern and Western Europe the signs of a new revolutionary movement. Debord would read them together with the leading theorists of what Lenin had once described as the "infantile disorder" of left-wing and workers-council communist thought of a previous era: Lukács, Karl Korsch (1886–1961), Anton Pannekoek (1873–1960).[3] This would culminate in the text that is Debord's masterpiece: *The Society of the Spectacle* (1967), which is above all a détournement of the texts circulating in the radical milieu of the time.[4]

In deciding between the competing Marxist currents, there are many paths not taken. Debord would be close to, then estranged from, the veteran Marxist philosopher Henri Lefebvre. He would also encourage and collaborate for a time with Asger Jorn on the development of a distinctive Marxist project. Jorn's pamphlet *Critique of Political Economy* (1960) was published with a cover to match Debord's *Report on the Construction of Situations* (1957), as if to give it the same status as a statement of Situationist research results. It seems some of the copies were seized by customs agents, so it never achieved the level of circulation intended for it.[5] In this often overlooked text, Jorn tries to draw together his earlier pataphysical rewritings of Marx with the results of the Letterist International's experiments, in a new synthesis which goes beyond the project of the construction of situations to a new theory of value that might embrace them.

The burden of Jorn's critique of political economy is to show that something is left out of Marx's equation of labor with value. It is not labor alone that creates value. On the one hand Jorn restores a role for nature, for materiality. On the other, he insists on the role of another class in the creation of value, even if he does not quite have a language with which to describe it. This other class he occasionally calls the *creative elite*, in contrast to "the delicious name of the power elite."[6] *The Power Elite* by C. Wright Mills (1916–62) is a powerful restatement, in the teeth of the cold war, of the existence in the West of a ruling class, in control of modern means of production and communication.[7] Mills exposes corporate, state and military power as an integrated nexus, in the hands of a ruling caste with a consistent world view. The same people circulate through the commanding heights of all of the institutions at the disposal of the power elite. Democratic governance is a sham. The mass parties no longer control their leaders. One-way communication has usurped the space of civil dialogue.

Jorn's creative elite is something else. It has no power, but its significance is that it can give form to value. It renews the form of things. The term creative elite seems at first ill-chosen, even for Jorn, who has very little time for the elites of the art world. The sources of creation in Jorn are popular. He happily describes himself as a vulgar Marxist—after *vulgus*, of the people.[8] Where Marx identifies himself with another class—the proletariat—and reconstructs the world from its point of view, Jorn sees the world from the point of view of his own class, or at least from his own milieu—the bohemia of Saint-Germain that Bernstein documents and the extensive network of other creative bohemias with which the peripatetic and multilingual Jorn was intimately familiar.

Like William Morris (1834–96), and drawing on his own anthropological studies, Jorn thinks something has come between art and life. Unlike Morris, his response is a socialism that is not utopian, nor is it quite what Marx and Engels would recognize as scientific. Rather, Jorn's socialism is *experimental*. Where Marx begins with a critique of bourgeois economics, Jorn begins with a critique of socialist economics. Unlike most critics of the Stalinist regimes from the left, Jorn sees them not as wrong in implementation, but in essence. The Trotskyites saw them as deformed workers' states. The Socialism or Barbarism group dispensed with this formula, but not (yet) with the socialist ideal. Probably without knowing it, Jorn picks up the critical thread of Marcel Mauss and others who thought the problem with the socialist states was not just a political deformation, but fundamentally economic.[9]

Marx was fascinated by capital, almost seduced by it.[10] He marveled at its astonishing productivity, its vast accumulation of wealth. While denouncing its violence and inequity, Marx could still love capital's productivity, which the revolution would deliver to the proletariat as its rightful inheritance. Jorn sees capital quite differently. He thinks it has not increased but abolished true wealth, which is variability in consumption. In abolishing difference, the wage relation and the commodity form impoverish the world. For Jorn, the bourgeois revolution of 1789 and the proletarian revolution of 1917 were "two sides of the same affair."[11] Jorn makes the astonishing claim that in their effort to abolish poverty, socialism abolishes wealth along with it. Socialism is a permanent politics of devaluation. This was not inevitable. This was the significance of Gallizio's industrial painting: it showed, experimentally at least, that difference was not incompatible with abundance.

For Marx, wealth and value are the same, and value is derived from labor. Jorn sees Marx's writings as a critique only of the capitalist form of value, not of value in general, and certainly not of value-forms to come. Jorn wants a concept of value more in line with the pataphysical writing on natural science he developed in the 1940s and '50s. Marx's theories assume a nature in which form, complexity and difference can be spirited away by the white-hot flame of reductive analysis. Marx's scientific socialism rests on a materialist worldview which reduces the complexity of forms to an underlying essence. Jorn's materialist attitude to life intuits the possibility of a science of forms, and of the centrality of this science of forms in connecting natural science not only to social science, but to an experimental practice. Elements of such an experimental practice persist in modern art, but its roots are ancient. It continues a communism of the collective making and unmaking of forms.

Marx lacks a sense of the materiality of forms. The concept of form is never placed in relation to that of *substance*. Marx thinks instead of form and *content*. A content is what is enclosed in a form. Marx insists that the content of the form of value is always labor. Labor is the truth hidden within the form. In Marx, "The transition from use value to exchange value happens by the devaluation of the article of utility's material actuality." Use value and the article of utility are the same. But, says Jorn, "if we accept that the use value is the commodity's actual substance, then it is impossible to perceive an article of utility as being identical with a natural form. An article of utility is not a natural form but a cultural form."[12] The question of form cannot be discarded like an old tin can.

Use value is the same as the article of utility for Marx. In Jorn, use value is the opposite of article of utility. Use value is the negation of an article of utility, of its form. Use value is the using up, the consumption of an article of utility. Use value is a negation of a quality. This brings us to Jorn's most striking conclusion: "The market value of things is not conditioned by their quality, far less by their amount. It is conditioned by their *differences*, their variability."[13] Form is not a husk to shuck off, revealing some essence that is an independent content, the universal essence that is labor. "The exchange value of two commodities is thus not their equivalence but their dissimilarity." Jorn restores the claim of form, and at two moments in the production process: natural form and the form of the article of use.

Having dispensed with Marx's dialectic of form and content, he does not pursue the complexity of Marx's value theory much further. Rather, he unfolds his own subtle analysis of value. One is tempted to say that Jorn's value is as subtle as Marx's, but that would of course mean in Jornian terms that, being equivalent, it had no value. The point might be rather to stress its incommensurable difference. If Marx discards the question of form, Jorn stresses it. There are many kinds of form in Jorn. Money as pure equivalence is actually valueless, except as a form. It is empty form. The form that matters to Jorn is the form of substance, but there are others, notably container form and cultural form.

Jorn replaces political economy with aesthetic economy. He does not want to reduce the appearances of value as form to the content of labor, and in so doing make the working class the exclusive heart of economy. The working class is present in Jorn. Unlike bourgeois economics, he does not want to hide them away behind the surface-effects of exchange. Rather, he shifts attention away from exchange to production; not to production as quantity, but production as quality, as difference. The key to this is not labor as the universal content of value, but form as difference, as the production of differences. Labor may be the content of value, but creation is its form. There is both a laboring class and a creating class. Capitalism is the alienation of labor from creation.

In short: substance is value, value is process, and process is difference. Substance is something that can't be measured. It is a materiality of differences, without number or dimension. Dimension is the quantity of a particular quality. Value is a particular quantity of qualities undergoing a process or change. Natural form becomes substance in a process that makes not quantity but other kinds of form, or qualities. Substance is the material reality of the change or transformation. Substance is the ornamentation of natural form. Tintomara's turn is the transformation of natural substance into aesthetic substance.

To complicate things somewhat, Jorn proposes seeing substance as having its own form, or rather, that substance is potential for *transformation*. In an article of utility, the volatile form of substance is held in a certain tension with another kind of form, what Jorn calls container form. Jorn reads Marx as seeing all form as container form, a form which, analytically at least, can be opened to reveal a universal and homogenous substance—labor. But not all form is container form. Substance has its own form which is different from container form and works against it. A substance form is volatile; a container form, relatively inert.

"A substance is a possibility of value." But only a possibility. Value is not a state of things, but comes and goes. One cannot own value. Quality is an attribute of matter; value is the dynamics of matter. "The value of a form … thus depends upon the ease with which one can dissolve the form and liberate its latent energies, whilst its character of quality consists in its resistance to this."[14] Form as container is thus only a special case of form, an instance where value can be easily produced, the quality of the thing readily overcome.

Viewed in quantitative terms, container form seems desirable. Containers yield their contents readily. Container form maximizes the amount of value that can be extracted. But for Jorn the failure of socialist economics lies in actually attempting to realize Marx's conceptual separation of value from form as mere container. Socialist economies measure their progress in terms of rising quantities, all the while presiding over a massive devaluation. The extinction of difference, of the qualities of substances, is an impoverishment of the world. Jorn's critique might apply in attenuated form to socialist economies. Now that most of these have ceased to exist, the salience of Jorn's critique for capitalist economies is all the more acute.

Jorn challenges the central tenet of socialist thought: that the worker alone makes value, that value is labor power. He even claims that mechanical and industrial work is without value at all. The equivalence of units of labor time under industrial conditions, for all its efficiency, does not make more value, it abolishes value altogether. It is not labor, but time that is alienated from the worker. "Surplus value is not created in the work but in the variability of the work."[15] Difference is value. Who creates difference? The creative elite. There are two classes that make value. One is exploited by commodity production; the other marginalized. Jorn's is a recognizably romantic critique of the modern world, but what is distinctive is how far into the realm of the economic Jorn is prepared to pursue it.

Jorn's is perhaps a perverse kind of Leninism. It is not the party that brings class consciousness to the workers from without, but bohemia. The nucleus of a radical form of action is not the specialists in political praxis, but the connoisseurs of the free use of time (Gilles and Carole, wandering the labyrinth of the city at night). Theirs is not a politics of work, but an aesthetics of leisure. Both capitalism and socialism make free time over in the image of work. Sounding a theme that will be a major one in Debord's *Society of the Spectacle*, Jorn claims that the industrial worker's life is eventless, as she does not transform or change things. Leisure time has the same quality, or rather lack of quality, as work. Leisure is as much a sham as work.

Both socialist and capitalist societies have parallel ideologies of form: that container form abolishes differences. The container appears to function as a unit, making substance forms equivalent. Differences are—apparently—abolished as the units increase in number. Jorn calls this "tin can philosophy."[16] It equates the abolition of difference with progress. Both socialist and capitalist societies specialize in the efficient delivery in uniform containers of what has no value. In place of this, Jorn wants an ecology of forms.

The article of utility becomes a commodity when the producer has no use for it. It can either be given away as part of a gift economy of rivalry and recognition, the potlatch, or it can be exchanged. Either way, the problem is what to do with the surplus. Jorn's economics, like that of Georges Bataille, is not about economizing or efficiency, but expenditure, or wealth. Not scarcity but abundance is the key to his thinking: "wealth is surplus, abundance, multiplicity."[17] Where he differs from Bataille is in this emphasis not just on quantitative surplus, but a surplus of difference. Bataille sees both capitalist and socialist economies as distinct from all hitherto because they accumulate rather than disperse surplus, thereby reproducing the problem of surplus at ever higher levels. Jorn sees both capitalist and socialist economies as distinctive for their impoverishment of surplus as multiplicity.

The politics Jorn practiced is also about surplus rather than scarcity. Politics is surplus fellowship. For Jorn, the state is an anti-politics. The statesman is the prototype of the *manager*, and whatever else they may be, socialist states are fanatically managerial. In Engels's phrase, in socialism, the administration of men ought to be replaced by the "administration of things." It became the management of men as if they were things, not least during what Henri Lefebvre called "Stalin's assault on the universe." The socialist vision, from Alexander Bogdanov (1873–1928) forward, is for cybernetics to replace politics. "Statistical robots will compute, guided by effective soundings of public opinion, in accordance with the wishes or otherwise of the majority." Socialism abolishes the state only to make it universal, a container for everything. The socialist goal is in opposition to working-class interests, "for bureaucracy is the container system of society."[18] As Debord was increasingly turning towards a political conception of praxis, Jorn was turning away from it. The parting of the ways, this time, would at least be amicable.

If there is a Situationist praxis, it has to take time in a quite different sense to a Marxist one. It is not just that capital quantifies time and cheats the worker of the value of it. Rather, it is that the quantification of time suppresses the qualitative aspect of the transformation of one substance into another. The slogan "live without dead time" comes to mean something quite specific here. It is not that the situation is the spontaneous irruption of a pure event, severing all ties with the past, freeing itself from the grip of technologies, built spaces, all the massive forms of dead labor. As Debord wrote to Jorn: "I am in agreement on the question of time. To put the accent on non-preserved art or all other deliberately 'direct' situationist activity is not — has never been — a choice between amnesia and refusing history."[19] But this leaves open the question of what a *progressive* orientation might be, if it is neither the purely quantitative piling up of wealth, nor the sudden revolutionary break that abolishes the old world in an instant.

For all their differences, Jorn and Marx are in love with a notion of progress, and this is instructive. It is perhaps the key to resisting the slide of critique towards certain kinds of conservatism, not to mention mere resistance. It's a question of redefining what progress might mean. In Jorn, progress is transport; progress is movement. "In order to give possibilities of orientation, progressive movement must be movement collected from within in relation to the surrounding element."[20] Orienting action is like turning the rudder of a boat in a swift and uncertain current. It is not an act of domination, of imposing a will on time. It is an act which works both with and against the current of the times, ornamenting it.

8   The Thing of Things

Henri Lefebvre is swimming in the ocean one sunny day. He is alone, and the waves are choppy. He swims far, far out from the shore. Clouds obscure the sun. Anxiety grips him. He turns back. While swimming hard against the rip, a vision unfolds, born of real danger, and of quite a different order to the spectacle of waves and sun. It becomes "a shifting totality, roaring, buffeting, overwhelming: the sea." He no longer looks at the waves, he is among them, "each new one taking up the terrifying void left by its forerunner." And yet this ocean of danger is not formless void. "The duration of each wave is strictly determined by its objective logic, which leaves us with an indeterminable wealth of contingencies, accidents, appearances, and—I was about to say—ornaments. Logic and splendor. Before me, around me, I have space-time."[1]

Henri Lefebvre (1901–91) was a contemporary of Jacques Lacan (1901–81), but their trajectories could not be more different. In the late twentieth century, Lacan would become the king of secular bourgeois thought, raising the practice of psychoanalysis to a high pitch of Delphic profundity. Meanwhile, Lefebvre would leave the Communist Party by the rarely used leftward exit. Lacan sought to acquire the dignity of the status of philosopher; Lefebvre pushed philosophy out into the streets. And while Lefebvre was at his most influential in the blazing years of the 1960s, Lacan would eclipse him in the long dark decades that followed.

If there is one abiding purpose to psychoanalysis, it is to make bourgeois lives seem fascinating, at least to those who live them. That it is a form of bourgeois thought is attested by the status of *the real* in Lacanian doctrine. The real is always something terrible, formless, lawless, which the *symbolic order* tries to shield from awareness, but which keeps slithering in, unbidden. It is a modern version of the serpents that in

Jorn's account Apollonian thought has to slay, again and again. The symbolic preserves for the ruling class, to whom it classically belongs, an order that keeps at bay the self-ornamenting powers of nature and labor, working together, writhing and worming their way into the cracks in Apollonian form.

In Lefebvre the real is the fulcrum of action rather than an apprehension of terror. His vision of it comes to him while swimming against the current, the body acting on raw need to survive. "The real can only be grasped and appreciated via potentiality."[2] It is by attempting to transform everyday life that the contours of the real are encountered. The real is not entirely formless, even if its forms are not an order that reveals itself in the clear light of day. The encounter with the real, because it is active, informs the *imaginary*. From the struggle in and with the real emerges an imagining of what might be possible. The object of study for both Lacan and Lefebvre is in a sense always everyday life, but in Lefebvre study is a stage in the project of transforming it.

From the Landes department, in the western Pyrenees, Lefebvre joined the Communist Party in 1928. He was active in the Resistance during the war in the countryside near where he was born. An unofficial blacklist kept him from returning to teaching after the liberation, so his friend and contemporary Tristan Tzara found him a job working in radio in Toulouse. It was not until 1961 that he became a professor at Strasbourg, before moving in 1965 to a post at Nanterre, on the outskirts of Paris, a suburb of "misery, shanty towns, excavations ... housing projects ... a desolate and strange landscape," which would become one of the flashpoints of May '68. His was a lively, diverse, but hardly orthodox career.[3]

He was fifty-six when Debord met him in 1957, via Lefebvre's girl-friend (and typist) Evelyne Chastel, who knew Michèle Bernstein. Lefebvre was at the time the most talented philosopher of the French Communist Party, if hardly the most trusted. He left the party in 1959, the year he published *The Sum and the Remainder*, in which he sets out his theory of *moments*. Lefebvre's moment is closely related to Debord's turn towards the situation. Lefebvre starts from the observation that the leading strategists of advanced capitalism recognized the futility of clinging to colonies such as Algeria, and advanced instead a strategy of colonizing everyday life. Formerly outside the sphere of capitalist social relations, everyday life had become a new site of both commodification and its contestation. Out of everyday life, even in its commodified form, crystallizes a series of moments — of work, but also of play, love, rest, justice, contestation — each of which presses towards the absolute realization of a specific possibility. The moment is "the absolute at the heart of the relative."[4]

A welder welding and a weaver weaving perform quite different acts, but Marx had shown in elaborate detail how the qualitative particulars of such concrete labors became the quantifiable substance of abstract labor through the imposition of the wage relation, the commodity form and the *general equivalent* of money. The Situationists wanted to create what one might call the *specific non-equivalent*, and their name for this was the *situation*. But the very word resisted becoming a concept. The relationship between Lefebvre and the Situationists would dissolve before they got very far with their parallel investigations and experiments with it. It was, as Lefebvre later said, "a love story that ended badly, very badly."[5]

Shortly after his encounter with the Situationist International, Lefebvre published two books which invoke them. The second volume of the *Critique of Everyday Life* (1961) opens with Debord, and *Introduction to Modernity* (1962) closes with the Situationist International. The books are as different as day and night. The former is almost a classic of the sociology of culture, as systematic and structured as anything Lefebvre ever wrote. The latter is a wild ride, a romantic medley of genres, mixing memoir, critique, essay, letter, myth and even science fiction. Between them can be found the practical results and problems of the Situationist International raised to the level of method, and comprehended in the long, deep context of the moves and movements that try, in Rimbaud's words, to change life.

The second volume of the *Critique of Everyday Life* was a book for which Lefebvre had high hopes. He wrote to his friend Norbert Guterman: "So, the book of all books comes to an end. Since the beginning of December, 1,600 handwritten pages, 800 typed (Evelyne only charged me 12–15 per page) ... Now I can see what will hinder this book from being the book of all books, the total book of this era. I can see the errors and the flaws. I now understand what should have been done. Now it is too late. There is no way of stopping the machine now."[6] *Introduction to Modernity* maps the uncharted coast that the *Critique* had yet to reach.

Lefebvre the sociologist invents hypotheses and images as much as concepts, and nothing in his writing matches the formal beauty of Lacan the psychoanalyst's topological knots. The proof or refutation of Lefebvre's ideas lies not in the elaboration of a coherent discourse, but in *transduction*, in which the practice of encountering the necessities and contingencies of the real elaborates on it in the direction of the possible. "To know the everyday is to want to transform it."[7] Knowledge is a strategy whose tactics are concepts, forged for discovering the options latent within the everyday. Lefebvre's work of this period encompasses at least five concepts, around which others cluster, which respond to and inform the Situationist project: the everyday, totality, moment, spectacle and the total semantic field.

Freedom is not the opposite of necessity in Lefebvre. Freedom is born out of *need*, and the starting point is a theory of needs.[8] Without the experience of need, there can be no being. Needs are few; desires are many. There is no desire without a need at its core. Need can be intense: hunger, thirst, lust. Need without desire, without play, artifice, luxury, superfluity, is no longer human. It is human poverty. Desire abstracted from need loses vitality, spontaneity, and ossifies into the mere accumulation of things. It is abstract and alienating, another kind of poverty. Lefebvre's critique aims to bring together a presentation of needs and a determination of desires to arrive at a theory of situations, as they arise in the everyday.

The *everyday* overlaps with what Martin Heidegger (1899–1976) calls the *ontic*. But rather than bracket it off in favor of a more fundamental ontology, Lefebvre takes the trivial and seemingly superficial aspects of the everyday seriously. "Either philosophy is pointless or it is the starting point from which to undertake the transformation of non-philosophical reality, with all its triviality and its triteness." His project is an overcoming of the internal limitations of both philosophy and the everyday. "The everyday is a philosophical concept and cannot be understood outside philosophy ... it is not the product of pure philosophy but comes of philosophical thought directed toward the non-philosophical, and its major achievement is in this self-surpassing."[9] Everyday life might be a concept internal to philosophy, but it directs philosophy to that which it excludes in the interests of a coherence, the achievement of which renders it null and void.

If the *everyday* is a problem for philosophy, so too is *life*. Eugene

Thacker: "Every ontology of life thinks of life in terms of something other than life."[10] The thing other than life through which life is thought can take one of three forms. One: life is spirit. It is interiority and exteriority. It is an incorporeal essence that remains the same, or immaterial essence common to all forms and moments of life. Two: life is time. It is affirmation and negation, movement and change. It is dynamic and self-organizing. Three: life is form. It is additive and subtractive. It is boundaries and transgressions. For Jorn life is form, for Lefebvre it is time, and for nobody in the Situationist orbit is it spirit.

If the central question for antiquity was being, and for modernity the death of God, then the central question today is life. And yet the metaphysical problem remains of identifying "an animating principle of the world that is not itself reduced to its own attributes." What Lefebvre's turn to everyday life, like Jorn's to the attitude to life, accomplishes, is an opening towards new fields of practice which do not require a retreat to ancient regimes of the *care of the self.* The fissures within the concept of life yield not just a critique but the seeds for new forms and tempos of living itself, and perhaps also a fourth category of the thing other than life through which life is thought: matter. Life as surplus and scarcity, as need and desire, a way of (thinking about) life not reducible to biology yet completely outside the grasp of theology. Life is *praxis.*[11]

The everyday can be a realm for forms and times of life, if it yields situations for a collective praxis. Praxis here might mean a coming-into-being through the encounter with something other, an encounter which necessitates a moment of both transformation and reflection. Labor is a form of praxis, but not a privileged one. Praxis is the struggle to overcome need, but also the game of creating and satisfying desires, of desires collapsing back towards need, and so on. In modern times the free creation of relations between desire and need has come to an end. Lefebvre: "As Guy Debord so energetically put it, everyday life has literally been 'colonized.'"[12] The imposition of the commodity form on one aspect of everyday life after another breaks the tension between desire and need. Those unable to discover a relation between need and desire are cut off from their own being, alienated from an active encounter with the real. Hence the need for negative concepts, for *negation,* to reveal not just what everyday life is, but what it isn't. It isn't all that praxis can be imagined as becoming.

The everyday is a mediating level. It is where people appropriate for themselves, not nature, but a second nature of already manufactured articles. It is where needs confront goods. It is not just a functional sphere of consumption and the reproduction of labor power. Nor is the everyday a prisoner of any pervasive disciplinary power, of cops and social workers, psychologists and sociologists intent on prying into people's lives. There is always something unformed in the everyday, something that exceeds and escapes both commodity and power. It is a strategic terrain for experimenting with practices and possibilities. "Today," writes Lefebvre, "what is the aim of utopian investigation? The conquest of everyday life, the recreation of the everyday and the recuperation of the forces which have been alienated in aesthetics, scattered through politics, lost in abstraction, severed from what is possible and what is real."[13]

Two kinds of time meet and mingle in the everyday. One is a linear time, the time of credit and investment. The other is a cyclical time, of wages paid and bills due. This is how class makes itself felt in everyday life. Linear temporality is ruling-class time; cyclical temporality is working-class time. The workers spend what they get; the bosses get what they spend. Cyclical time is the time of needs and the struggle to meet them. But it is also the experience of a certain kind of desire, for example in the patient waiting for the festival to return, and with it the gorgeous consumption of goods in the name of desire. Linear time imposes its own distinctive necessities, its booms and recessions, and this is not the least aspect of the colonization of the everyday by the commodity form. It introduces a distinctive kind of desire as well, desire deferred, not until festival time and its potlatch of goods, but in the interests of accumulation.

The everyday also has a third kind of temporality, the time of adventure, which is perhaps a remnant of aristocratic time. A notable characteristic of the Letterist International, which persists in the Situationist International, is a longing for this time of adventure. It is not because they are titled knights and ladies that they expend time freely in search of adventure; it is because they expend time freely that they consider themselves entitled to style themselves with a certain louche nobility. This is not the least aspect of them that would appeal to the Lefebvrian sensibility. "On the horizon of the modern world dawns the black sun of boredom, and the critique of everyday life has a sociology of boredom as part of its agenda."[14] Adventure is nothing if not the practical refutation of boredom.

What could the everyday become? "Could it be some sort of grand game without any precise objective?"[15] The colonization of everyday life by the commodity form diminishes the role of collective experience, yet groups persist. Within groups, individuals have tactics and strategies, as the early years of the Situationist International makes abundantly clear. Groups also have tactics and strategies in relation to other groups. The everyday is the level of tactics; history, that of strategy. Whether or not traditional societies were governed by the gift, as Mauss and Bataille thought, Lefebvre thinks modern societies are governed by the *challenge*. "Challenge is a means of exerting pressure beyond the group, but its actions reverberate within it."[16] The classical bourgeoisie loved a challenge. It overcame feudalism while staving off the challenge of the working class. Postwar technocrats seem challenge-averse. They prefer to manage challenges, rather than confront them. Not the least pleasure of Lefebvre is his sense, won from his own remarkable experience, that history had still more challenges up its sleeve.

Lefebvre sees everyday life as a mix of *agôn* and *aléa*, of contest and chance. "In the beginning was action; in the end action is recognized … Every human life is a progress or a process toward a possibility, the opening up or closing down of what is possible, a calculation and an option based upon random events and the intervention of 'other people.'"[17] As with linear and circular time, there is a class basis to the experience of the everyday as contest or chance. Experiencing life as a contest to which to apply strategies is a view far less available to the individual members of the working class. Only through collective action can the proletariat enter history at the level of strategy. In decline, its forces lose their grasp on the game of history. All that remains are the tactics of the everyday.

If there is a distinctive experience of modern life, it is the *aleatory*. It is rather like pinball, or Gallizio's industrial painting, a mix of necessity and chance. Confronted by the aleatory, people gamble and gambol with their lives, making moves in a game that may be based on tactics and even strategies, but where the variables are not all known, and the outcomes are far from predictable. Few moves in this game could be considered a *rational choice*. This is the lesson Lefebvre takes from game theory and other technocratic attempts to annex the everyday to social science. They reduce the experience of the everyday to signals and calculations. They describe what everyday life is not: a rational totality. Rather: "Everything becomes disjointed, yet everything becomes a totality, everything becomes reified, yet everything starts disintegrating. The aleatory is triumphant."[18]

Johan Huizinga believed that vigorous civilizations have the capacity to elaborate new forms of play. In decadent ones, play becomes codified into more formal games. Lefebvre differs from Huizinga in that he thinks modernity is a time in which play can flourish. "But it is certainly rather surprising that it should be our era, the era of functionalism and technology, which has discovered homo ludens."[19] Writing at the high watermark of rational and functional social science, Lefebvre thinks history is still capable of objective irony, of confounding order and revealing contingency. History is a game in Lefebvre, the rules of which are never clear and in any case keep changing. It is not a machine or a structure, but neither is it random. It is more like the flocking of starlings. Groups play each other with more or less awareness of the local rules of the game, though not of how their moves swarm together and affect the historical stakes.

Within everyday life, groups challenge one another, and not the least part of the challenge is the tactic of appearances. "The secrets of groups, their opacities, which are what give the illusion of substance, are made up of anxieties or audacity with regard to what is possible, of entrenchments or offensives, of retreats and advances in relation to other groups, of courage or of weakness of will in response to problems."[20] Here Lefebvre and the Situationists are very close, and close also to Huizinga, for whom play always has an element of the secret about it. The game within the group ought not to be apparent to the group's rivals.

Play is a misunderstood aspect of praxis. Play "uses appearances and illusions which—for one marvelous moment—become more real than the real."[21] Through the concept of play, Lefebvre manages to bypass two of the great theoretical fetishes of his times: *structure* and *sign*. Structure is just a reified apprehension of play, its fossilized remains. "Structure itself is nothing more than a precarious and momentary success, a win or a loss in a complex gamble."[22] The sign is just one aspect of play, that which a player brandishes, the better to conceal a secret—and to display that a secret is concealed.

The concept of *totality* would become the great boo-word of late twentieth-century thought, linked, through a rather casual association, to the *totalitarian* state of the Soviet Union. Particularly for the so-called new philosophers, totality reeked of the gulag. Some genuine conceptual objections were bent to the service of legitimating the status quo. For Lefebvre, totality has a somewhat different sense. Not totality as an achieved philosophical system, but as an orientation for praxis. "Discourse strives for totality. It must strive for totality, yet it is never more than incomplete." What Lefebvre calls *totalization* is praxis revealing itself in terms of its tendency. Every praxis wills its own totalization. "Every totalization which aspires to achieve totality collapses, but only after it has been explicit about what it considers its inherent virtualities to be." The concept of totality directs research. "If there is no insistence upon totality, theory and practice accept the 'real' just as it is, and 'things' just as they are: fragmentary, divided and disconnected."[23] Totality is a negative concept, it is the gap between what is possible and what is impossible. The critique of everyday life hinges on thinking certain moments within it as far as they will go.

Groups acting within everyday life pursue their strategies as far as they will go. Praxis is at once repetition and creation. Creation emerges out of repetition. Inventiveness is born from the everyday, through the action not of individual genius but of collective play. "Could not inventiveness—or the seeds of inventiveness—be a product of the limited and daring praxis of small-scale groups: sects, secret societies, political parties, elective groups, laboratories, theatrical troupes, etc?"[24] As in Jorn, the sources of creation are popular, but this does not lead to an uncritical celebration of all things popular. The everyday is vital for what it can be, not for what it is.

Praxis has its dangers. What was once a living form of collective self-discovery and self-invention can harden into a thing-like routine. It can, in short, become *alienated*. Lefebvre differs from much of the Hegelian Marxist writing of the time in thinking of alienation as something less than a total, remorseless, one-dimensional and one-directional descent into a nicely equipped hell. Modern life is not all alienation. Rather, it's a game in which certain tactics prove dis-alienating for a time, then fall short of their own totalization, cease to work, forcing groups to either come up with new tactics or lose sight of their self-affirming praxis. Praxis can fail both by falling short in its totalization and by exceeding it. "Beyond a certain limit, the negative becomes a fetish, a vision of nothingness; radical critique becomes hypercritique, and nihilism is established as a truth without that truth having been legitimated."[25] It's a critique that could be applied with some justice to the Situationist International after the exclusion of the artists.

Everyday life is to be transformed according to its own tendencies. When a group discovers a dis-alienating practice in everyday life, it may crystallize into a *moment*. Possible moments might include love, play, rest, knowledge, although nothing prevents the creation of new moments. Philosophy might be nothing other than making contemplation into a moment. The moment emerges out of the cyclical time of repetition, but creates a time of its own. The moment constitutes its own kind of space, and enables the stabilizing of determinable relations with otherness. A moment is constituted in space and time by a decision which singles it out from ambiguity.

The moment weaves itself into and out of the everyday. The moment tries to achieve the total realization of a specific possibility. It exhausts itself in the act of pursuing its own goal to the very end. "It wishes to perceive the possibilities of everyday life and to give human beings a constitution by constituting their powers, if only as guidelines or suggestions."[26] The moment wants to endure. It wants to gather its own temporality. The moment requires a certain amount of ritual and ceremony. It makes for itself a special time and place. It creates its own specific form of memory.

These forms the moment creates run the risk of repeating themselves, of no longer serving the moment but enclosing it. The moment provokes its own specific alienation. The gamer or the lover becomes obsessed. A Korean man expired in 2005 after playing the game *Starcraft* in an internet café for fifty hours, with only brief naps and toilet breaks.[27] The gamer forgets to eat, to sleep, commits everything to beating a level. The lover spends sleepless nights thinking about the object of affection. At this point alienation is complete, and the moment disappears.

Moments may have different scales. *Festival* might be the grandest scale to which the moment can aspire, a historical scale. "Festival only makes sense when its brilliance lights up the sad hinterland of everyday dullness, and when it uses up, in one single moment, all it has patiently and soberly accumulated."[28] Lefebvre thought of the prewar leftist

Popular Front—with its mass demonstrations, equal parts celebration and desperation—as festival. At quite a different scale, he writes movingly of a working-class painter from his hometown whose work was shunned even by the provincial museum, but who was a decisive influence on the young Lefebvre. "There are men who are not artists and not philosophers, but who nevertheless emerge above the everyday, in their own everyday lives, because they experience moments: love, work, play, etc."[29] Just as there is a tomb for the unknown soldier, there could be one for the unknown artist, whose moments are unrecognized and fade clean away.

Situation is a persistent concept in philosophy, if usually a marginal one. From Hegel to Kierkegaard to Sartre it designates a zone in which otherwise different elements confront each other.[30] Those elements can be isolated, defined, made into concepts, but the situation within which they meet and mix has a singular quality. Lefebvre's procedure is in some respects the other way around. "The moment is not exactly the same as a situation. The result of a decision or a choice—of an endeavor—the moment creates situations." Thinking aloud in a letter, Debord tries to specify the situation in its difference from Lefebvre's moment: "The difficulty of the 'situationist' moment is … marking the exact end (its reversal? And another), its transformation into a different term of this series of situations that (can?) constitute such a Lefebvrian moment."[31]

Here, in this hesitating language, Debord gropes towards an understanding of the Situationist practice of creating collective experiences of space and time that have their own singular coherence, but neither collapse back into the dead time of routine, nor ossify into mere artifacts. Unlike the moment, the situation "must unify falsely separated categories (love, play, expression, creative thought). And each of these formations—as conscious and calculated as they can be, that is to say, brought into play with superior chances—inevitably move towards their own reversal, because each one is entirely lived in time along with its negation and permanent supersession."[32] For Debord all of the singular moments, of love, play, work, knowledge, can be combined within a situation.

Between writing *Critique of Everyday Life, Volume 2* and *Introduction to Modernity*, Lefebvre appears to lose faith in the possibilities of the moment.

> You used to think that an auto-critique of everyday life through its own transpositions was possible: a critique of the slimy animal by its delicate shell and vice versa—a critique of the everyday by festivals, or of trivial instants by moments, and vice versa—a critique of life by art and of art by life, of the real by its double and its reverse image: dreams, imagination, fiction. The times change. Technology began penetrating everyday life. There were new problems.[33]

Modern life might not give rise to its own critical agent of transformation—what Lefebvre terms *modernity*—and praxis might be foreclosed, and with it being, the engagement with the real. "It is not that God is absent, but something worse: modernity is like a shell to hide the absence of praxis ..." Modernity is the "ghost of revolution."[34]

What forecloses the possibility of praxis is what Lefebvre, citing Debord, calls the *spectacle*. The spectacle makes totality visible, but only in fragments, and visible only within the space of the private. It does not make the private social as well. The spectacle is a one-way street, the public privatized. "It is the generalization of private life. At one and the same time the mass media have unified and broadcast the everyday; they have disintegrated it by integrating it with 'world' current events in a way which is both too real and utterly superficial."[35]

Lefebvre calls the spectacle the great pleonasm, the Thing of Things. Thought in terms of its totalizing tendency, "it would be a closed circuit from hell, a perfect circle in which the absence of communication and communication pushed to the point of paroxysm would meet and their identities would merge." What is real is what is known; what is known is what is real. The illusion of permanent novelty occludes the possibility of surprise. It is a world of incessant redundancy. Everything is always the same, only better. It makes the same special offer to everyone, all the time: "the faked orgasms of art and life."[36]

The challenge of the colonization of the everyday by the spectacle calls for a reassessment, not just of tactics but of strategy. Lefebvre takes a step back to the terrain on which the challenge appears, the *total semantic field*, of which the spectacle is an alienated form. Everyday life takes place not just in the streets, but also in the total semantic field. It has three registers: signals, signs and symbols. *Signals* form closed systems of redundant messages which appear mostly in the form of commands. A traffic light is a signal. It commands the driver to stop or

go. *Signs* form a region within the semantic field of relatively open networks, a mix of information and redundancy. *Symbols* cannot command
and are not particularly legible. They irrupt into the semantic field as
noise. Symbols may have faded and gone into hiding, but they can still
be glimpsed through the spectacle. The total semantic field is "complex,
differentiated, polarized, alive with the fluxes and tensions which come
and go from one pole to the other. Language tries to equal this totality,
but is never more than one of its parts."[37]

Cybernetic theories totalize the whole of the semantic field as signals,
and imagine it can be made self-regulating. Semiotic theories totalize
the semantic field as if it were composed entirely of signs and governed by the grammar of their combination. Lefebvre's strategic move
is to counter the spectacle's growing reduction of communication to the
level of signal and sign by moving onto the terrain of the symbol, or
rather by treating the whole semantic field as the space of the challenge:
signal, sign and symbol together. "Communication in depth implies the
totality of the semantic field. The more it incorporates that totality, the
more aesthetic it becomes."[38]

The legacy on which Lefebvre draws is a certain understanding of
romanticism, which might be the memory of a series of practices for
crystallizing the total semantic field itself into moments. Lefebvre is
sometimes thought of as a Hegelian Marxist, but his understanding
of romanticism owes more to Stendhal. From Stendhal's *Racine and
Shakespeare* (1823), Lefebvre draws out a theory of the romantic as the
precursor to a critical modernity, and like it the product of defeated revolutions. Romanticism brings everything into art. Everything classical
art excluded is drawn into it, to the point of exhaustion. Romanticism
occupies the total semantic field and gravitates particularly to the pole
of the symbolic, to stimulate the creation of works of art. The artwork
in turn condenses the total semantic field. "Living romanticism reveals
a totality."[39]

If there are symbols through which the romantic and its antithesis,
the classical, might first be approached, they are the knight and the
king. The king stands first and last for order, if also for an unknown
range of things in between. The knight is the figure of adventure,
driven by a certain goal but of uncertain outcome. The knight submits
to a vow and lives his life in the name of an ideal, but one which is
constantly challenged by circumstances. The knight's horse raises him

above earthly things, but when he falls he comes crashing down into the shit. The knight is a figure of the aleatory, standing for all those who live in an ambiguous or shadowy milieu, which perhaps explains Debord's taste for *Prince Valiant* comics.[40]

The classical assumes a legitimate order, revealed by the light of the sun. God's in his heaven, the king's on his throne, all is right with the world. And what goes wrong can be rectified. Like Le Corbusier's plans, classicism favors the right angle and the straight line. It favors the form of the myth, in which order is destabilized, restored, legitimated. Its privileged medium is architecture. Its method is *imitation*. Everyone imitates the one above them in the social order, just as the king imitates God, and the whole social order imitates nature. Classical humor, from Molière to Sacha Baron Cohen, ridicules failed attempts at imitation. In Molière's satirical attack on the Precious movement, provincial ladies shun some noblemen as beneath them, so these retaliate by having their grooms pretend to be Precious sophisticates. Hilarity ensues, but classical humor serves order.

The romantic is a corrosive fluid that attacks the classical on every front. It is a refusal of obedience. It lurks in the dark, in the mist, within the eclipse. Time is out of joint. It favors the wave, the vibration, the curlicue. It mixes forms, detaches symbols from myths, and puts them in play against all that is legitimate. Its medium of greatest affinity is music. Its method is *creation*, which it claims as a human potential, not a divine attribute. For Lefebvre the romantic intersects with a certain strand of irony. Unlike Jorn he idolizes the achievements of the Greeks, not least Socratic irony, which is the undoing of any order of belief. The subjective irony of Socrates anticipates the objective irony of history, which sweeps order away in its aleatory currents.

Romanticism can be both pre- and post-revolutionary. Lefebvre acknowledges that most notable French romantics sided against the revolution. Its key tension is between the ideal of bourgeois life, and its pallid reality. Romanticism became a bourgeois art in the sense that they were the class that consumed it. This kept romantic artists from pursuing romanticism to its logical conclusion. The romantic lives outside bourgeois society yet within it, "like a maggot in a fruit."[41] Or like the grit within the oyster, forcing it to make the classical pearl. The fate of the romantic gesture is—if not obscurity—to become classical, to calcify into *the good form* (something Jorn identifies in Max Bill, for example).

From the symbolic pantheon, romanticism draws on figures who rarely occupy central and active roles in classical culture: the knight, the prince, the seer, the child, the witch, the devil, the stranger, not to mention some even more strange, like Tintomara. Those who can't find their place in the classical world—the marginal, the minor, the delinquent, the weird—might find it here. But while one aspect of romanticism is otherworldly, an escape from this alien planet to one more hospitable, the symbols drawn from the total semantic field can also be brought back to the everyday. They can be lived. And while isolation might be one practice favored by romanticism, it is also an initiation into deviant or secret groups. Although Lefebvre does not use the term, its homeland is *bohemia*. Romanticism includes a desire for communion in some kind of lived utopia. A desire which, at the limit, feeds into utopian socialism.

Lefebvre: "The best man of action is one who chooses his moment well … His decision simplifies the complex situation and the ambiguity, and by the very act of simplifying them, transforms them."[42] If Guy Debord was not that man, it was certainly what he aspired to be, at a time when even the aspiration was becoming rare. The Situationists were not the only group working over the remains of romanticism in postwar Europe. But if there was a dominant strategy, it was to pursue the romantic exploration of the total semantic field only so far, before turning back and setting up a new classicism in the resulting ruins. This was the trajectory of absurdist theatre, modern jazz, Robbe-Grillet's *nouveau roman*, or new wave cinema. What the Situationists acquired from Isou and the Letterists was a commitment to pursuing a certain romantic decomposition to the limit, if not his claim to build a new classicism of entirely new forms on the ruins. What Lefebvre perceives as the open path is to pursue the romantic further, in two directions: further into the semantic field, and further back, not into new art forms like Isou, but into everyday life. "The most brilliant Situationists are exploring and testing out a kind of lived utopianism."[43]

The romantic strategy is not without difficulties: "contradictions are thick-skinned, and their bones are even thicker."[44] Lefebvre identifies contradictions between cosmopolitanism and nationalism, between futurism and the middle ages, between religiosity and revolt, and between subjectivity and the outside world. These all pass through the Situationist International. These contradictions are traceable to a central tension between two worldviews: an anthropological nature and a cosmological nature. The roots of anthropological nature lie in the enlightenment philosophies of eighteenth-century France, articulated by Buffon and others. It is optimistic, it stresses human perfectibility and equality. The worldview of cosmological nature is more German than French. Here nature appears as wildly other, as an inaccessible external world. It enters the French semantic field in force relatively late, with surrealism. Can what is real become rational? Can what is rational become real? Such might be the terms of this irresolvable tension. It infuses the entire scope of possibilities for our species-being.

In playing with the devil of romanticism and its symbols, the Situationist International inherited its contradictions, which would play out through the movement in the splits and fissures of the 1960s. The relationship with Lefebvre was also a casualty of the tensions of the times, both personal and political. And yet not only did he provide the Situationists with the concept of everyday life, he also engaged with them in thinking through the two key concepts of the spectacle (or pleonasm) and the situation (or moment). And while it was not a welcome insight, Lefebvre as seer foresaw the necessity for the formation within the everyday of multiple forms of group action. The monolithic party of labor would not have as its counterpart a single party of play, but rather a number of fractious groups, playing off and against one another, challenging one another. In the twenty-first century, when so many intellectuals seem unhealthily obsessed with the ubiquitous thought of an omniscient power, Lefebvre, even in his less ebullient moments, radiates a sense of possibility. He still swims against the current. The following chapters trace the detours and deviations of the most interesting attempts to appropriate from the early versions of Situationist thought and practice, and open up new possibilities, to recall them and not let their moments pass.

9   Divided We Stand

"Newell Street, London, E14 7HR. £1,250,000: A beautiful Grade 2 listed house formerly headquarters of The British Sailors Society. Built circa 1802 for one of Horatio Nelson's captains, the property retains many naval features including one of London's only Victorian swimming pools, originally built to teach sailors to swim. The property is laid out over three floors and consists: large entrance hallway, drawing room, conservatory, four bedrooms, two bathrooms, studio room, sauna, private garden and two parking spaces. The property has also been used for filming, including *Beginner's Luck* and *Dead Cool* and has been graced by stars such as Rosanna Arquette, Liz Smith, and Julie Delpy."[1]

It's easier to sell a property with a story, but beneath these stories lie others. The ad neglects to mention that the same address formerly housed the homeless, or that it was once disgraced by the anti-celebrities of the Situationist International. In preparation for the 1960 London conference, Debord and Jorn embarked on a dérive of the city looking for a suitable venue. They settled on this hall in the Limehouse district, mythologized by Charles Dickens as a seedy warren of opium dens.[2] With them was Jacqueline de Jong (b. 1939), one of the handful of women who, like Michèle Bernstein, was able not only to put up with men like these, but make vital contributions of her own. "I mean, no washing the dishes and things like that."[3]

De Jong's was a sophisticated family from provincial Holland. Her father's company made seamless stockings for Dior. When the Nazis invaded Holland, two-year-old Jacqueline crossed over the Jura Mountains with her mother, while her father hid out in Amsterdam. After the war de Jong moved to Paris, where her father found a position for her at Dior. She met Jorn in the company of her father, when he bought one of Jorn's pictures. The family collection included works by several Cobra artists, a Franz Kline, and many other fine contemporary works. In 1957 de Jong was in Holland, working as an assistant to Willem Sandberg at the Stedelijk Museum. The Situationists were involved in a somewhat fraught collaboration with the Stedelijk, which brought de Jong into contact with them.[4]

The Spur Group (1957–66) was one of the stronger signs of life in postwar German culture. It formed in 1957 in Munich. De Jong joined Spur in 1959. "Jorn thought very highly of them," she says. He found them a dealer and brought them into the orbit of the Situationists. They would not return the favor. "If you pick a strange baby, don't be surprised if it craps on you!" Or so the artist Roberto Matta advised his friend when Jorn became their champion.[5]

To Spur, art was the last free domain from which to oppose the rationalization of social life. Spur defended art against attempts to rationalize it as well, a last redoubt against administered life. They had read their Theodor Adorno (1903–69), and while the cardinal of critical theory would hardly recognize them, they were his mutant offspring. "We are against truth, against happiness, against satisfaction, against good conscience, against fat stomachs, against HARMONY," their manifesto declares.[6]

Many postwar German artists looked back to the 1920s as a time from which to start building a new German culture, but for Spur the roots of Nazism also lay in the ambiguities of that period. They wanted to make contact with history, but theirs was a détournement of 1920s expressionism, rather than an imitation. There they found the resources to mobilize against both the lingering Nazi presence in postwar Germany and also the amnesia of a modernizing, technocratic state. They cast their lot with Jorn's creative elite rather than Debord's renewed interest in the proletariat.

To escape both the Nazi past and techno-statist future in Germany, Spur tried to occupy a transnational avant-garde space, and this cosmopolitanism was not the least thing about them that caused offense in their homeland. They spurned not only the state and its official culture, but also the proletariat. Where the Communist leadership in the resistance cast an aura over the idea of the French working class, Spur saw their German brothers and sisters as compromised by Nazism and coopted by Social Democracy. Spur took refuge in art as precursor to another kind of labor, a free play in which a psychic surplus could feed back into self-production.

Spur became the German section of the Situationist International in 1959, and found themselves caught in the same tensions as the Italian section around Gallizio. The artists might see their creative efforts as aligned with the Situationist International, but artists need collectors, and to find collectors they need dealers. To the dealer, an artist's adherence to a movement merely gives the work a certain glamor, not to mention some free publicity. To the dealer the actual aims of such a movement are neither here nor there. To the extent that the movement promotes the artist and the artist succeeds, the artist is then pulled out of the orbit of the movement and into that of the art world—dealers, collectors, curators, critics. This would happen to Spur as it did to Gallizio. Vincent Kaufmann: "If a ... Situationist art exists, it functions as an invisible model: all representation is treason, including when it is the product of a real ... Situationist."[7] Or rather: art could only function tactically, as provisional instances of a total project.

The prevalence of artists tilted the Situationist International towards their particular concerns. So Debord gathered the forces that would enable him to dispense with their nettlesome presence. The Brussels-based writers Attila Kotányi (1924–2004) and Raoul Vaneigem (b. 1934) replaced Constant as the anti-art left wing of the movement.[8] The tensions between the mostly Francophone theorists and the mostly German-speaking artists were papered over at the London conference, where de Jong was both translating and taking the minutes. The French were turning towards the proletariat, just as the Germans were abandoning the idea of its revolutionary force. The conference did manage to unite in support of Alexander Trocchi, facing serious drug charges in New York.

While in London the Situationists made a farcical appearance at the Institute for Contemporary Arts (ICA), something of a replay of Debord and Trocchi's appearance there three years earlier to show Debord's film *Howls for Sade*.[9] De Jong: "The event was just one big joke, snubbing the public." After the London conference, the energetic and able de Jong found herself active on the central council of the Situationist International at twenty-one years of age. After the exclusion of the group around Constant, she effectively was the Dutch section. She proposed to the central council that it needed an English-language journal. The others agreed, and appointed her co-editor with Trocchi. It never appeared—at least not as planned.

She also made a pilgrimage to Alba. "Pinot asked me to come and work with him. He became completely impossible. Anyway, my whole idea was not to stay very long, to make as many meters of industrial painting as I could, then roll them up, take them away and see what I could do with them. He wanted me to leave them. Later, when he made an exhibition with them, he told me that was my payment for my stay! So I do understand Debord, who was pretty well fed up with Pinot. For me it was finished. A week doing this industrial painting and you've had it! It was industry, literally. But the idea of industrial painting was fantastic. Very Beuys-like, although Joseph Beuys was later."

In an extraordinary letter of 1960, Jorn discussed the status of his donation to the movement should he leave it:

> My interest in the situationist movement is purely personal and passionate, in a direct fashion, and, if the inevitable developments of social circumstances necessitate my exclusion from the movement this changes absolutely nothing in my purely economic attitude towards this movement. The economic surplus that my social situation, insofar as I am a painter, gives me is best placed with the situationist movement, even if this movement is obliged to attack me for being in a situation from which I can't escape, but which embarrasses the movement.[10]

Jorn declares himself a strategic ally of the Situationists even if the Situationists turn against him tactically. Jorn left the Situationist International, officially at least, in 1961, and with him went his nimble fencing between aesthetic and theoretical practices. It was time to move on. As Debord wrote to Jorn in 1962: "I only want to work on a 'moving order,' never constructing a doctrine or an institution." Then he détourns Jorn back at himself. It's a question of "creating veritable disequilibria, departure points for all [future] games."[11]

The Reeperbahn district of Hamburg is best known today as the place where the Beatles really learned to play. While a young George Harrison (1943–2001) was probably on stage somewhere, playing with a toilet seat around his neck, Debord, Kotányi and Vaneigem decanted the "Hamburg Theses," although they were not so much hammering out theses as getting hammered. Debord wrote soon after to Vaneigem:

> As a profound theoretical justification of our indolence ... we agreed not to write the "Hamburg Theses," so as to impose all the better the central meaning of our entire project in the future. Thus, the enemy cannot feign to approve it without great difficulty. Moreover, one can certify that this is the height of avant-gardism in the formal presentation of ideas, perhaps opening the way for the explication of Lautréamont's *Poésies* by schoolboys? One adds the most fortunate confusion to all this if one bears in mind that it will be necessary to rank among the authors of this constellation of situationist theses (a very nebulous theoretics, out of reach and imprecise where its frontiers are concerned, but nevertheless bright and shiny) Alex Trocchi, who follows the same path but without being in nor being seen in Hamburg, at least not at the moment.[12]

Nineteenth-century revolutionaries like Louis-Auguste Blanqui plotted in secret. Marx and Engels chose instead to declare their aims to the world. With the "Hamburg Theses," the remaining rump of the Situationist International took the novel path of openly declaring that henceforth they would maintain certain secrets.

Art was now officially anti-Situationist. Spur were expelled. There was no procedure, no consensus. They were out. The timing wasn't brilliant, as Bavarian police had just seized copies of the *Spur* journal and arrested the group. De Jong shared some of Debord's reservations about the quality of Spur's journal, but she resigned from the Situationist International over the high-handed way in which a faction within it had routed them out. The nature of the movement was changing. As de Jong observes in retrospect: "This wanting to have very serious people and also clowns is in the beginning, right from the start,... It's a pity it stopped being like that."

Together with Jorn's brother Jørgen Nash (1920–2004) and Swedish ceramic artist Ansgar Elde (1933–2000), she wrote a protest against Debordian treachery. The letter sets the stage by describing the Paris of 1962 as a "cauldron of political instigations and demonstrations, armored cars in the streets, the bloody shadow of the Algerian war ... strikes, police raids, censorship ... shootings and reprisals."[13] This is the atmosphere in which they accuse Debord's faction of turning on their own comrades. And yet about all that Spur, de Jong and Nash had in common was a rejection of Debord's style of organization of the Situationist International. De Jong eventually lost patience with the mercurial Nash. She was certainly not pleased to discover him forging paintings by his more famous brother, Asger Jorn.

The Second Situationist International put together by Nash, Elde and other Scandinavian Situationists, whose founding document de Jong also signed, claimed that "now everyone is free to become a Situationist without the need for special formalities." Gone were the structural forms: the sections, the central council, the direct democracy, the vetting of potential members, and above all the principle of exclusion. While this seems in some respects a step forward, something is also lost. The possibility of exclusion binds a member to a group in a quite particular way. The game is not the same.

This founding text, "The Struggle for the Situcratic Society" (1962), was philosophical about the split between what it saw as the French and Scandinavian approaches. While the "First" Situationist International denounced the "Nashists" in harsh terms, the latter did not return fire. They identified Debord's practice as one of *position*, as opposed to the Scandinavians'—one is tempted to say Jorn's—of *mobility*. "In the argument neither side can claim to have a monopoly on the right ideas."[14] The distinction does not seem quite right. Perhaps it is rather one between an analytic conception of mobility in a fixed space, and a ludic conception of mobility in an open and variable space. Here the so-called Second International seems justified in its self-awareness as a fragment of a wider movement. Combining a low theory with a critical practice that might evade, if not avoid, capture by the institutions of art and the academy remains a challenge.

The Second International hung together for a decade or so, producing extraordinary work and one or two interesting situations.[15] They took the practice of art directly into everyday life, to create situations as experiments in ways of behaving and being together. Among them was Jens Jørgen Thorsen (1932–2000). An artist and anarchist, he was also for a time a tabloid journalist, and had a knack for provocations that could puncture the routine of the spectacle. He proposed a relational approach to art, with "the disappearance of the spectator and his replacement by the participator. A communicative art is an art which lives between. In the space between people."[16] With Thorsen's help, the Second Situationist International carried off at least two great feats of communicative art.

Out on an island in Copenhagen harbor sits the iconic statue by Edvard Erikson, the *Little Mermaid*. In 1964, the head mysteriously disappeared.[17] The Second Situationist International put out a press release claiming to know its whereabouts. They invited the media to a beach location. A diver swam towards them from a boat, but paused midway on a reef where in view of the assembled media he dropped a bag, containing a heavy object, into the sea. In 1968, when anarchists picketed the Venice Biennale, Thorsen and friends used fake press passes to get through and occupied a pavilion, complementing the siege without with an occupation within. They issued a statement denouncing the art concentration camp, which concluded with the slogan "divided we stand."[18]

The Second Situationist International set itself up as both a rival and a replacement for what it called the "First" Situationist International. Their sophistication was at the level of participatory experiments. As Thorsen said, "The situationist idea is based on utilization of art and the forces of creativity within art being used directly in the social environment." Nothing in their writing bears comparison to what T. J. Clark once called the "chiliastic serenity" of Debord's key texts.[19] And while the contempt of Debord was a given, they also managed to lose the support of Jorn, who disapproved of Thorsen's antics. While no doubt fun at the time, the *Little Mermaid* and Venice Biennale pranks do not seem to advance much beyond the Notre Dame affair the Letterists pulled off back in 1950.

In a handwritten note about the improper expulsion of the Spur group, de Jong wrote, perhaps addressing Debord: "I'm proud you call us gangsters, nevertheless you are wrong. We are worse: we are Situationists."[20] She goes on to articulate, for the first time, an accurate formula for the impasse into which the Situationists had wandered: "The Situationist International has to be considered either as an avant-garde school which has already produced a series of first-class artists thrown out after having passed through their education, OR as an anti-organization based upon new ideology which is situationist and which has not yet found in details its clear formulations in the fields of science, technique, and art."[21] The Situationist International had indeed functioned as a school for scandal, through which many fabulous (one would not say distinguished) writers and artists passed. But it could not function as an anti-organization.

De Jong adds the first principle of the new anti-organization to come: "Everybody who develops theoretically or practically this new unity is automatically a member of the situationist international and in this perspective the *Situationist Times*."[22] Here de Jong dispenses with the notion of organization altogether. The Situationist International could henceforth be taken as just one player of a collaborative game that could be challenged by another, or triangulated by a third. De Jong: "That was my idea. The important thing is: no interpretation and the freedom for anyone to join in." Perhaps it was more of a détournement of the form of the organized avant-garde than an avant-garde. Here a new kind of relation appears, perhaps with new dangers. If the Situationist International acquired the vices of collective being, anti-organization might be just one step towards the vices of an all too familiar individualism. The *Situationist Times* would head that off for now by documenting a network of related experiments, steps towards what it called the *situcratic society*.

Revenge is a dish best served from a great height. The *Situationist Times* that de Jong edited from 1962 to 1967 is a remarkable set of documents. The early issues were edited jointly with Noël Arnaud (1919–2003). A hospital administrator by profession, he was a member of Dada and surrealist groups, of Cobra and Oulipo, a satrap of the College of Pataphysics, and Boris Vian's biographer.[23] Collaborating with him suggests de Jong's awareness that the Situationists' recuperation of their own immediate avant-garde past was by no means complete. The *Situationist Times* would pointedly include texts by François Dufrêne, who left the Letterist movement in 1964 to start the Second Letterist International with Gil Wolman and others.[24] There is also a text by Piero Simondo (b. 1928) who started a new institute in Turin in 1962 to further the researches begun at Alba. Produced outside of the Situationist International and without Trocchi, the *Situationist Times* turned out to be a somewhat different beast. It was multilingual, and even its English-language texts were written in what one might now call *netlish*—transnational English unapologetically cast as a second language patterned after the writer's first language.[25] The era of French as the lingua franca of the avant-garde was over.

The *Situationist Times* pursued a different course to the experimental practice of the excluded artists and the strategic logics of the Debord faction. It offered resources for thought, action and creation, rather than a consistent line. It was more about suggesting possible connections than pronouncing on fault lines. De Jong was interested in a logic of images, of concepts that might be discovered and presented through visual conjunction. If one took seriously Lautréamont's injunction that "poetry should be made by all," then perhaps a journal—any reproducible media—should distribute both finished art and raw materials with which others could make art. Or perhaps there could be no difference between a raw material and a finished work.

Each issue contained the statement, consistent with established Situationist practice, to the effect that "all reproduction, deformation, modification, derivation, and transformation of the *Situationist Times* are permitted." This was similar to the *copyleft* statement published in *Internationale Situationniste*, and connects Situationist practice with the hacker and pirate practices of twenty-first-century struggles around free culture as a fitfully acknowledged, still barely understood, precursor.

The first issue of the *Situationist Times* defended the Spur group, expelled from the Situationist International at a time when charges were being brought against them for their allegedly licentious publication. In a little dossier of texts is included a strong editorial from Arnaud, a statement by Debord and others, and some fragments of a comic strip called "Spur: Paintings and Sculptures." It includes a panel with a Situationist last supper, the elements of which include: Bauhaus, shit, violins, birds, beauty, belches, mercilessness, coffee, and kisses. The issue also documents the expulsion of the "Nashists" of the Second Situationist International with a crude détournement of pages from the *Internationale Situationniste* journal.[26] There is a letter in Danish from J. V. Martin, the only Scandinavian to remain loyal to Debord, attacking Nash. Where the *Internationale Situationniste* always aims at a consistent line, the *Situationist Times* is interested in the relationships between players.

Several issues present what remained of *Mutant*, a post–Situationist International collaboration between Jorn and Debord that turned away from the then-current spectacle of the *space age* towards a prescient intervention in the technological transformation of earthbound life.[27] Never set foot in a fallout shelter, *Mutant* advises, for "it is better to die standing with all the cultural heritage of humanity, the perpetual modification of which must remain our task." Nuclear weaponry's main function is to deter not the enemy but the state's own population. Contrary to the Ban the Bomb movement, this position sees not nuclear annihilation as the main threat, but the disarming of critique. The channeling of critical energy into the anti-nuclear cause serves the interests of existing political forces. Hence: "I ... pledge myself not to expect the necessary upheavals of society [to be effected] by any of the existing formations of specialized politics." One wonders how much the twenty-first century's obsession with things environmental might likewise play a demobilizing role.

A consistent project in the *Situationist Times* is the investigation of *topology*, in keeping with one of Jorn's abiding interests.[28] The mathematician and surrealist collage artist Max Bucaille (1906–96) contributed a whole series of texts on the subject. Topology is a geometry of transformations, and it exercised a fascination over a number of postwar artists, architects, and writers, including Henri Lefebvre, who were looking for a more modern understanding of space than perspective drawing. Topology seemed to better describe the geometric imagination of folk art, with its knots, rings, spirals and labyrinths, all of which the *Situationist Times* documented with copious photographs from cross-cultural sources. While many were interested in its formal properties, here it points towards a way of diagramming practices in space and time, a *situology* of singular and variable forms. De Jong: "That is the beautiful thing about topology, that everything can be changed at any time."[29]

Following his withdrawal from active participation in the Situationist International, Jorn took on some ambitious new projects. His great interest at the time was in documenting what he took to be a Nordic spatio-temporal folk culture, quite at odds with the formal geometry bequeathed to modern art and science by the Renaissance. For this purpose he created yet another organization, the Scandinavian Institute for Comparative Vandalism (1961–65). According to Jorn's friend and collector Guy Atkins, "the unattractive name was deliberately chosen to put off art lovers."[30] It referred to graffiti found in Normandy churches in which Jorn saw the hand of peoples migrating from the North, leaving their mark, so to speak, on European culture.

More generally, *comparative vandalism* named an understanding of popular cultural creation that could appreciate the way it flowed along migration routes, subtly defacing the edifice of every cultural center it encountered. Jorn was interested in the traces left by the dérive of whole peoples over centuries and continents. Jorn thought that the wandering attitude to life of different migrating groups might have produced comparable understandings of space and time, expressed in similar visual iconographies.

Jorn co-authored a book on the church graffiti, but the main part of the project was the documentation of the distinctive symbolic and ornamental forms of the northern world.[31] The project was to culminate in a massive book series — *10,000 Years of Nordic Folk Art* — but little was published at the time. Jorn may have run into difficulties with his academic partners, state officials or his collaborator, the noted photographer Gérard Franceschi (1915–2001). De Jong, who worked closely with Jorn on the project, says that "the trouble started with Franceschi, who wanted more money and more credit." While the project acknowledged traditional archaeological classifications, Jorn was also interested in applying his comparative method to the visual forms, tracing patterns of modification and borrowings across place and time. Jorn: "Through my art I have learned to see and find meaningful relationships where others might not see them."[32] The volumes were to contain articles by specialists, but the meat of them is Jorn's organization of Franceschi's photographs into stunning, elaborate, purely visual essays.

When *10,000 Years of Nordic Folk Art* stalled, Jorn used the Institute for Comparative Vandalism as the vehicle for another extensive publishing project, this time of his own writings. The Institute began issuing his manuscripts as reports: *The Natural Order* (1962), *Value and Economics* (1962, including a revised version of his earlier *Critique of Political Economy* of 1960), *Luck and Chance: Dagger and Guitar* (1963), and *Thing and Polis* (1964). What the Marquis de Sade was to the surrealists and the Comte de Lautréamont to the Situationists, Emanuel Swedenborg (1688–1772) was to the Jorn of the Comparative Vandalism period. From the Swedish mystic Jorn took the principle of correspondences and turned it into the literary technique of *triolectics*, in which he would triangulate any three concepts, and through analogies, puns, transpositions, permutate them in unexpected directions.

This procedure for navigating flocks of concepts, arranged in threes, combined a precise discipline with limitless movement. To Jorn it was a topological approach to the concept, a way of thinking concepts via spatial transformation, in a "polydimensional cosmos of the surface." Or as he said elsewhere: "all my outpourings of words are just one long defense of a world to which words have no right of entrance." In these texts, Jorn taught himself to swim atop Lautréamont's old ocean. Peter Shield: "Jorn's texts are a work of art."[33] Works that have yet to find a domain of critical reception.

De Jong made her own use of the extraordinary photographs Jorn collected for his researches on comparative vandalism in the *Situationist Times*. They are a key part of the journal's attempt to gather materials for a situology to come, a critical practice in time and space no longer dependent on the language and forms of art or politics. The Situationist International had surprisingly little to say about actual situations. Drawing on Jorn's extensive researches, the *Situationist Times* would at last attempt a more explicit inquiry. Perhaps the abandonment of the more rigid geometry of the organization, with its static national sections, opened up the possibility of a variable field of collaboration.

"Situation: Life space or part of it conceived in terms of its content (meaning). The life space may consist of one situation or two or more overlapping situations. The term situation refers either to the general life situation or the momentary situation."[34] Situation is (Satrean) a hinge between subject and objective space. "Situation, overlapping: Two or more situations which exist simultaneously and which have a common part. The person is generally located within this common part." Once space and time are thought in terms of situations, then an assessment of the potential of such spaces and times is possible. "Space of free movement: Regions accessible to the person from his present position. The space of free movement is usually a multiply connected region. Its limits are determined mainly by (1) what is forbidden to a person, (2) what is beyond his abilities." Situations and the regions they compose can be not only thought but appropriated according not to boundaries of function or ownership, but relations of contiguity and continuity. "Structure of a region: Refers to (1) degree of differentiation of the region (2) arrangement of its part regions, (3) degree of connection between its parts." The *Situationist Times* is, among other things, elementary research into space and time that can be self-composing.

A situology might be a theory and practice of intervening in the currents of a turbulent time, an art of the event, a politics of the event, but one that seeks out the limits of art and politics. With the irrevocable split between Paris and everyone else, the conditions were not ripe for sharpening such practices and experiments against the blade of critique. Howard Slater writes:

> In many ways the conflicts with Spur and the [Nashists] were to some degree encouraged and used by the First Situationist International to prune itself of contradictions that may have eventually led to a deepening of the theory of the spectacle, a politicization of the practice of art and a productive extension of its notion of class ... The problem of creativity — the right to productive socialization as a countervalue — was not resolved, it was polarized.[35]

Or perhaps Debord did everyone a favor by forcing the issue, by choosing paths, rather than allowing the movement to sink, like so many others, beneath the weight of its incoherence.

The contradictions the Situationist International attempted to prune may well be those inherent in romanticism, the strategy that Lefebvre thought was the headwaters of the movement. The Situationist International never worked through the terms of this tension. It relied on the romantic staple of a poetics to bring together an anthropological and a cosmological nature. The tension proved too great. Debord and Constant stuck close to the project of an anthropological nature, indeed Constant made the entire world over in its image. Nash and Spur head in the opposite direction, where a wild and woolly cosmological nature can irrupt into the social.

Only Jorn and de Jong come close to appreciating the necessary tension between an anthropological and a cosmological nature, although in Lefebvre's terms, Jorn's Dionysian proclivities rule out the possibility of superseding the tension between them. Lefebvre: "the Dionysian dance is not always a round." Sometimes it destroys rather than creates. Jorn found a writerly procedure, a spatial or topological logic of the concept, for navigating the difference between reason and nature. Lefebvre really thought that the Situationists had opened a new path, extending romanticism in a new direction. Perhaps he was, and is, right: "The most brilliant Situationists are exploring and testing out a kind of lived utopianism."[36] In the pages of the *Situationist Times* are carefully documented many the irreconcilable elements strewn about by the implosion of the Situationist International, together with not a few innovations contributed by adjacent avant-gardes.

Perhaps it can all be put best allegorically. In the *Situationist Times* No. 5, de Jong reproduces the "Parable of the Three Rings" by Gotthold Lessing (1729–81). Saladin, ruler of Jerusalem, summons Nathan to his court, and asks him which of the three faiths of the city is the true one. Nathan can hardly tell a Muslim ruler that Christianity or his own Judaism is the true faith, and in any case he suspects Saladin's real intention is to milk him for cash. So he answers with a parable. Once upon a time lived a man who possessed a ring which made its bearer beloved by man and God. He had three sons, so he had copies of the ring made, and bequeathed the three rings to his three sons. At once the sons set to fighting over which was the real ring. When the case came before the judge, he observed that all three sons had nothing but enmity for each other, which led him to conclude that none of the rings was the real one, that each was a détournement. Perhaps the father had lost it, and given all the sons copies. Or perhaps the father did not want one ring to dominate the others, and so made copies so exact nobody could tell the difference.

The judge exhorted the three descendants each to live as if he possessed the real ring, thus demonstrating that he would be worthy of it. Saladin was pleased with this tale, and dismissed Nathan. Before taking his leave, Nathan tactfully offered to leave a substantial sum on deposit with his ruler, who after all had the power to judge between the three faiths of Jerusalem and determine their fortunes. It is not immaterial to this story that Jorn was the patron of all of the descendants of the Situationist International, usually through donations of his rather valuable paintings. He supported them all for a time. Nor was this unusual behavior for Jorn, who by hewing to the principles of the gift economy accumulated a remarkable collection of modern art, most of which now constitutes the collection of the Silkeborg Museum, an enduring monument to potlatch.

In *For Form* (1958) Jorn was largely critical of contemporary architecture and design, which he thought had usurped the role of art as a critical and creative practice. Yet the book offered one image by a living architect: an elevation drawing for his submission to the Sydney

Opera House competition by his Danish contemporary Jørn Utzon (1918–2008). Utzon at one time wanted to commission some of Jorn's colorful ceramic tiles for the Sydney Opera House. This did not come to pass, but Jorn returned the favor when he asked Utzon to design his museum at Silkeborg. Utzon presented plans and a plaster model for the project in 1964. Bulb-shaped galleries three stories high, buried underground, with crocus-like protrusions above ground, clad in brilliant ceramic, the proposal combined curved shapes with mass-produced components. Visitors would enter the caverns on curling ramps, strolling past hanging artworks lit by natural light filtering in at odd angles from above. While there could be no such thing as a Situationist art museum, Utzon's proposal certainly embodied Jorn's aesthetics of pliable form.[37]

Housing his gift would take more than potlatch. The Utzon plans for Silkeborg never materialized because Jorn couldn't raise the funds. But perhaps there was something premature in even such a fitting mausoleum for Jorn's life and work. Considered as the husk of a once-viable unitary project, Situationist materials may yet have some juice in them that has not been sucked dry in a three-way necrophilia with the museum and with scholarship. But there might be other projects, spun off out of internal tensions with the Situationist International, that also might be considered as materials for a future critical practice. Two such projects exemplify the possibilities and limitations of a practice after art. Both were nurtured within the Situationist International, and both extend beyond it. One is mostly a project for the overcoming of literature, the other for the overcoming of architecture. They are otherwise quite different and are the product of former members who had very little to do with each other. Indeed, both revealed significant differences from the Situationist International.

After literature comes project sigma, whose instigator was Alexander Trocchi (1925–84). After architecture comes New Babylon, the life-work of Constant Nieuwenhuys. Constant and Trocchi were roughly contemporaries. They were both products, among other things, of Saint-Germain. About the only other thing they had in common was that at one time they had earned Guy Debord's respect—and he had earned theirs. Just as Nash and de Jong parted ways with Debord and spun off into their own collaborative practices, so too did Alexander Trocchi. Or at least he gave it a go.

10   An Athlete of Duration

Better known as a novelist, Trocchi tried and failed to form a much more ambitious movement. He called it project sigma, after the mathematical sign that can stand for the sum or the totality. He thought it "free of bothersome semantic accretions." He set out his sigma project in two luminous texts, "The Invisible Insurrection of a Million Minds" and "Sigma: A Tactical Blueprint." "Revolt is understandably unpopular," he writes, and generally conceived in a somewhat backward way. Just as Leon Trotsky knew enough to seize the railways and the power stations while the old guard persisted in defending the offices of the state, "so cultural revolt must seize the grids of expression and the powerhouses of the mind." Rather than a frontal confrontation, Trocchi suggests a more subtle practice of installing the material basis for a new practice of creation. It is no longer a question of a new journal or art movement. "Art can have no existential significance for a civilization which draws a line between life and art and collects artifacts like ancestral bones for reverence."[1] It's a question of new relations of creation.

The key Trocchi finds in a stray quote from his contemporary Raymond Williams (1921–88), a pioneer of cultural materialism and British cultural studies: "The question is not who will patronize the arts, but what forms are possible in which artists will have control of their own means of expression, in such ways that they will have relation to a community rather than to a market or a patron."[2] Williams is best known today for the project of democratizing the practice of critical reading. Here he takes up the production side of the creation of a people's culture. This appealed to Trocchi, who found proletarian culture rather more stifling than did Williams. In what must have been a charming thought to Debord, Trocchi wanted to bypass the brokers of the culture industry—the publisher and art dealers. In an extraordinary mix of the practical and the sublime, he plots the means of creative autonomy within capitalism itself.

Trocchi's project sigma is partly inspired by Black Mountain College (1933–57), the famous North Carolina school, where Franz Kline, Robert Creeley, Merce Cunningham, John Cage and so many other transformative figures of the American avant-garde once taught. Trocchi also conceives of sigma as "a continuous, international, experimental conference."[3] Spaces of free creation, of ongoing and unfolding situations, could be based just outside metropolitan areas, a network of experimental sites in constant communication.

The actually existing university has become a microcosm of spectacular society. It reproduces and reinforces a strictly functional approach to creation. Trocchi mentions a contest at Cambridge University to come up with a use for its neglected chapels. Many are quite beautiful and once functioned as the unitary heart of their respective colleges. The winning suggestion was to turn them into canteens or student housing. Trocchi thought brothels would at least be a more spiritual solution. The postwar university was rapidly becoming a mere functional support for the spectacle, training the mediators who would manage its desires. What was lacking was a point at which to start making situations.

The sigma texts are part manifesto, part manual. The practical side to Trocchi's proposal is the means of funding it. Project sigma is not just a university, it is also an agency for what Jorn called the creative elite. Those who join it become part of an agency controlled by the creators themselves. Sigma lives off residuals, patents, commissions, even what one would now call consultancy fees. Its network of spontaneous universities function as advertisements for themselves. One might almost say that they are brands. Trocchi's solution is a weird kind of Leninist dual power.[4] An autonomous, self-managed, unalienated power of seamless creativity exists alongside the old commodified spectacle until such time as it can subsume it within its new means of creation. It is both science fiction and a business plan, a utopian future and an almost exact description of sophisticated spectacular business in the twenty-first century. It could almost be the model for the Blue Ant agency of Hubertus Bigend (b. 1967), the fictional son of a Situationist in the novels of William Gibson.[5] It is a summation of Trocchi's own extraordinary experience, yet it is also a program he was in no sense fit to carry out in person.

Trocchi survived a genteel-poor upbringing in Glasgow. During the war he sailed on convoy ships taking supplies to the Soviet Union. After a stint at Glasgow University he took advantage of a scholarship to ship off to Paris. He was an editor of the English-language journal *Merlin* (1952–54), which coexisted in friendly rivalry with the *Paris Review* of George Plimpton and friends. In Paris he fell under the spell of Samuel Beckett and managed to get Beckett published, together with Jean Genet and Eugène Ionesco, with Olympia Press, a Paris-based, English-language imprint best known for its porn. Like more than a few expats, Trocchi wrote porn novels for Olympia's charming but deeply dodgy impresario Maurice Girodias.[6]

The best of Trocchi's porn novels is *Helen and Desire* (1954). Growing up in the far north of Australia, Helen is a bored teenager with only her own immediate sensations to amuse her. "I count the sea as my first love … it was an impersonal one." She embarks on the adventure of renouncing her own will, her subjectivity, her interiority. Instead she allows herself a terrible and ungovernable thirst for annihilation. And yet Helen remains a writer. The book purports to be a found manuscript, a diary not of a person but of a process of depersonalization. The body becomes a surface for the replacement of self with sensation: "Riven now at twin poles of delight, my glistening torso slithered under discs, flats, and surfaces, under flanges of containment and protusion, all seeking the weld of female union. My breasts, charged with ambiguous alluvial sensations, slipped to and fro under their counterparts …"[7]

Helen's writing recounts the steps by which the very possibility of authorship is undone. Her diary ends when there is no longer a subject to be writing it: "And gradually the whole desire to commit my experiences to history has been outflanked by the terrible pleasure I experience in approaching the unconscious state of an object … It is indeed doubtful whether I can still usefully use the word 'I.'"[8] Helen gives herself over to the situation, and abolishes the act of writing, the possibility of literature as a separate art, in the process.

Self-destruction seemed preferable to self-construction, to the institutional forces that pinned the self in place. Trocchi wrote about such institutions in a short story for his *Moving Times*, a literary journal that was supposed to appear as posters in subway stations:

At the third jolt the patient's body was seen to shudder like a tall jelly within the leather harness, and a wisp of blue smoke issued from his nostrils, a reaction generally regarded as a symptom of what, in technical nomenclature, is called "reintegration." The patient reintegrated slowly, the shuddering subsided gradually over a period of two and a half hours, after which he was returned to the deep freeze as a precaution against pong.[9]

The construction of the stable subject requires a huge effort of disciplinary force, but it is not as if there were a natural self which such techniques suppress. Rather, it's a choice between two kinds of process, between the psychiatric techniques of the subject, or the crafty whittling of the body into sensate being within the unstable, unfolding embrace of the situation. As the social and medical sciences claim the body as their own, Trocchi finds resources for the body's self-experiments in writing.

As a writer Trocchi connects Beckett to William Burroughs, and both to Debord. His great, *Cain's Book* (1960) is often considered a Beat classic, but it is rarely read as a Situationist text. Debord was an admirer of Malcolm Lowry (1909–57), author of *Under the Volcano* (1947), with whom Trocchi had at least two things in common. They both produced only one book that was a literary success, and they both preferred to destroy themselves rather than inflict more literature on the world. Lowry was an alcoholic; Trocchi a drug fiend. Both explored in depth the practice of playing with time, with time outside of both labor and leisure. Trocchi's advice to ambitious writers: "Let them dedicate a year to pinball and think again." Both were adepts at what Trocchi called "the chemistry of alienation."[10] Both found the limits to becoming a professional in the art of intoxication.

"Tomorrow is an age of Doctors," Trocchi says prophetically. By 2007 the American Environmental Protection Agency will announce that what it calls the *emerging contaminants* in drinking water come mostly from anti-depressants, painkillers, antibiotics, hormones and blood pressure remedies.[11] It's the effluent of the affluent world of spectacular medicine. The disintegrating spectacle has inadvertently medicated whole populations, not only of humans but of other species too, a whole biosphere rendered comfortably numb. It's a by-product of constantly reintegrating the human body into the uniform time of production and consumption, for a time that repeats the same steady intervals without end; and rendered efficiently, without the blue smoke.

The central character in *Cain's Book* avoids work as best he can, and takes to its extreme the practice of playing with his own life. This play is far from a joyful distraction. It is an immersion in one intensity after another. "To mean everything and for everything to be a confidence trick, tasting power coming into being for others; I had often thought that only through play could one taste that power safely, if dangerously, and that when the spirit of play died there was only murder."[12] From Sartre, Trocchi took the idea of being condemned to freedom. Unlike Sartre, he did not limit himself to discussing banal situations in which one might be confronted by this freedom. Rather, new situations had to be created. For Debord this creation of situations was always a collaborative project, of love and play and boisterous rivalry as a means of effacing bourgeois consciousness. For Trocchi it was a much more grim and solitary business, a lone self-purgation amid the purgatory of other people.

Cain's Book was, for all its brilliance, something of a dead end. It lacks the self-annihilating power of *Helen and Desire*. It allows itself the one masochism the earlier book did its utmost to refuse: that of becoming the plaything of *literature*. Its failure to put an end to literature led the critic James Campbell to declare with smug satisfaction: "The novel didn't die, after all, but, following *Cain*, Trocchi's part in it did."[13] This is not the least reason that Trocchi's post-*Cain* writing calls for a fresh appreciation. He borrowed in part from his friend and contemporary Wallace Berman (1927–76) and his attempt to redefine circuits of communication for poetry and visual art with his homemade journal *Semina* (1955–64). Trocchi shifts attention from form as a question of arranging words on the page to form as the question of the medium and economy by which words are communicated.[14]

While *Cain's Book* is now a captive of its own literary success, the same cannot be said of the *sigma portfolio* (1964). The *portfolio* allowed Trocchi to abandon literature and yet keep writing. It's a project he hatched in New York, but brought back to London with him, "close under his eyelids, an electronic load, an unwritten book, a plan in four dimensions, a shadow one, including time ..." This puckish, punkish project would be self-generating and self-published. "The *sigma portfolio* is an entirely new dimension in publishing, through which the writer reaches his public immediately, outflanking the traditional traps of publishing-house policy, and by means of which the reader gets it, so to speak, 'hot' from the writer's pen, the photographer's lens, etc."[15]

Through a probably deliberate misunderstanding, Trocchi presents the early Letterist movement as being based, not on chipping writing down to the letter in the typographic sense, but on the sending of letters in the postal, or perhaps topographic sense. He borrows from the Letterist International the name *Potlatch*, but to designate what he calls an *interpersonal log*. It is to be an open-ended series of simple typed and duplicated documents. "This gambit, a round robin which includes *n* participants, an interpersonal experiment in expression; a man responding as and when he pleases; copies of his response at once roneo-ed for circulation; individuals chiming in, checking out at any time."[16]

Trocchi calls it a *log* to stress the temporal aspect, the sequence of statement and rejoinder: "it should literally discover many things, including the dialectical process of its own growth." Where the book puts an end to the transformations of the text and sets up a distinction between author and reader, the interpersonal log keeps transforming itself, and makes of its readers writers and of its writers readers. "Essentially ludic, and calling, it seems to me, for a particular kind of gesture, it might be called *potlatch*." It might also be called *blogging*.[17] Trocchi invented a web of logs before there was even an internet.

Or it might be called sigma, that blank, elusive, all-embracing one-word poem that Trocchi put at the heart of the enterprise. "For, sigma is a word referring to something which is quite independent of myself or of any other individual, and if we are correct in our historical analysis, we must regard it as having 'begun' a long time ago."[18] The term sigma stands in for a process, without beginning or end, without subject or goal, and yet which is not a mere abstract force, but something experienced within the lived time of everyday life. This willful and collaborative play within and against creative forces is the thread that becomes lost under the conditions of spectacular society.

And so "it is the object of sigma to bring all informations out into the open." The *sigma portfolio* is a kind of residue of a process, which leaves behind a diagram of the ephemeral forces that make and unmake situations. Passing through the interstitial spaces of spectacular society, not least its literature, the *sigma portfolio* finds light, cheap, temporary means to bypass the spectacular and yet, for all its evanescence, to become an exemplary instance of the new power at work in the world. Sigma is a new power which is at the same time the ancient power of homo ludens, joining in with the ineffable play of the world.

Trocchi quotes Debord: "Everything being connected, it was necessary to change it by a unitary struggle, or nothing." Trocchi's sigma texts abound in tactical maxims: the round robin of Roneoed texts is an outflanking gesture, which exploits a loophole in the technical apparatus of mechanical reproduction. But where Debord's tactics are always elusive, seductive, Trocchi wants to create a center, which he sometimes calls the *box office*, as if it offered tickets to the endgame of the spectacle itself. "The box office will be a primitive micro-model of a possible future." This plan for a consciously constructed environment includes audiovisual media as well as *futiques* (future antiques), objects designed for open-ended play. The resources of all the arts are to be integrated into the conscious construction of situations.

The portfolio includes Trocchi's détourned version of a "Situationist Manifesto." What he adds and subtracts from the *orthodox* Situationist document is instructive. Like Constant, he stresses the role of automation in clearing the way for a ludic world. "Automation, and a general 'socialization' of vital goods will gradually and ineluctably dispense with most of the necessity for 'work': eventually, as near as dammit, the complete liberty of the individual in relation to production will be attained." In place of surplus value, a play value. But play meets resistance. Just as the church resisted the festival, so the authorities seize *Cain's Book*. The unions resist automation and defend work. Sigma has to take place outside of all forms of existing power: "we propose immediate action on the international scale, a self-governing (non-)organization of producers of the new culture beyond, and independent of, all political organizations …"[19]

No matter how euphoric his theory, Trocchi's practice is modest in scale: "so long as our techniques for the passing on of informations grow with the passage of time more and more effective, etc., our insurrection will snowball of its own momentum."[20] The means of dissemination for sigma was the stencil duplicator, or mimeograph machine. Ironically enough it was a popular medium for the kinds of organization sigma eschews, such as churches, schools and social clubs. It was the original medium for science fiction fanzines. Trocchi found that this low-tech device also afforded a means for making low theory. Duplicating was an easy and cheap means of making copies by the hundreds without recourse to a professional printer. Popular makes included Gestetner and Ditto. Trocchi used another trademark as a verb—to Roneo—although strictly speaking this brand worked by a slightly different process.

Trocchi claims at least some sigma texts were composed directly on the stencil. He would have taken the ribbon out of the typewriter, inserted the stencil and typed away. The stencil was a stiff sheet of card backed with wax, and attached to it a thin sheet of tissue paper. The impact of the keys cuts the letters into the wax, with the residue sticking to the tissue paper. Judging by the *sigma portfolio*, Trocchi was a good stencil cutter: type too hard, and the enclosed spaces within the letters turn to black blobs. Once Trocchi cut the stencil, he removed it from the typewriter and attached it to the drum, which was filled with ink. He would then turn the crank by hand, each rotation drawing a sheet of paper under the drum, through the pressure rollers, copying his text in the process. On most duplicators, it takes a bit of fiddling with various settings to get good copies. Judging by surviving copies, Trocchi and his sigma associates mastered it. Martin Heidegger: "the typewriter makes everyone look the same."[21] Perhaps not, if one looks closely enough.

Trocchi was not exactly master of his own life. Constant: "Freedom is the most difficult way of living that man can lead. For freedom can only be realized in creation and creation means discipline."[22] The quest for extreme situations quickly collapsed into the sheer habit of junkie life. When he was living in Venice Beach, California, hanging out with the Beats, he was visited one day by Irving Rosenthal (b. 1930), who wrote down his impressions of Trocchi's materialist and experimental attitude to life there in his very own Musée Imaginaire:

> Everything functional had been drafted into the service of art, taken apart and reassembled, and many things looked subjected to more than one transformation, as if the lust to create had been so overpowering as to become cannibalistic, or as if each object of art, once created, became as stupid as a lamp or bookend, and had to be destroyed and built anew. The whole room seemed to belong

to another world, to whose inhabitants these uncanny furnishings were the beds and chairs of everyday life.

Rosenthal quickly soured on Trocchi and his miniature version of unitary urbanism: "Even the little true beauty I picked up there, to pop in my mouth and suck on, was mixed with a slow-acting poison to make the eyes opaque and dreamless ..." It would not be long before the whole place burned to the ground.[23] Trocchi was an addict, and like many addicts, left a wake of casual violence behind him. The poet, artist and jazz musician Jeff Nuttall (1933–2004), who assisted him for a time, left a portrait that has the rare quality of being critical but nonjudgmental: "Trocchi once told me he first took heroin for the sense of inviolability it gave him. If the cool hipster is severed from identificatory processes and thus from other people's pleasure and pain, he is nevertheless an athlete of time. ... No user is punctual."[24] This queer athleticism has nothing to do with stopwatches and world records. It is not an athleticism of measurable time. Rather, it is an extreme sporting with duration, with immeasurable time itself.

In his novel *Tainted Love* (2005), Stewart Home (b. 1962) is not so kind.

> Alex liked women, but clearly he preferred getting them fucked up on drugs to any kind of physical intimacy. Trocchi got a kick out of watching a beautiful woman like Lyn spiraling downwards through endless cycles of degradation. And when Lyn did die Alex was mortified, and it seemed to me that he'd been killed either with or before her. Trocchi no longer simply took drugs; he had become heroin. Alex was dead and didn't yet know it. I liked and admired Trocchi, he was a visionary who'd written two brilliant novels, but when it came to his relationship with other people he could be a complete cunt.[25]

This is written from the point of view of a young woman who is herself hustling for heroin, who is the mother of the novel's narrator, and who dies in dubious circumstances. It's a timely reminder that not everyone survives bohemia, and that those who rise to it from delinquency rather than fall into it out of privilege have rather a hard time of it. The romance still clinging to Rosenthal's version is here—almost—expunged.

For someone like Constant, the failure of Trocchi's project sigma had less to do with Trocchi's personal limitations than with objective necessity. The spectacle required a structural transformation which no mere passing of *informations* between disaffected hipsters could ever achieve. New Babylon placed its bets on changing the forms within which everyday life is experienced. Constant: "The culture of New Babylon does not result from isolated activities, from exceptional situations, but from the global activity of the whole world population, every human being engaged in a dynamic relation with his surroundings."[26] In an era that would become absorbed with the permutations of cultural superstructures, Constant's obsession with infrastructure was a rare corrective.

11 New Babylon

Frankfurt [in 1950] was indescribable. I'd borrowed a studio from a painter who was himself in Paris. I was working there for an exhibition in the Zimmergallerie Frank, and every morning I took my son to school. The walk to the school was across an enormous bomb site. A greap heap of rubble, with here and there some places that had been flattened so you could walk over them like paths. There were some outer walls of houses still standing. A doorway, and some stretches of wall. It was a surreal landscape ... If you walk through a town that lies in ruins, then the first thing you naturally think of is building. And then, as you rebuild such a town, you wonder whether life there will be just the same, or what will be different.[1]

Perhaps for Constant very different.

Constant built a future out of offcut Plexiglas and bicycle spokes. Later he would say that his marvelous models of New Babylon were appreciated in much the same way as African masks were in surrealist times, as interesting forms, but stripped of their significance for everyday life. What is lost from New Babylon is a passion gone from the world, a desire to seize the world itself as the object of desire, to find a form for the whole of life.[2]

Constant had photographs made of New Babylon, and a film. He produced a newspaper for it, and he gave his famous lecture-performances. All to conjure into being a landscape that envisioned what was possible right here and now, but was held back by the fetter of outdated relations of production. It was not a utopia. "I prefer to call it a realistic project, because it distances itself from the present condition which has lost touch with reality, and because it is founded on what is technically feasible, on what is desirable from a human viewpoint, on what is inevitable from a social viewpoint."[3] The question that lingers is not whether New Babylon was merely a dream, but whether actually existing built form is really a nightmare.

Modern architecture, begun with so much promise, had found its default setting in functionalism. It divided the city between the functions of work, transport, leisure and the home. Its ruling passion was *efficiency*. The city was a machine for the free circulation of capital, labor, materials and products. Planners merely accepted existing social relations as given. They accepted the division between public and private. On the one hand, private property, the bourgeois family, and the car. On the other, pathetic little Bantustans of public life, hived off to the margins.

New Babylon is a détournement, not of art or literature, but of modern architecture and town planning. Jorn: "Why are we, free artists, so interested in the doctrines of modern architecture? Because they exclude us." Even more troubling, architects co-opt artists, or claim the role of artist for themselves.[4] If there is a key architect whom New Babylon can be read as détourning, it is Constant's friend, mentor and patron Aldo van Eyck (1918–99). While caught up in the modern movement, van Eyck was critical of architecture as a pseudo-science, and critical of modern built form with its "miles upon miles of organized nowhere."[5] He took his inspiration more from modern art and physics than architecture. Like Jorn and Gallizio, he saw art and science as creative experiments that shattered the last vestiges of a Platonic universe of static order and eternal forms. Once famous for the hundreds of children's playgrounds he built in Amsterdam, he was also an original theorist. He extended the momentum of what he called the "great riot" of modernism into built form.

The key architectural form for van Eyck is the threshold, which he imagines not as dividing one space from another, say public from private, but as connecting one possibility to another. Rather than an efficient division of space by function, he imagines a landscape of place, occasion, threshold, an architecture in which to tarry. As he writes in the *Situationist Times*, "a house is a tiny city, a city is a huge house." The key is to think built form more in terms of time than space, a time that can't be measured. For people who can linger there, the city enables times of full participation and rich experience. The city is when "associative awareness changes and extends perception, rendering it transparent and profound through memory and anticipation." The urban malingerer becomes aware of *duration*. Here time acquires depth and subtlety, and "awareness of duration is as gratifying as awareness of the passing instant is oppressive. The former opens time, renders it transparent, whilst the latter closes time, rendering it impenetrable."[6]

The sensation of duration is the sense of being itself. Architecture should make us at home in duration, not enclose us in space, nor in time measured out as if it were space. Van Eyck does not want to build a dwelling for *being*, but a nexus for a homecoming. Such in-between places, or thresholds, can "resolve the conflicts which exteriorize man from time (thereby closing the door on himself)." The people make places, but not with the space of their own choosing. Van Eyck wants an architecture that can imply the capacity for making meaning, for turning space into places. This is why his playgrounds contain only abstract forms, which play makes meaningful in its own inimitable ways. Constant radicalizes van Eyck's program. He extends the playground over the surface of the earth. The problem, he realizes, is total, and if the architect-planner does not take on the totality of built form, then, as van Eyck says, "people will spread over the globe and be at home nowhere."[7]

While Constant borrows his program from van Eyck, the architectural language that he détourns comes from French utopian architects of the postwar years. There were at least three such utopias. The Architecture Principe group built on the bunker archaeology of Paul Virilio (b. 1932). They proposed massive forms, sloping floors, all to create a conserving architecture that would arrest and congeal the rapid flux of contemporary life. The Utopie group, which included Jean Baudrillard (1929–2007), took the opposite tack, favoring a temporary and playful architecture of inflatable pods (if not of blow-up dog turds). Meanwhile, architects like Yona Friedman (b. 1923) proposed building space-frames in the air, hoisted aloft on pylons. Like Le Corbusier, Friedman thought this form allows for the separation of networks that move different things at different speeds.[8] This was the form Constant favored too, even though he used the elevated spaceframe for quite different ends.[9] Of all these seemingly utopian projects, Constant's is the only one for which a transformation in built form can only come out of a transformation of social relations.

Rather than demolish the old world to build a *radiant city*; rather than build a *garden city* on greenfield sites, Constant cantilevers new spaces up above, leaving both city and countryside untouched. Automated factories would be underground, the surface level is for transport, while up above stretches a new landscape for play, a massive superstructure of linked *sectors*, within which everything is malleable, changeable at whim. Considered vertically, as an elevation, New Babylon makes literal Marx's diagram of base and superstructure. Its airy sectors are literally superstructures, made possible by an infrastructure below ground where mechanical reproduction has abolished scarcity and freed all of time from necessity. It is an image of what Constant imagines the development of productive forces has made possible, but which the fetter of existing relations of production prevents from coming into being.

New Babylon responds both to the expansion of material resources and the expansion of population. Like a suburban family that adds a new story when the second kid is born, Constant builds a second deck—for the whole planet. Rather than suburban sprawl inserting itself into any and every terrain, he leaves much of the old world intact—including, interestingly, the classic spaces of the dérive in the heart of the old cities such as Paris and Amsterdam. The Les Halles of which Abdelhafid Khatib was so fond would remain. This is a new world that expands, not horizontally but vertically. It is a "a new skin that covers the earth and multiplies its living space."[10] Not the least charm of New Babylon is that Constant thinks the planet is a robust enough foundation on which to build such a bold addition.

Like many others at the time, Constant was influenced by the *cybernetic* theories of Norbert Wiener (1894–1964), particularly his notion of a second industrial revolution. Wandering the streets of London and Manchester, Friedrich Engels movingly recorded the human misery that resulted from the first one. It confounded modern artists, who felt compelled to either reject industry or embrace it. The alternate utopian visions of William Morris and Edward Bellamy represented these two seemingly incompatible options.[11] As Lefebvre might say, they détourned the resources of romantic dissent against the rise of capitalism, drawing respectively on its visions of a cosmological and an anthropological order. But this debate was now moot. The first industrial revolution had given way to the second, a revolution in the use of information as a means of control.

Cybernetics might just provide the means of mitigating the damage of the first industrial revolution, while building on its enormous expansion of productive potential. Or it could result in what Wiener called the "fascist ant-state."[12] Constant takes to heart Engels's formula that communism reduces the state to the administration of things. Cybernetics as control is relegated below ground, to the world of administered things. Cybernetics as freedom, as the ability to connect anywhere, anytime, is in play up above. Constant pushes the debate about technicity to both extremes at once: total control and total freedom. By exacerbating the instrumentalizing tendencies of cybernetic control, freedom from necessity appears in the realm of the possible.

Constant was not alone in imagining cybernetic automation to be a transformative development, but he was in rarer company in seeing it in the context of a social revolution. "Well then, how could such far-reaching automation be achieved without social ownership of the means of production?"[13] Automation changes the relations of production, which in turn change social structures. The increase in productivity wrests freedom from necessity, but generates a surplus which needs dissipating somehow. New Babylon addresses the prospect of a new kind of necessity. As Constant says, "automation inevitably confronted us with the question of where human energy would be able to discharge itself if not in productive work."[14] New Babylon addresses a major theme of Georges Bataille: that surplus presents more fundamental problems for human societies than necessity. Where for Bataille the solution tends to involve orgiastic sacrifices to an impossible absolute, for Constant it is more a question of enabling playful and challenging social relations to take place. Constant takes to the limit the Lefebvrian play of need and desire.

Meanwhile, in the twenty-first century we appear to inhabit, automation lives within the old relations of production rather than prompting new ones. Nearly two-thirds of automated machine tools use controllers made by a secretive robotics company called FANUC. This near-monopoly allows FANUC to reap the lion's share of profits from automation. "FANUC's headquarters, a sprawling complex in a forest on the slopes of Mount Fuji, looks like something out of a sci-fi flick … FANUC lore holds that the founder, Seiuemon Inaba, believed yellow 'promotes clear thinking.' Inside the compound's windowless factories an army of (yes, yellow) robots works 24/7." On a factory floor as big as a football field there might be only four workers—also in yellow.[15] FANUC does its business by fax, paranoid about the new digital networks and their roiling seas of piracy. The promise of automation has come down in the twenty-first century to just another kind of monopoly.

Constant's multilevel layout borrows a recognizable figure from modern architecture. The space-frame suspended in the air on pylons appears in the work of Le Corbusier, and becomes an image of utopian form in Yona Friedman. Constant greatly expands its significance. In his hands it becomes the image of a world in which the time of free movement takes priority over the space of private property. Fencing off one space from another as private property is for Constant a "dehumanization of the earth," against which New Babylon presupposes "the socialization of the earth's surface."[16] Rather than lines that make borders, Constant's *experimental geography* proposes lines that make connections. His vast aerial sectors, the size of little cities, link up and spread out over the landscape like reinforced-concrete crabgrass.

Owning property affords someone a house in which to be at home, at the price of being homeless in the world. Dispense with property, dispense with separation, and the feeling of being merely thrown into the world goes with them. Our species-being can give vent to its wanderlust, at home in a house-like world. Constant thought modernity was already accelerating a return to a nomadic existence. New Babylon is nomadic life fully realized. It is an architecture of duration, of thresholds, of collaborative place-making, writ large. Freed from the fixity and uniformity of property, space could again have its qualities. A short trip in New Babylon should offer more variety than the most interminable journeys through the concentrated city of spectacular society. "Life is an endless journey across a world that is changing so rapidly that it seems forever another." The New Babylonians could wander over the whole surface of a world that was in flux. "New Babylon ends nowhere (the earth is round)."[17]

Beneath the ground, the automatic factories; across the surface, endless highways; and up above—a global network of superstructures, within which play takes place. Without borders, without centers, without a state, it snakes and forks all over the map. New Babylon "is organized according to the individual and collective covering of distance, of errancy: a network of units, linked to one another, and so forming chains that can develop, be extended in every direction."[18] And above that, figuratively at least, up in the ether, is another network, of communication. Constant intuits some things about what will turn out to be the internet. "The fluctuating world of the sectors calls on facilities (a transmitting and receiving network) that are both decentralized and public. Given the participation of a large number of people in the transmission and reception of images and sounds, perfected telecommunications become an important factor in ludic social behavior."[19] Interestingly, Constant's vertical arrangement also corresponds to his friend Henri Lefebvre's total semantic field, with cybernetic signaling at the base and symbolic play at the summit.

Through a decentralized network of communication, a nomadic species of play-beings coordinates its frolicking, designs and redesigns its own habitat, and creates a life where "the intensity of each moment destroys the memory that normally paralyses the creative imagination."[20] Constant experiments with a geography for a world beyond spectacle, where dérive and détournement are generalized practices, and indeed become the same practice. Both physical space and the space of information belong to everybody, and are resources for a life without dead time. It's a world not only made for but made by *homo ludens*, whose species-being is play. The only question is whether we are, or could become, such beings. New Babylon may very well be a posthuman critique of the limits of our species as we know it.[21]

Writing in the 1930s, Johan Huizinga offered homo ludens as a way of thinking our species-being that was outside of the *homo economicus* of political-economic discourse. We do not contend with each other to maximize our utility, whatever that means, but for the pleasure of the game, for the renown a good move brings.[22] Huizinga also opposed his figure of homo ludens to the *homo politicus* of Nazi jurist Carl Schmitt. For Schmitt contest cannot be playful, it is to the death. But, says Huizinga, if victory is total, who remains to *recognize* the victor? Constant's contribution is to propose in spatial form the conditions under which contestation can be playful rather than fatal, by distinguishing contest from control of resources, or desire from need. Automated production makes the surplus available for all, not just the victors. A playful dissipation of surplus energy can then become a pure game, its stakes only recognition, not domination.

Huizinga also opposes homo ludens to *homo faber*, the productivist worker-ant of Stalinist discourse. But as Constant discovers—more through aesthetic experiment than textual scholarship—what Marx always had in mind was the reconciliation of quantity and quality, of the substance of labor with the creation of forms. The productive surplus generated by the industrial revolution could restore, at a higher level, the qualitative being of the premodern world. In short, something closer to homo ludens. The struggle of the proletariat reduces the working day, from ten hours to eight, and—why not?—down to six, four, two, zero. As time becomes free, why should not space be freed also? Homo ludens will no longer make art, but will create everyday life, altering the ambience of the world, as easy as programming the jukebox in a Saint-Germain café.

Here is the architecture that Guy Debord and Ivan Chtcheglov only dreamed of as they wandered the streets of Paris: "Every square mile of New Babylon's surface represents an inexhaustible field of new and unknown situations, because nothing will remain and everything is constantly changing." Constant wanders far beyond his erstwhile comrades, if at the risk of an absolute euphoria. For Constant, the Situationist International "did not constitute a real movement. The adherents came and went and the only view they shared was their contempt for the current art practice."[23] He does credit the movement with contemplating the end to culture conceived as scarcity and property, and pursuing this possibility to its conclusions. "Unlike other Situationists, I realized straight away that the theory of unitary urbanism was not primarily concerned with micro-structures or with ambiences. On the contrary, these depend largely on the macro-structure ..."[24] Those who design the future by halves plot their own graves.

In the 1960s, New Babylon came to seem very out of step with the times. "Spontaneous, direct action struck many people as more important than analytical study." Favorite paperback reading included not just Marx but also his anarchist antagonist, Mikhail Bakunin. Constant: "This mentality continued until the mid-60s and achieved its apotheosis, but also its end, in ... Amsterdam with the appearance of Provo, an anarchic movement that took delight in making the establishment look ridiculous and which attracted international attention."[25] In the early 1960s the Provos, like the Second Situationist International, created a style of direct action as performance art, and no matter how much the Situationist International despised them, they embodied a certain spirit that was recognizably their own. While they claimed Constant as an inspiration of sorts, and he contributed to their publications, their projects were different.

"I had given priority to the structural problems of urbanism while the others wanted to stress the content, the play, the 'free creation of everyday life.'"[26] Looking back, peering through the ruins of the disintegrating spectacle, it appears that Constant was right to be skeptical about the political effusions of the sixties. New Babylon is the most thorough negation, not of the world of the late twentieth century, but of a world which is only just now coming into being. It is Constant who seems in touch with the real historical development of the twentieth century, and closer to the possibility of leaving it. He understood the transformative power of the second (cybernetic) industrial revolution, and that its consequences would be a vast reconfiguring of space. In the absence of a social revolution, this transformation of the means of production produced quite the opposite result, New Moloch rather than New Babylon. Welcome, then, to New Moloch, a global division of functions, which banishes the factory to the sites of cheap labor in China and elsewhere, while massively concentrating control over networks in the overdeveloped world. The fascist ant-state has gone global.

New Babylon looks less implausible that many of the landscapes that are now supposed to actually exist. "Her first day on the job, Min turned seventeen. She took a half day off and walked the streets alone, buying some sweets and eating them by herself. She had no idea what people did for fun."[27] Like a hundred million others, Min came down from the country to find work in one of China's new industrial cities. (Rural labor is cheaper than FANUC's controlled robots.) She came to Dongguan, a city of some ten million people in the Pearl River Delta. She thought it would be fun to work on an assembly line, with people talking and joking, but it was not that way at all. Factory work is noisy, tiring and boring. Factory dorms are full of petty crime, gangs, cliques and doomed romances. All that keeps anyone in touch with anyone is the mobile phone. When she lost her phone she lost her friends. Time is governed by shifts on machines and the global shopping calendar. When the nights are warm and the days are long, Americans think it time to buy sneakers.

Like so many others in China's early-twenty-first-century boom years, Min changes jobs often, but keeps finding much the same thing. It's not so different to the 1960s in Europe, only on a vastly greater scale. Young people weaned away from the provinces, from the farm, become proletarian, and discover that factory life dulls not just the muscles, but the mind. Yet the break has been made. Cast out of the old life, they make up the new as they go along. The difference is that unlike so many of the young people of the '60s, Min has never heard of Chairman Mao. The local museum manages not to mention him. When the boom bust, the Chinese government committed billions to propping up New Moloch with vast projects, aimed at building more of the same. Who would have thought, back in the middle of the twentieth century, that in the early twenty-first century, the fate of global capital might hinge on the prudent stewardship of the Chinese Communist Party?

Perhaps Mao's portrait could come down from Tiananmen Square. Perhaps a more appropriate figurehead would be the great swindler Charles Ponzi. Even the *New York Times* has to admit that these days the disintegrating spectacle looks like a giant Ponzi scam: "We have created a system for growth that depended on our building more and more stores to sell more and more stuff made in more and more factories in China, powered by more and more coal that would cause more and more climate change but earn China more and more dollars to buy more and more US T[reasury]-bills so America would have more and more money to build more and more stores and sell more and more stuff that would employ more and more Chinese."[28] This disintegrating spectacle built no great pyramids: the best it could manage was a great pyramid scheme.

Is it possible to imagine collective human agency as productive of something playful, joyous, communal, even beautiful? "The culture of New Babylon does not result from isolated activities, from exceptional situations, but from the global activity of the whole world population, every human being engaged in a dynamic relation with his surroundings."[29] New Babylon extends the ethos of the dérive to its limit, to world history. It is ultimately a philosophical work. "New Babylon is not a town planning project, but rather a way of thinking, of imagining, of looking at things and at life."[30] It is the disintegrating spectacle in negative. The great abundance really came to pass, only rather than free itself from labor, our species-being decided to labor making more and more things. "The growing presence of excess human energy has started to make itself felt."[31] But rather than outlets for joy—outlet malls. The disintegrating spectacle in which we actually live is the most utopian world of all, because of its savage insistence that it has abolished the very possibility of utopia for all time.

Walter Benjamin once drew a distinction between the fascist tendency to aestheticize politics and the revolutionary potential of a politicized aesthetics.[32] Constant retrieves the formula for an era way past the promise of art. It's a choice between a techno-fascist technologizing of aesthetics and the possibility of an aestheticizing of technology. Constant does not make a fetish of technology, as either saving grace or iron cage. Rather, it's a question of thinking the possibilities of social and technical transformation together.[33] The essence of technology is nothing technical. But could it be something playful? Could it be a way, not of instrumentalizing nature, but of producing a new relation to it, as a totality? Such was the scale of Constant's ambitions, the ambitions really of a whole way of life. One which leaves behind beautiful objects as unreadable as African masks.

12 The Beach Beneath the Street

There is a sixties to suit every taste. It's a truly versatile era. There is a psychedelic sixties, a Provo sixties, a cybernetic sixties, an anti-colonial sixties. There was the Prague Spring. There was the Watts rebellion. August 1965: the Black population rises up. Debord: "But who has defended the rioters of Watts in the terms they deserve?" Before Watts, there was Newark, July that same year. Ronald Porambo (1939–2006) wrote a first-rate book about it, *No Cause for Indictment: An Autopsy of Newark* (1971).[1] In it Porambo takes the hard-boiled American style of journalism to delirious, obsessive lengths, slotting together facts, quotes and anecdotes to create an unrelenting portrait of relentless oppression in a podunk town ruled by what Dashiell Hammett used to call the cops, the crooks and the big rich.

The book was not the hit that Porambo imagined. America in the 1970s preferred the *new journalism*. The ruling tastes ran more to the minutiae of status details than to Porambo's hard-luck stories. But this is where it gets interesting. Like Pierre-François Lacenaire before him, Porambo would have preferred a literary success, but, failing that, chose the infamy of a life of crime. Not just any crime. He robbed drug dealers. A dealer died in an aborted attempt at one such robbery, and a week later someone shot Porambo in the head. Arrested and tried for the murder, Porambo drew a life sentence rather than the Pulitzer Prize. He died in jail. The prison says he choked on an orange. Criminal acts, as Constant says, are "an expression of a frustrated will to power."[2]

The Situationists did not write about Porambo, or Newark, but Debord wrote about Watts. "The Los Angeles revolt was a revolt against the commodity," he said. It was at least partly so. "The flames of Watts consumed consumption." The spectacle, diffusing itself throughout society, presenting back to it the image of the abundance of things, could only appear as a cruel reminder of inequity to Black America. Just as the spectacle ranks its objects in order of desirability, so too it ranks its subjects. Its Black subjects saw through it: "they demand the egalitarian realization of the American spectacle of everyday life." Some among them negated the commodity through the unwitting gift. They saw the swag on offer—and looted it.

There is a lot that is missing from Debord's account: the thirty dead, the thousand injured, the four thousand arrests. Nor was he aware that here, unlike in France, the context is not the strength but the weakness of the old left, of the Communist Party and its union and popular-front forces. The red purge of the 1950s created a gap that the Black nationalists would fill with a quite different theory and practice. Still, it might have interested the Situationists when later investigations upheld their hunch that while the riots were leaderless, they were not without organization. Impromptu meetings in the park after dark coordinated movements. Safe-conduct hand signals, of gang origin, allowed looters to move outside their home turf. The areas burned and looted correspond to key gang territories. Gerald Horne: "the Watts Uprising was decentralized; it was a mass uprising and not organized in inception and conception."[3] It was a Lefebvrian festival, at least until the police opened fire.

It all happened again in 1992: fifty deaths, sixteen thousand arrests. The strenuous efforts of the state to prevent a recurrence were overturned with gas and a match. One scholar sums it up in a statement of the kind that only those who dream of being close to the policy process could love: "Present policies of selective imprisonment are not only the most expensive solutions but also the most counter-productive in the long run."[4] And it happened again, in Paris, November 2005. The biggest riot in Paris since May '68, the papers said. One dead, three thousand arrests. It spread to over two hundred towns.

The signature Situationist concept for such—recurring—events is *potlatch*. Where Marx compared the transformation of the object of labor into a commodity to a transubstantiation, the Situationists were interested in a kind of reverse miracle, by which the thing lost its status as commodity and became the gift. The looted object is no longer a commodity. But the perversity of the gesture is that its seizure does not break the spell of exchange and return to things their value. Rather, looting takes the spectacle at its word. In the spectacle, what is good appears and what appears is good.[5] The looter jumps the gap between desire and the commodity. The looter takes desires for their necessity, and necessity for their desires, but freeing the commodity from exchange does not expunge exchange from the commodity.

The riot contains a quite contrary movement as well—arson. The arsonist is not the same as the looter. The arsonist's is a negative relation to what appears, particularly to the built environment. The arsonist's actions are marked by the refusal of spectacular form. Constant: "Enormous energy is being withdrawn from the labor process and it finds no other outlet than in aggression prompted by dissatisfaction."[6] In the riot, that aggression turns against two of its sources: against the time of the commodity form; against an alienating urban space.

Looting and arson are recurring events within what René Viénet calls the "overdeveloped world." They are the mark of overdevelopment, of the quantitative expansion of production outstripping the qualitative transformation of everyday life, of desires spinning their wheels, without traction in the elaboration of needs. The proximate causes may vary, and are usually to do with the thuggery of the police and the indifference of the state. What the Situationists point to is the consistency and persistence of what follows, the twin forks of seize it all or burn it down. Sometimes the riot takes a different form, and moves towards rebellion, even towards revolution, or perhaps those in the middle of it think it does. This is why May '68 has a special place in not only the theory but also the mythology of the Situationists. It was more than a riot. It was the fabled *general strike*.[7]

The Situationist account of May '68, *Enragés and Situationists in the Occupation Movement* (1968) was issued under the name of René Viénet, although it was probably something of a collective effort. The son of a dockworker from Le Havre, Viénet (b. 1944) came in contact with Debord in 1961 via an affair with Michèle Bernstein's sister. When he came to Paris to study Chinese, he joined the Situationists. In 1965 he went to China, and saw the beginnings of the Cultural Revolution before being expelled in 1966. As Debord wrote of him, somewhat prophetically: "René's often fallible turn of mind—resolving problems by trenchant extremism—becomes obviously just and timely when the real conditions are such that it is necessary to envision being truly trenchant."[8] It was probably Viénet who wrote some of the more startling of the famous graffiti of May '68, including: "Beneath the pavement, the beach."

In Viénet's version, the proximate cause of May '68 is the provocation on the Nanterre campus by the Enragés, a group who had already made contact with the Situationist International. Viénet: "The agitation launched at Nanterre by four or five revolutionaries, who would later constitute the Enragés, was to lead in less than five months to the near liquidation of the state."[9] It's a hyperbolic statement, but what is distinctive about Viénet's little book is that it is a subjective account of history, and seen from the point of view of an active subject. Like the *Memoirs* of the Cardinal de Retz—one of its literary models—it preserves and extends the moment of insurrection with a form of memory specific to it.[10]

Nanterre at the time was a bleak spot in the western suburbs of Paris. Viénet: "The scene was perfect: the urbanism of isolation had grafted a university center onto the high-rise flats and the complementary slums. It was a microcosm of the general conditions of oppression, the spirit of a world without spirit." Dominique Lecourt: "The whiff of cordite hung over the desolate campus adjoining the shantytown, far from the Paris elites." Lefebvre called it "a place of damnation."[11] And so it proved: in 2002 Richard Durn opened fire with two Glock pistols at the end of a town hall meeting, killing eight councilors. Durn: "Because I have by my own will become a kind of living-dead, I have decided to end it all by killing a small local elite which is the symbol of, and who are the leaders and decision makers in, a city that I have always detested."[12]

Bernard Stiegler makes of this pointless massacre an emblem for what he calls a loss of *individuation*. To constitute the self requires collective belonging, and what the spectacle erodes is both the collective and the individual, or rather the situations that make both together. "Today we are enduring an enormous suffering of this individuation."[13] The situations that assure individuation are not far removed from the Situationist inventory of the forms of praxis: dérive, détournement, gift, and finally potlatch. The spectacle makes all of time homogenous—*synchronized*, in Stiegler's terms. The spectacle does not require that we think alike, dress alike or act alike, merely that we act within the same time in relation to the same form, the commodity form, which synchronizes our actions. The triumph of the spectacle erases what Stiegler calls the *diachronic*, or what van Eyck called duration, and the Situationists, play. It forecloses the connection of actions through time. May '68 was a critique in advance of the impoverishment of individuation.

Back in 1968, that handful of Nanterre agitators were brought before a disciplinary committee of the University of Paris. By trying to break up the support meeting in the courtyard, the authorities provoked the movement into action. Workers and lumpenproles joined in, daubing slogans on the walls and throwing up barricades. Viénet: "The construction of a system of barricades solidly defending an entire quarter was already an unforgivable step towards the negation of the state." Chlorine gas grenades overcame the barricades. Meanwhile events on the street acquired their inevitable spectacular double. Daniel Cohn-Bendit (b. 1945) became the spokesmodel for the revolt, an honest but limited revolutionary, as the Situationists would characterize him. He was the one who could speak acceptably about the unacceptable.[14]

The movement occupied the Sorbonne and called for a general strike. The Gaullist Prime Minister Georges Pompidou, who was no fool, freed arrested students and withdrew the police. His strategy was patience rather than confrontation. The Sorbonne became the scene of a wide-ranging discussion which attempted to create out of itself some kind of self-organization. The Situationists and the Enragés formed a joint committee. They made posters denouncing the remnants of art, warning against recuperation, and calling for the disinterment of Cardinal Richelieu, which would have warmed the ghost of his sometime antagonist Cardinal de Retz. When it came time for the general assembly to elect delegates, eighteen-year-old Enragé René Reisel gave a rousing speech proclaiming that the struggle was not just about the university, and that sociologists and psychologists were the new cops. It ensured his election to the occupation committee.[15]

Elsewhere, workers seized the opportunity with wildcat strikes and occupations of their factories. The Communist union federation tried to limit this development, and to steer it towards the routine demands of wages and conditions. They did their best to prevent contact between striking workers and students. Meanwhile, the Sorbonne Occupation Committee proved ineffective, or as Viénet says, "showed itself incapable of self-respect." The Situationists, Enragés and friends withdrew, and convened their own uninterrupted general assembly at the National Pedagogical Institute in the rue d'Ulm. They set up standing committees for liaisons, printing, and requisitions, the latter to keep it fueled with money, vehicles, food and wine. It was not just a student group. Among its thirty-odd members were Guy Debord (1931–94), Alice Becker-Ho (b. 1941), René Viénet (b. 1944) and René Reisel (b. 1950).[16]

There is a certain charm to groups such as astronomers and professional footballers declaring themselves for *self-management.* The general air of tolerance made it hard to resist the antics of some other professional groups, such as film-makers and museum directors, who recast the revolt as a pretext for reviving some warmed-over *radical aesthetics.* They preferred changing their métier to the métier of change. What is of genuine interest lay elsewhere: "in the space of a week millions of people had cast off the weight of alienating conditions, the routine of survival, ideological falsifications, and the inverted world of the spectacle."

For Viénet, this is an idyllic situation. "People strolled, dreamed, learned how to live." Time assumes a measureless quality. "For the first time youth really existed. Not the social category invented for the needs of the commodity economy by sociologists and economists, but the only real youth, of life lived without dead time …"[17] The outpourings of popular creativity showed just how much of what Jorn called surplus fellowship actually existed. Cars now attracted only the match. People modified the landscape to suit themselves—a spontaneous critique of urbanism. Police stations at Odéon and rue Beaubourg were "enthusiastically sacked," as was the stock market. It was as if a blind but determined force was undermining the foundations of Gaullist order. As Viénet says, "the 'old mole' spared nothing."[18]

It was not to last. "The Stalinists began to despair of the survival of Gaullism." The chain reaction of wildcat strikes could not be sustained as a general strike. The unions channeled the inchoate desires of the strikers towards specific demands on wages and conditions. The Trotskyites, the Castroites and the Maoists all wanted to replay one or other revolution they had missed, rather than the one they were in the midst of actually having. They drew their lessons from past defeats.

"The state was ignored for the first time in France." But the odds weren't good. "Everything was to hang on the power relations in the factories between the workers, everywhere isolated and cut off, and the joint power of the state and the trade unions. The movement was dismantled strike by strike, either by negotiations or by force." The movement divided was rapidly conquered. The occupied factories lacked the means to remain in communication with each other. They would not know what to say even if they were. Viénet puts it down to "backwardness of theoretical consciousness," but surely it was more than that.[19] The means were lacking to create social relations of a new kind. The state banned certain leftist organizations while making discreet overtures to the far right.

Theory lags behind the situation that calls for it. These days one wonders if the moment of theoretical consciousness arrives at all, or is short-circuited by brutal acts like Durn's. Hegel's owl of Minerva no longer flies at dusk, because the shotgun of Dick Cheney fired at first light.[20] If Viénet's problem in writing about May '68 was how to remember it, then our problem is how to remember that remembrance. Perhaps one way to start is as Maxim Gorky does, at least on Lukács's reading, or the reading of Vali Myers. Start with supposedly *minor characters*, the Viénets and the Porambos, whose actions are neither famous nor typical, but who in their extremity embody, and are embodied in, the extremes of the situation itself.

With the failure of the revolution, Viénet turned away from the critique of urbanism and towards the other pole of Situationist action—détournement. *Can Dialectics Break Bricks?* (1972) takes a kung fu action film, reorders some scenes, and replaces the subtitles with Viénet's own, making of its narrative a rather more pointed allegory for the co-option of radical desires by the supposedly leftist wing of spectacular power. In one scene, two Stalinist bureaucrats lounge in a hot tub. One says: "It seems their latest discovery is to détourn the mass media." The other replies, "That, old man, is the beginning of the end." And the first concludes: "They are capable of reducing our own wooden language to sawdust." In Viénet's hands, détournement is a Marxist chainsaw. It becomes a tool for remembering what was and forever could be.

It may seem quixotic, in the twenty-first century, to talk about Marx, and certainly much now escapes the contemporary reader—not only about the collective practices of the Situationists but also their theoretical obsessions. But perhaps there is something to be said for a Marxism the memory of which one cannot abandon, just as one cannot abandon the memory of a certain lover, or of one's home town. But one lives on. In place of the memory of that lover, another love. In place of the hometown, an adopted city. In place of that memory of the Marxists, the memory of the Situationists. Fidelity, or rather, the solidarity without faith that is détournement, outlives that with which it stands.[21] Not the least virtue of speaking at length about Situationist détournements of Marxism is that they form a bulwark against the collapse of their legacy into a disciplinary scholarship, into art history for instance, even Marxist art history.[22] Better to tilt at windmills than pawn the lance.

There is a passage by Marx that Lefebvre liked to quote:

> A philosopher produces ideas, a poet poems, a clergyman sermons, a professor compendia and so on. A criminal produces crimes. If we look a little closer at the connection between this latter branch of production and society as a whole, we shall rid ourselves of many prejudices. The criminal produces not only crimes but also criminal law, and with this also the professor who gives lectures on criminal law and in addition to this the inevitable compendium in which the same professor throws his lectures onto the general market as "commodities." This brings with it the augmentation of national wealth.[23]

Marx goes on to show how the criminal produces the police, the judiciary, a whole division of labor, "creating new needs and new ways of satisfying them."

Who says crime doesn't pay? Crime also produces technological improvement: "Torture alone has given rise to the most ingenious mechanical inventions." The criminal produces new necessities: criminology and even criminal law itself. The criminal produces new desires: popular entertainments such as novels and TV shows, from Balzac to Gorky to Vian to *The Wire*. Marx: "The criminal breaks into the monotonous yet secure everyday life of the bourgeoisie, provoking it out of stagnation. The illicit desire for the criminal life gives rise to that uneasy tension and agility without which even the spur of competition would get blunted."

The same could be said of delinquents, radicals, and perhaps especially radical delinquents such as the Situationist International, who keep a veritable industry alive, including the book you hold in your hands. Reduced to the logic of *productivity*, the activities of the Situationist International "augment national wealth" with the best of them. And if mere delinquent radicals can *produce* all this, what then of the social crime of a failed revolution? May '68 did not induce the revolution so much as a whole industry of commentary. Violence is the midwife of history publishing. Enough books entered the market to rebuild all the barricades many times over.

The trick might be to recall this legacy otherwise, to stimulate a quite different kind of production. Not just to quote it or imitate it, for quotation and imitation are classical forms of connecting past to present, here to there, this to that. Let's be done with nostalgia for '68 and all it represents. If there's a consistent lesson in the Situationist approach to history, it is to expect surprises. No doubt Prince Charles was surprised when his limo lost its escort one day in 2010 and he found himself surrounded by protesters angry about the privatizing of British higher education. Somebody shot it with paintballs. Comrades, the time of life is short, and if we live, we live to tread on kings![24] But in these spectacular times, when royalty is hardly royal, it might do to startle a prince, pink-faced and blinking, in the presence of cameras. The moment of surprise, when power ceases its phantom existence even for just a moment, is not limited to May '68. It recurs on all kinds of scales, all the time. Historical thought has the task of preparing the active subject for the emergence of promising situations within lived time. The art of détournement is a training ground for the appropriation of historical time itself.

In the novel *2666*, Roberto Bolaño (1953–2003) describes the phantom novelist Benno von Archimboldi (b. 1920): a possible candidate for the Nobel Prize, a "veteran, a World War II deserter still on the run, a reminder of the past for Europe in troubled times. A writer on the left whom even the Situationists respected. A person who didn't pretend to reconcile the irreconcilable, as was the fashion these days."[25] In literature and art, the Situationists are sometimes invoked as if to bestow a certain blessing on the proceedings, as if making a genuflection to the dangerous saints could preserve art and literature as they go about business as usual. Scholars search out the Situationists like the elusive Archimboldi, to finally pay back the gift, to be done with the unseemly *generosity* of what they offer, their unbidden donations of thought in action. This gnawingly unaccountable quality is the very thing with which to try to settle accounts.

"Philosophy," says Simon Critchley, "begins in disappointment." After the death of God, the end of Art, the failure of the Revolution, there's nothing left but philosophy, the moment of contemplation of the ruins. For Jacques Rancière, it is not that literature arises out of failed revolutions, but that revolutions are failed literature.[26] Certainly the high theory of the post-'68 era was born of the disappointments, not just of May but of the *red decade* of 1966–76, of which May was the high water mark. If other failed revolutions gave us Hegel and Stendhal, Marx and Baudelaire, this one gave us Foucault and Deleuze, Derrida and Lyotard. Whatever interest such thoughts may once have held, they are now no more than the routine spasms of an era out of love with itself.

Low theory returns in moments, not of disappointment, but of boredom. We are bored with these burnt offerings, these warmed-up leftovers. High theory cedes too much to the existing organization of knowledge and art. It is nothing more than the spectacle of disintegration extending into knowledge itself. Rather a negative theory that reveals the gap between this world and its promises. Rather a negative action that reveals the void between what can be done and what is to be done. Rather a spirited invention of genuine forms within the space of everyday life, than the relentless genuflection to the hidden God that is *power*.[27] For such experiments the Situationist legacy stands ripe for a détournement that has no respect for those who claim proprietary rights over it. There is still plenty of fruit to be gleaned from the vine.

Viénet: "Nothing is too beautiful for the Blacks of Watts."[28] That is why low theory pushes critique away from the relentless quotation and commentary on itself. Low theory takes critique gently by the neck and leads it outwards, towards the labyrinth that is the production of situations, including the production of new forms for critique itself. It is not too embarrassed to turn up as shopgirl philosophy or on delinquent mixtapes: "Our ideas are on everybody's mind." Even before May '68, Viénet wanted critique to détourn new forms, including comics, chick lit, cinema, pirate radio, porn. He thought every Situationist should be able to make films. One could translate that today to mean that the low theorist should know not only how to détourn some Hegel but also some code, or should at least be able to throw up a decent website or viral video, but without making a fetish of such media practices.

"Up till now our subversion has mainly drawn on the forms and genres inherited from past revolutionary struggles, primarily those of the last hundred years. I propose that we supplement our forms of agitation with methods that dispense with any reference to the past," says a twenty-three-year-old Viénet. Ah, youth! Or perhaps: use the past as a reservoir of tactics, not to imitate, but from which to learn the tactical arts, and not least how all tactics fail in the end. The Situationist project, as an instance of low theory at work, made some rare moves. Among other things, it advanced a new romantic agenda on the least likely terrain, that of architecture, the most steadfastly classical of forms. As Lefebvre shows, many of the tactics that worked, if only for a time, were themselves détournements of romantic game plans.

Here are some techniques for discovering the way into the total semantic field that they détourned, alone or in combination: alcohol (Debord), opium (Trocchi), psychosis (Chtcheglov), mania (Spur), synaesthesia (de Jong), fatigue (the dérive), obsession (Constant), love (Bernstein), revolution (May '68), solitude (late Debord). Many of the tributaries into which the Situationist project flowed found one or other of the alibis that Lefebvre identified for avoiding the question of how to supersede aesthetics and ethics in praxis: aestheticism (Jorn, de Jong, Spur); technicism (New Babylon); moralism (the Situationist International sans artists), nihilism (Trocchi again). Every spent tactic is a lesson in how to make new ones. And unlike the romantics, the Situationists made the fateful leap beyond subjective revolt to class struggle. They were not content to play merely within the total semantic field, within the economy of tolerable middle-class dissent. Détournement challenges that very economy.[29]

It's still a fine slogan: Never work! Perhaps we could add: Never play! For play is becoming as co-opted as work, a mere support for the commodity form.[30] Just as the Situationists adjusted romantic tactics to suit new situations, so too Situationist tactics can be adapted at will. To the dérive, psychogeography and unitary urbanism, what could one add but the question of scale? Where now does the space of the city end?[31] Détournement is now a whole social movement in all but name, able to sample anything and everything but unable to know its own provenance. With the commodity form extending even into *social networks*, what could be more pressing than Jorn's contemplation of an extreme aesthetics, an invention of forms as something other than mere containers? With the end of the Situationist International as an organization, its fantasy of being the vanguard of organized form died with it, but not perhaps the experiment with social form. Let a thousand internationals bloom! Each with their own provisional rules of labor and donation, inclusion and exclusion, initiations, rituals, forms of remembrance.[32]

Shorn of its chemical romances, project sigma is still a signal instance of creating a counter-network. New Babylon, for all its supposedly utopian grandeur, looks a whole lot more endurable than the new Moloch that was actually built in its stead. The *Situationist Times* is still a remarkable precedent in creating an intercourse between languages, and between languages and different visual practices, within which to propose a new kind of knowledge and practice of form. Speaking of forms, Jorn opens up novel ways of thinking about the severing of the production of quantities from the production of qualities as a class division.[33] Supposedly superseded by the structural turn in both philosophy and urban thought, Lefebvre's body of work seems far richer than either its fans or detractors credit. Perhaps everyday life offers ways of escaping the prison house of *biopower*.[34]

In an age which still worships eternal love—albeit with a frenzy that belies a still unacknowledged waning of belief—what could be more telling than Bernstein's amorous tactics? And speaking of tactics, was not Debord brilliant at the tactics of knowing when things should end? When to split from Isou, when to break up the Letterist International, when to be done with the artists in the Situationist International: he knew when to move on. The terrain changes, the disposition of force changes, and so the tactics change. Just as Debord, with the founding of the Situationist International, accepted the tactic of positioning the movement within rather than against the art world, perhaps today one might take up a defensive position within higher education rather than against it. The Situationists are often taken as offering dogmas when really they practiced something else: tactical mobility combined with the ruthless criticism of all that exists. There's a constant non-identity of tactics and theory. Extremist theory, put directly into practice, leads to quietism; provisional tactics, translated directly into theory, aren't theory at all. The difference is the thing.

The world has only changed philosophy. The point, however, is to interpret it. Is philosophy that domain to which the project of transforming the world retreats? Or is it rather premised, as Critchley says, on disappointment with this world and what it lacks? If the latter, then perhaps critical theory needs to chart another path through the aftermath of May '68, one that does not take one or other royal road back to philosophy. The archive too is a space for dérive. There are turning points where the monuments of the critical theory canon intersect with more interesting back alleys: take the streets named Lefebvre, not Lacan; Jorn, rather than Althusser; Debord, not Foucault. Or: praxis, not therapy; form, not structure; situation, not power. The renewal of critical theory as critical practice might take these or other alternate pathways through the twentieth century, if it is to find its way back to the labyrinth rather than end up on the steps to the Panthéon.

The contributions of Situationists and ex-Situationists by no means ended with May 1968. The organization disbanded in 1972, but there were other projects, other adventures. Writing about those will have to wait for another moment. What continues unabated, regardless of what anyone writes, is the détournement of the Situationist project. Beneath the pavement, the beach. Wherever the boredom with given forms of art, politics, thought, everyday life jackhammers through the carapace of mindless form, the beach emerges, where form is ground down to particles, to the ruin of ruins. There lies what the old mole is always busy making: the materials for the construction of situations. These too might be recuperated into mere art or writing some day, and sooner rather than later, but not before their glorious time. Our species-being is as builders of worlds. Should we consent to inhabit this given one as our resting place, we're dead already. There may be no dignified exits left to the twenty-first century, the century of the flying inflatable turd, but there might at least be some paths to adventure. The unexamined life is not worth living, but the unlived life doesn't bear thinking about.

Notes

Introduction

1 *Guardian*, August 12, 2008. Thanks to the *Colbert Report*, August 20, 2008; F. T. Marinetti, "The Futurist Manifesto," in *Critical Writings*, edited by Günther Berghaus, Farrar, Straus, Giroux, New York, 2006, p. 8.

2 See Karl Marx, "Estranged Labor," *Early Writings*, Penguin Books, Harmondsworth, 1973, p. 322 ff. The concept of species-being is not common in Situationist writings, but René Viénet picks up the term in *Enragés and Situationists in the Occupation Movement*, Autonomedia, New York, 1993.

3 Guy Debord, "On Wild Architecture," in Elizabeth Sussman (ed.), *On the Passage of a Few People through a Rather Brief Moment in Time: The Situationist International 1957–1972*, MIT Press, Cambridge MA, 1989, p. 174.

4 On the contemporary in relation to the modern, see Terry Smith, Okwui Enwezor and Nancy Condee (eds), *Antimonies of Art and Culture: Modernity, Postmodernity and Contemporaneity*, Duke University Press, Durham NC, 2008 and Terry Smith, *What Is Contemporary Art?*, University of Chicago Press, Chicago, 2009.

5 On the career of high theory, see François Cusset, *French Theory*, University of Minnesota Press, Minneapolis, 2008; Sande Cohen and Sylvère Lotringer (eds) *French Theory in America*, Routledge, New York, 2001. Symptomatic of the moment when high theory tries to appropriate low theory might be: Edward Ball, "The Great Sideshow of the Situationist International," *Yale French Studies*, No. 73, 1987.

6 "The Idea of Communism," Birkbeck Institute for the Humanities, March 13–15, 2009, and Slavoj Žižek et al, *The Idea of Communism*, Verso, London, 2010. The various revivals of the figure of the *communist*, by Slavoj Žižek, Alain Badiou, Antonio Negri, might not be the least reason to revive the attempt to supersede it in the figure of the *situationist*.

7 Luc Boltanski, in Daniel Birnbaum and Isabelle Graw (eds), *Under Pressure: Pictures, Subjects and the New Spirit of Capitalism*, Sternberg Press, Berlin, 2008, p. 66. Boltanski's lecture here summarizes Luc Boltanski and Eve Chiapello, *Le nouvel esprit du capitalisme*, Gallimard, Paris, 1999. On the politics of the memory of May–June 1968, see Kristin Ross, *May '68 and Its Afterlives*, University of Chicago Press, Chicago, 2002.

8 The specific problem implied in writing about the Situationist International is raised at the end of Frances Stuckey, "Surviving History: A Situationist Archive," *Art History*, February 2003. Some biographies: Christophe Bourseiller, *Vie et Mort de Guy Debord*, Omnibus, Paris, 1999; Andrew Hussey, *The Game of War: The Life and*

Death of Guy Debord, Pimlico, London, 2002; Vincent Kaufmann, *Guy Debord, Revolution in the Service of Poetry*, University of Minnesota Press, Minneapolis, 2010; Andy Merrifield, *Guy Debord*, Reaktion Books, London, 2005.

9 The more or less official history is Jean-François Martos, *Histoire de l'Internationale Situationniste*, Editions Lebovici, 1989. Useful counter-histories include: Roberto Ohrt, *Phantom Avantgarde*, Galerie van der Loo, Munich, 1990; Stewart Home, *The Assault on Culture*, AK Press, Stirling, Scotland, 1991. All those whom Debord rendered anathema are also excluded from the Martos, whereas Ohrt and Home have a tendency to champion the non-Debordist offshoots at his expense. *The Beach Beneath the Street* aims more to find the value in all of the various nodes of the Situationist network.

10 Debord's own commentary is *Comments on the Society of the Spectacle*, Verso, London, 1998. The two major works not discussed here are Guy Debord, *Society of the Spectacle*, Zone Books, New York, 1994, and Raoul Vaneigem, *Revolution of Everyday Life*, Rebel Press, London, 2001. I have already written about both books, if somewhat indirectly. McKenzie Wark, *A Hacker Manifesto*, Harvard University Press, Cambridge MA, 2004 is a détournement of *Society of the Spectacle*. McKenzie Wark, *Gamer Theory*, Harvard University Press, Cambridge MA, 2007, is, among other things, about how the radical potential of the figure of play has been foreclosed. In many respects *The Beach Beneath the Street* is a *prequel* to my two earlier books.

1   Street Ethnography

1 Simone de Beauvoir, *Force of Circumstance*, Paragon House, New York, 1992, p. 128.

2 See Boris Vian, *Manual of Saint-Germain-des-Prés*, Rizzoli, New York, 2005. His fake American crime novels are *I Spit on Your Graves*, Tam Tam Books, Los Angeles, 1998, and *The Dead All Have the Same Skin*, Tam Tam Books, Los Angeles, 2008. His *literary* novel *Autumn in Peking*, Tam Tam Books, Los Angeles, 2006, is perhaps his quasi-surrealist take on postwar culture, and *Foam of the Daze*, Tam Tam Books, Los Angeles, 2003, includes a delirious scene about the morbid enthusiasm for the celebrity philosopher Jean-Sol Partre.

3 For the Anglophone invader's perspective, see Elaine Dundy, *The Dud Avocado*, New York Review Books Classics, New York, 2007, p. 84 ff.

4 Simone Signoret, *Nostalgia Isn't What It Used to Be*, Harper and Row, New York, 1978, p. 43.

5 The classic study is Stanley Cohen, *Folk Devils and Moral Panics: The Creation of Mods and Rockers*, Routledge, New York, 2002. For a more contemporary assessment of the concept, see Catharine Lumby, "Sex, Murder and Moral Panic: Coming to a Suburb Near You," *Meanjin*, Vol. 58, No. 4, 2000.

6 Dick Hebdige, *Subculture: The Meaning of Style*, Routledge, London, 1988. Hebdige uses Jean Genet as his touchstone for a literature of subculture. The Situationists despised Genet, and not without reason, as his romance of negativity all too neatly worked as a spectacle of negation, rather than as negation of the spectacle.

7 Here moral panic could be read in the terms proposed by Slavoj Žižek, *The Sublime Object of Ideology*, second edition, Verso, London, 2009. The teen existentialists are a threat to bourgeois enjoyment either because they enjoy too much (sexual depravity, amorality, and so forth) or too little (political seriousness, asexual relations between the genders, and so on).

8 Quoted in Gianni Menichetti, *Vali Myers: A Memoir*, Golda Foundation, Fresno CA,

2007, p. 20. For Patti Smith's recollection of Myers, see her *Just Kids*, Ecco Press, New York, 2010. It seems appropriate for Myers to be reading Gorky. As Lukács once said of Gorky and his time, but in a way also applicable to postwar Paris and the Saint-Germain milieu: "neither the revolutionary nor the modern bourgeois ideology were born simply and immediately out of the dissolution of the old ideologies. On the contrary; as in every period of disintegration, the process begins with an ever greater perplexity of the great masses concerned; the weak sink into apathy or fritter away their strength in short-lived outbursts of senseless revolt." George Lukács, *Studies in European Realism*, Howard Fertig, New York, 2002, p. 212.

9 The dangers of appropriating the term *tribe* in such an urban context are neatly sidestepped in Wu Ming, *Manituana*, Verso, London, 2009. In this novel, Mohawk warriors visit London as representatives of the Iroquois Federation. The Federation has been loyal to the British Crown but seeks assurances that the alliance is mutual before joining forces against the American revolutionaries. While in London they are presented with an appeal from the London Mohocks, fierce exemplars of the dangerous classes, who suggest instead an alliance with them, as both have been dispossessed of their lands and their traditional way of life by British power. To be *tribal*, then, is not to exist in a state before colonial contact, but rather to have been dispossessed by that contact, whether at the antipodes of empire or at its very center.

10 Ed van der Elsken, *Love on the Left Bank*, Dewi Lewis Publishing, Stockport, UK, 1999, unpaginated. Tennessee Williams describes the Vali Myers look in his play *Orpheus Descending*. See *The Rose Tattoo and Other Plays*, Penguin Books, London, 2001, p. 252. For the Plimpton, Pomerand and the unattributed observation, see George Plimpton, "Vali," *Paris Review*, No. 18, 1958, pp. 43–47. For Plimpton and the permanent invader culture of Saint-Germain, see Nelson Aldrich (ed.), *George Being George*, Random House, New York, 2008, p. 83 ff; Juan Goytisolo, *Forbidden Territory: The Memoirs of Juan Goytisolo, 1931–1956*, translated by Peter Bush, North Point Press, San Francisco, 1985, p. 177. Goytisolo recounts in the same volume his wandering with Bernstein and Debord, pp. 205–6. Perhaps the most remarkable record of the time is Guy Debord, *Mémoires*, Editions Allia, Paris, 2004, in which Debord détourns both van der Elsken photos and a phrase from Goytisolo. See Boris Donné, *Pour mémoires*, Editions Allia, Paris, 2004. Also worth mentioning among memoirs of the time is Maurice Rajsfus, *Une enfance laïque et républicaine*, Editions Manya, Levallois, 1992.

11 *Class warfare*, Vian, *Manual*, p. 38; *closed group*, Ralph Rumney, *The Consul*, translated by Malcolm Imrie, City Lights, San Francisco CA, 2002, p. 63.

12 The Situationists spotted this convergence of the bourgeois and bohemian fairly early. See "On the Poverty of Student Life," in Ken Knabb (ed.), *Situationist International Anthology*, Bureau of Public Secrets, 2007, and Guy Debord and Giancarlo Sanguinetti, *The Real Split in the International*, Pluto Press, London, 2003.

13 The community of difference is advanced, though with considerably more subtlety than is possible here, in Maurice Blanchot, *The Unavowable Community*, Station Hill Press, Barrytown NY, 1988. Blanchot's reference points are Georges Bataille's Acéphale group, Breton's surrealists, and Marguerite Duras, a Saint-Germain identity not mentioned by Vian, for the obvious reason that she was still identified with the Communist Party, to which she adhered during the Resistance.

14 Jean-Paul Sartre, *What is Literature? And Other Essays*, Harvard University Press, Cambridge MA, p. 174; Georges Bataille, "La Divinité d'Isou," *Œuvres complètes*, Vol. 11, Gallimard, Paris, 1988, p. 379. See also André Breton, *Manifestoes of Surrealism*, University of Michigan Press, Ann Arbor, 1972, p. 298.

15　Isidore Isou, *L'Agrégation d'un nom d'un Messie*, Gallimard, Paris, 1947; Isidore Isou, *Introduction à une nouvelle poésie et une nouvelle musique*, Gallimard, Paris, 1947. It was Greil Marcus who really put Isou into this story, not least for Anglophone readers, but not without a certain embarrassment. On the Romanian connection in Dada, see Tom Sandqvist, *Dada East: The Romanians of Cabaret Voltaire*, MIT Press, Cambridge MA, 2006.

16　Isidore Isou, "Manifesto of Letterist Poetry" (1942), in Mary Ann Caws, *Manifesto: A Century of Isms*, University of Nebraska Press, Lincoln NE, 2001, p. 545. *American Speech*, Vol. 26, No. 3, 1951, notes references to Letterism turning up in *Time*, the *New Yorker* and the *Spectator* in the late 1940s. Isou's manifestos did not go entirely unnoticed.

17　Isou, "Traité de Bave et d' éternité (Venom and Eternity)", *Avant Garde 2: Experimental Cinema 1928–1954, Films from the Raymond Rohauer Collection*, Kino International, New York, 2007. This 111-minute version is based on the 1953 version produced by Raymond Rohauer and Leon Vickman, with 30 minutes of material restored from Isou's four-hour version. See also Allyson Field, "Hurlements en faveur de Sade: The Negation and Surpassing of Discrepant Cinema," *Substance*, No. 90, 1999, and Jacques Donguy's interview with Isou in *Art Press*, No. 269, 2001. Isou's relation to Dada is rather more complicated than there is room to explore here.

18　Gabriel Pomerand, *Saint Ghetto of the Loans: Grimoire*, translated by Michael Kasper, Ugly Duckling Press, Lost Literature Series No. 1, Brooklyn NY, 2006. Originally published as *Saint Ghetto des Prêts: Grimoire*, OLB, Paris, 1950. Needless to say the literal renderings of lines from the book which follow here hardly do it justice. Interestingly, Vian also draws a link between Saint-Germain and the Jewish ghetto, perhaps with less warrant.

19　Jules Romains, *Donogoo Tonka*, Princeton Architectural Press, New York, 2009. Romains started a movement called Unamism, based on the idea of collective consciousness and group behavior, and Pomerand's invocation of him is of interest in this connection as well as for his handling of the exotic. For an illuminating discussion of the relation between fiction and ethnography, see James Buzard, *Disorienting Fiction*, Princeton University Press, Princeton NJ, 2005.

20　Jean-Michel Mension, *The Tribe*, City Lights, San Francisco, 2001, p. 41. For a seminal if slightly later study of deviance, see Howard Becker, *Outsiders*, Free Press, New York, 1963. The most excluded among the Saint-Germain tribe were probably those taking ether, the aroma of which is all too telling.

21　Louis-Ferdinand Céline, *Journey to the End of the Night*, New Directions, New York, 2006, p. 5. This novel and its sequel, *Death on the Installment Plan*, New Directions, New York, 1971, describe the same miserable outer suburban Paris of Debord's early childhood. Céline had something of a paranoid break and turned anti-Semitic in the 1930s. He escaped execution as a collaborator and was back in Paris by 1952, where his outsider status, but not his political deliriums, gave him a certain alternative currency. Even after the war Sartre could write, only half joking: "Perhaps Céline will be the only one of all of us to remain" (*What is Literature*, p. 244). Debord détourns the epigram from *Journey* in his *Mémoires* (1958), reprinted in facsimile by Editions Allia, Paris, 2004.

22　On bohemia in general, see Elizabeth Wilson, *Bohemians: The Glamorous Outcasts*, Rutgers University Press, New Brunswick NJ, 2001. My thanks to Tony Moore for his insights into bohemian cultural formations.

23　Ivan Chtcheglov, "Formulary for a New Urbanism" (1953), in Ken Knabb (ed.), *Situationist International Anthology*, revised edition, Bureau of Public Secrets, San Francisco, 2006, pp. 1–8.

24 The Letterist International had two distinct phases with quite different memberships, which need not concern us too much here.

25 "Next Planet," *Potlatch*, No. 4, July 1954, in Libero Andreotti and Xavier Costa
(eds), *Theory of the Dérive and Other Situationist Writings*, Museu d'Art Contemporani
de Barcelona, 1996, p. 43; Guy Debord, *présente Potlatch*, Gallimard, Paris, 1996,
p. 32.

2 No More Temples of the Sun

1 Georges Bataille, "The Obelisk," in Allan Stoekl (ed), *Visions of Excess: Selected Writings 1927–1939*, University of Minnesota Press, Minneapolis, 1985, pp. 213 ff.

2 See Michel Surya, *Georges Bataille*, Verso, London, 2002. A particularly interesting
attempt to make Bataille relevant again as the philosopher of a symbolic, rather than
material consumption of surplus, is Alan Stoekl, *Bataille's Peak: Energy, Religion, and
Postsustainability*, University of Minnesota Press, Minneapolis, 2007.

3 A great account can be found in the seminal Greil Marcus, *Lipstick Traces*, Harvard
University Press, Cambridge MA, 1989, p. 279 ff. See Michel Mourre, *In Spite of
Blasphemy*, John Lehman, London, 1953. Like Dada founder Hugo Ball, Mourre
found his way in spite of himself back to the church, and to a position of power
within it. It recalls in its own way Sartre's story "Childhood of a Leader." As Marcus
says, "He sought a bolt of lightning and gained the right to light a candle."

4 Le Corbusier, *Towards an Architecture*, Getty Research Institute, Los Angeles, 2007,
p. 95. André Breton had polemicized against Le Corbusier long before Chtcheglov.
See *Position politique du surréalisme*, Editions du Sagittaire, Paris, 1935.

5 Jacques Rancière, *The Politics of Aesthetics*, Continuum, London, 2004, p. 12.

6 *Tigers in a cage*, Le Corbusier, *Towards an Architecture*, p. 97; *unifying management*,
ibid., p. 233. The Parthenon and Roman form feature more heavily in this book, but
Luxor rates a mention.

7 See also de Chirico's novel, *Hebdomeros*, Exact Change Press, Cambridge MA,
1992. Debord was also fond of the landscapes of Claude Lorrain. Céline already
makes literary use of Lorrain's landscape techniques in *Journey to the End of the Night*,
p. 66.

8 Lev Kassil, *The Black Book and Schwambrania*, translated by Fainna Glagoleva, Progress Publishers, Moscow, 1978, pp. 13, 20. On Kassil see Inessa Medzibovskaya's
essay in *Russian Children's Literature*, Routledge, London, 2008. On Kassil and
Chtcheglov, see Jean-Marie Apostolidès and Boris Donné, *Ivan Chtcheglov: Profil
perdu*, Editions Allia, Paris, 2006.

9 See Robert McNab, *Ghost Ships: A Surrealist Love Triangle*, Yale University Press,
New Haven, 2004, for a usefully geographic account of the surrealists' relation to
wandering, travel and colonialism. The seminal essay on surrealist ethnography is
in James Clifford, *The Predicament of Culture*, Harvard University Press, Cambridge
MA, 2002. See also the *Visual Anthropology Review* Spring 1991 special issue on ethnographic surrealism, and Martin Roberts, "The Self and Other: Ethnographic
Film, Surrealism, Politics," *Visual Anthropology*, Vol. 8, pp. 77–94, for a critique of
the rather depoliticized surrealism at work in Clifford.

10 Debord, *présente Potlatch*, p. 241; Andreotti & Costa, *Theory of the Dérive*, p. 60.

11 Knabb, *Situationist International Anthology*, p. 7.

12 Michèle Bernstein, "Dérive by the Mile," *Potlatch*, No. 9, 1954, Andreotti & Costa,
Theory of the Dérive, p. 47; Debord, *présente Potlatch*, p. 65. The dérive is different from
the amblings of the flâneur, a more exclusively masculine figure for whom the street

is to be seen as a thing apart, rather than a succession of atmospheres and adventures to participate in. See Griselda Pollock, *Vision & Difference*, Routledge, London, 1988. However, the dérive certainly derives from the flâneur as a vehicle for remaking literary form. See Eric Hazan, *The Invention of Paris*, Verso, London, 2010, p. 315 ff which traces a line from Restif via Balzac to Baudelaire.

13 Interview with Jacqueline de Jong, Algonquin Hotel, New York, October 17, 2009. See also Andrew Hussey, *The Game of War: The Life and Death of Guy Debord*, Jonathan Cape, London, 2001, p. 82.

14 Henry Lefebvre, *Critique de la vie quotidienne I*, L'Arche Editeur, Paris, 1977 second edition, p. 197; *Critique of Everyday Life, Vol. 1*, Verso, London, p. 182. This 1947 volume has much more to say about rural than urban life. Only after his encounter with the Situationists would the city emerge as the great theme of his writing. No wonder they accused him of plagiarism.

15 "On the Role of the Written Word," *Potlatch*, No. 23, 1955; Andreotti & Costa, *Theory of the Dérive*, p. 55; Debord, *présente Potlatch*, p. 203. The slogan was détourned from the Belgian surrealists.

16 Rumney, *The Consul*, p. 58.

17 Debord, "The Big Sleep and Its Clients," in Tom McDonough (ed.), *Guy Debord and the Situationist International*, MIT Press, Cambridge MA, 2004, p. 21 ff; Debord, *présente Potlatch*, p. 104 ff.

18 Patrick Straram, *Les Bouteilles se couchent*, edited by Jean-Marie Apostolidès and Boris Donné, Editions Allia, Paris, 2006, p. 17. The original version known to Debord was lost. This edition is a reconstruction by the editors. See also Patrick Straram, *Lettre à Guy Debord*, Sens & Tonka, Paris, 2006.

19 Straram, *Les Bouteilles se couchent*, p. 92.

20 *Critical practice:* the term is borrowed from friends at Chelsea College of Art and Design. The critique of the commodification of everyday life was taken up by Lefebvre's assistant Jean Baudrillard, among others. See *The System of Objects*, Verso, London, 2006.

21 Here we concentrate on the writing of the dérive. Perhaps its best expressions were maps and diagrams. See Simon Sadler, *The Situationist City*, MIT Press, Cambridge MA, 1999, p. 82 ff for a careful reading of Debord and Jorn's *Naked City* (1957).

22 On leisure and the labor movement, see Brian Rigby, *Popular Culture in Modern France*, Routledge, London, 1991.

23 See *Internationale Situationniste*, No. 8, January 1963, p. 42.

24 Friedrich Nietzsche, *The Gay Science*, Vintage, New York, 1974; *Thus Spoke Zarathustra*, Penguin, 1983. Both translations by Walter Kaufmann.

25 An influential source for nomadism is René Grousset, *The Empire of the Steppes: A History of Central Asia*, Rutgers University Press, New Brunswick NJ, 1970. Originally published in French in 1939, it was reissued many times after the war.

26 Gilles Deleuze and Félix Guattari, *Anti-Oedipus: Capitalism and Schizophrenia*, University of Minnesota Press, Minneapolis, 1983, p. 2. The connection between Situationist and what would be known in English as Post-structuralist thought is developed in Sadie Plant, *The Most Radical Gesture: The Situationist International and After*, Routledge, London, 1992. On dérive in relation to surrealism's Freudian legacy, see Tom McDonough, "Delirious Paris: Mapping as Paranoid-Critical Activity," *Grey Room*, Spring 2005.

27 See Kristin Ross, *The Emergence of Social Space*, Verso, London, 2008, on the politics of geography, and on the counter-school of the communard and anarchist Elisée Reclus. Debord does not appear to draw on Reclus directly, but Ross makes an

excellent case for a continuity of spatial practices and concepts. See also John P. Clark and Camille Martin (eds), *Anarchy, Geography, Modernity: The Radical Social Thought of Elisée Reclus*, Lexington Books, Oxford, 2004.

28 An earlier expedition had produced Michel Leiris's *L'Afrique fantôme*, Gallimard, Paris, 1981. In a literal way, the Situationists *pass over* the interest in exoticism of the surrealists.

29 See Rolf Lindner (ed.), *The Reportage of Urban Culture: Robert Park and the Chicago School*, Cambridge University Press, Cambridge, 1996.

30 Bataille, *Visions of Excess*, p. 34. Here Bataille compares Icarus, soaring up above, with the old mole, burrowing underground.

31 See Anthony Vidler, "Terres Inconnues: Cartographies of a Landscape to Be Invented," *October*, No. 115, Winter 2006; Tom McDonough, "Situationist Space," *October*, Vol. 67, Winter 1994; Brian Newsome, *French Urban Planning 1940–1968*, Peter Lang, New York, 2009; Paul-Henry Chombart de Lauwe, *Paris et l'agglomération parisienne*, Presses Universitaires de France, Paris, 1952.

32 See also Walter Benjamin, "Surrealism," in *Selected Writings, Vol. 2*, Harvard University Press, Cambridge MA, 1999, pp. 207–21.

33 *Abstract*: letter from Constant, quoted in Aldo van Eyck, *Writings: Collected Articles and Other Writings*, Sun, Amsterdam, 2008, p. 64; *Saint-Germain*: see Mark Wigley, *Constant's New Babylon: The Hyper-Architecture of Desire*, Witte de With Center for Contemporary Art and 010 Publishers, Rotterdam, 1998, p. 134. Constant was on the mailing list for free copies of *Potlatch*.

34 *Las Vegas Review-Journal*, May 3, 2003. See also Mike Davis, *Dead Cities*, New Press, New York, 2003.

35 The moving city is from: "Unitary Urbanism at the End of the 1950s," in Sussman, *On the Passage of a Few People*, p. 144; *Internationale Situationniste*, No. 3, December 1959, p. 13. An early, avant-garde incarnation of this ecological model would be Paolo Soleri, *Arcology: The City in the Image of Man*, MIT Press, Cambridge MA, 1973.

36 Borrowed (or burrowed) from *Hamlet*, Marx used the figure of the old mole most famously in the "Eighteenth Brumaire of Louis Bonaparte," in Karl Marx, *Surveys from Exile*, Penguin, 1973, p. 237. Bataille contrasts the old mole to "Icarian" thought, such as Hegel's, which soars above materiality, surveying it from outside. See Bataille, *Visions of Excess*, p. 32 ff. It also appears in Viénet, *Enragés and Situationists*, pp. 15, 73.

37 On Siasconset: *New York Times*, July 8, 2007; George E. Stuart, "The Timeless Vision of Teotihuacan," *National Geographic*, Vol. 188, No. 6, December 1995, p. 11.

38 Guy Debord, "Introduction to a Critique of Urban Geography," in Knabb, *Situationist International Anthology*, p. 10. It originally appeared in the journal edited by Belgian surrealist Marcel Mariën, *Les Lèvres Nues*, No. 6. September 1955. The complete run is reprinted by Editions Allia, Paris, 1995.

39 Sadler, *Situationist City*, p. 15. This could be the place to mention Owen Hatherley's defense of the brutalist wing of social democratic urban planning, *A Guide to the New Ruins of Great Britain*, Verso, London, 2010. While quite possibly informed by Chtcheglov and Constant, New Brutalist architects like the Smithsons developed their own critique of the failures of modernist social housing, coming up with networks, labyrinths, intersections and other means of producing social experiences. As Hatherley shows, such building, whatever its limitations, was a damned sight better than the more recent policy of turning over social housing to the private sector. Hatherley shows how the punk and postpunk critique of social housing in Sheffield and Manchester led mostly to property development and speculation,

whereas it is to the credit of social housing that, when combined with a certain subcultural knowledge, it once gave rise to whole creative scenes of much greater interest than the "creative industries" real-estate scams that replaced it.

40 Knabb, *Situationist International Anthology*, p. 9.

3   The Torrent of History

1   *Slate*, January 11, 2002; *New York Times*, February 23, 2002.

2   Comte de Lautréamont, *Maldoror and the Complete Works*, Exact Change Press, Cambridge MA, 1994: *old discoveries*, p. 313; *direction of hope*, p. 260; *one can be just*, p. 249; *plagiarism is necessary*, p. 240; *pyramids*, p. 85; *umbrella*, p. 193, *starlings*, p. 159.

3   See Tom McDonough, *The Beautiful Language of My Century*, MIT Press, Cambridge MA, 2007, and Maurice Saillet, *Les Inventeurs de Maldoror*, Les temps qu'il fait, Paris, 1992. This section was inspired by a paper McDonough gave at Binghamton University in 2001, and is indebted also to his book.

4   Paul Nougé, *Works Selected by Marcel Mariën*, Printed Head, Volume 3, No. 8, Atlas Press, London, 1985. See also Patricia Allmer and Hilde van Gelder, *Collective Inventions: Surrealism in Belgium*, Leuven University Press, Leuven, 2007.

5   Gil J. Wolman, "The Anticoncept," in Marc'O (ed.), *Ion: Centre de Création*, No. 1, April 1952, reprinted by Marc-Gilbert Guillaumin, Paris, 1999, p. 167 ff. This translation is by Keith Sanborn. See also Jean-Michel Mension, *The Tribe*, City Lights Books, San Francisco, 2001, pp. 61–64; Gérard Berréby and Danielle Orhan (eds), *Gil Joseph Wolman: Défense de Mourir*, Editions Allia, Paris, 2001 and Bartomeu Mari and João Fernandes, *Gil Wolman: I Am Mortal and Alive*, Museu d'Art Contemporani, Barcelona, 2010.

6   Guy Debord and Gil J. Wolman, "Pourquoi le Lettrisme?", in Debord, *présente Potlatch*, p. 175.

7   Lemaître, who speaks English, claims the status of co-inventor of Letterism under the nose of Isidore Isou, who clearly can't understand a word that Lemaître and Welles exchange. Thanks to Allan Stoekl for the Welles suggestion.

8   Molière, *Les Précieuses Ridicules*, Hachette, Paris, 2006.

9   Détournement may be less about surrealist collective imagination and closer to a conscious practice of what Halbwachs called collective memory. See Maurice Halbwachs, *On Collective Memory*, University of Chicago Press, 1992.

10   Karl Marx and Friedrich Engels, "Manifesto of the Communist Party," in Karl Marx, *The Revolutions of 1848: Political Writings Volume 1*, edited by David Fernbach, Penguin Books, Harmondsworth, 1978, p. 71. See Martin Puchner, *Poetry of the Revolution: Marx, Manifestos and the Avant-Gardes*, Princeton University Press, Princeton NJ, 2006. Puchner gives an excellent account of the influence of the Communist Manifesto on its avant-garde successors. Less convincing is his reading of the Situationists in the context of Tel Quel poetics.

11   McDonough, *The Beautiful Language of My Century*, p. 49. On Letterist and Situationist détournement, see Astrid Vicas, "Reusing Culture," *Yale Journal of Criticism*, Vol. 11, No. 2, 1998. On intertextuality, see Julia Kristeva, *Desire in Language: A Semiotic Approach to Literature and Art*, Columbia University Press, New York, 1980. Debord's "Mort de J. H. ou Fragiles Tissus (En Souvenir de Kaki)" (1954) is reproduced as plate 043 in Stefan Zweifel, et al. (eds), *In Girum Imus Nocte et Consumimur Igni: The Situationist International (1952–1972)*, JRP, Zurich, 2006.

12   *Times*, London, January 13, 2008. Tom McCarthy's *Remainder*, Vintage, New York, 2007, is a novel that could be read as a detailed working through of the consequences

of quotation, rather than détournement, being the dominant form of acknowledging the past in the space of the present.

13 Michel Foucault, "What Is an Author?," in *Language, Counter-Memory, Practice*, Cornell University Press, Ithaca NY, 1977.

14 This is the difference between détournement and the creative commons approach. See Lawrence Lessig, *Remix*, Penguin, New York, 2008; Yochai Benkler, *The Wealth of Networks*, Yale University Press, New Haven, 2006.

15 The question of history in Marxist thought is handled with considerably more subtlety in Martin Jay, *Marxism and Totality*, University of California Press, Berkeley CA, 1984.

16 Richard Barbrook, *Imaginary Futures: From Thinking Machines to the Global Village*, Pluto Press, London, 2007. Barbrook's historical narrative encompasses not only the American and Soviet versions of history, but also the social-democratic "third way" versions. As he shows, all draw on a common Marxist stock to very different ends.

17 Gregory Elliott, *Althusser: The Detour of Theory*, Verso, London, 1987, is a rare account of Althusser which includes the Maoist context for his thinking. Régis Debray, *Praised Be Our Lords: The Autobiography*, Verso, London, 2007, presents in condensed form Debray's own account of his adventures and misadventures. For a critique of these deviations from Marx's economic thought, see Meghnad Desai, *Marx's Revenge: The Resurgence of Capitalism and the Death of State Socialism*, Verso, London, 2004. Jean-François Lyotard, *The Postmodern Condition: A Report on Knowledge*, University of Minnesota Press, Minneapolis, 1984, is famously where Lyotard abandons the Marxist *grand récit* of history.

18 For the script see: Guy Debord, *Complete Cinematic Works*, translated and edited by Ken Knabb, AK Press, Oakland CA, 2003. On this first film in the context of Debordian cinema, see Tom Levin's classic essay "Dismantling the Spectacle: The Cinema of Guy Debord," in McDonough (ed.), *Guy Debord and the Situationist International*. And in the context of Debord's other early works, see Vincent Kaufmann, *Guy Debord: Revolution in the Service of Poetry*, University of Minnesota Press, Minneapolis, 2006, pp. 1–78, in the course of which he describes the Situationist project, not without justice, as "like a rereading of Marx by Peter Pan" (p. 6).

4 Extreme Aesthetics

1 Of course it is Plato who puts this figure in the mouth of Aristophanes: Plato, *The Symposium*, translated by Christopher Gill, Penguin, London, 1999.

2 C. J. L. Almqvist, *The Queen's Tiara*, Arcadia, London, 2001. "When, however, Jorn identifies the development of [eroticism] he does not follow this through, as he does with other essentially aesthetic emotions, into a consequent curiosity which, by exploring the unknown, would make it feasible to expand the possibilities and awareness of sexual identities. In effect, he imposes an unnecessary a priori upon himself." Peter Shield, *Comparative Vandalism: Asger Jorn and the Artistic Attitude to Life*, Ashgate, Aldershot, 1998, p. 202. Not that this should stop us.

3 T. J. Clark, *Farewell to an Idea*, Yale University Press, New Haven, 2001, p. 389. A passing remark in the context of an extended discussion of Jackson Pollock. An exception would be Peter Wollen, *Raiding the Icebox: Reflections on Twentieth-Century Culture*, Verso, London, 2008. Fabian Tompsett and Stewart Home have also done much to promote the memory of Jorn in various avant-garde circles.

4 On Cobra, see Willemijn Stokvis, *Cobra: The Last Avant-Garde Movement of the Twentieth Century*, Lund Humphries, London, 2004.

5 See the autobiographical novel by Christian Dotremont, *La Pierre et l'oreiller*, Gallimard, Paris, 1955, p. 172.

6 Max Bill, *Form, Function, Beauty = Gestalt*, Architectural Association of London, London, 2010: *Bauhaus principles*, p. 42; *concrete design*, p. 9; *from the spoon to the city*, p. 9; *good form*, p. 31; *parasite*, p. 46; *art is an order*, p. 47. See also *Max Bill: No Beginning, No End: A Retrospective*, Museum Marta Herford & Verlag Scheidegger & Spiess, 2008, and Nicola Pezolet, *Le Bauhaus Imaginiste contre un Bauhaus Imaginaire*, Université Laval, Quebec, 2008. On Jorn, Bill and the Letterists, see Craig Saper, *Networked Art*, University of Minnesota Press, Minneapolis, 2001, p. 91ff.

7 Asger Jorn, *Pour la forme: Ebauche d'une méthodologie des arts*, Paris, Editions Allia, 2001, pp. 34–44. The following quotations are from Alan Prohm's translation of the chapter "On the Cult of the New in Our Century," in *Crayon*, No. 5, 2008, pp. 216–31. I am indebted also to his commentary.

8 On Sottsass, see Barbara Radice, *Ettore Sottsass: A Critical Biography*, Norton, New York, 1993, although his connection to Imaginist Bauhaus is passed over in silence. See also Mirella Bandini, *Pinot Gallizio e il Laboratorio Sperimentale d'Alba*, Galleria Civica d'Arte Moderna, Turin, 1974.

9 Graham Birtwhistle, *Living Art: Asger Jorn's Comprehensive Theory of Art between Helbesten and Cobra*, Reflex, Utrecht, 1986, p. 57. A work to which this chapter is heavily indebted. See also Peter Shield, *Comparative Vandalism:, op cit.*

10 Birtwhistle, *Living Art*, p. 85. For Apollo and Dionysus, see Friedrich Nietzsche, *The Birth of Tragedy*, translated by Shaun Whiteside, Penguin, London, 1994. A striking contemporary version of the Apollonian as fear of popular power is Christoph Spehr's film *Free Cooperation* (2004).

11 Birtwhistle, *Living Art*, p. 63. Jorn could be usefully compared to Brian Massumi, *Parables of the Virtual: Movement, Affect, Sensation*, Duke University Press, Durham NC, 2002.

12 Friedrich Engels, *Anti-Dühring*, Progress Publishers, Moscow, 1975. Engels's scientism plays a controversial role in both Eastern and Western Marxism. See Helena Sheehan, *Marxism and the Philosophy of Science*, Humanity Books, Amherst NY, 1993. What is distinctive about Jorn is that he is more interested in a parallel aesthetic practice, alongside science as practice, than in a philosophy of either art or science.

13 One could make an interesting comparison here between Jorn's genealogy of a radical modernism and that of another former Situationist with a deep interest in art history: T. J. Clark's *Farewell to an Idea*. Unlike Clark, Jorn at mid-century still thought of an affirmative role for aesthetic practice. It could be more than the spectacle in negative.

14 Friedrich Engels, *Socialism: Utopian and Scientific*, International Publishers, New York, 2004, p. 51.

15 *New York Times*, January 5, 2009.

16 *Entangled and chaotic truth*, Birtwhistle, *Living Art*, p. 69; *transformation of nature*, ibid., p. 72.

17 Ibid., p. 97. Jorn's attempt at a mystic materialism self-consciously recalls that of another Scandinavian artist in Paris: August Strindberg, *Inferno*, Penguin, Harmondsworth, 1979.

18 Birtwhistle, *Living Art*, p. 76.

19 *Art of naïve adults*, Birtwhistle, *Living Art*, p. 181. On the Modifications show, see "Modifications Peinture Détournée", in Gérard Berréby (ed.), *Textes et Documents Situationnistes 1957–1960*, Editions Allia, Paris, 2004, p. 102 ff; Claire Gilman, "Asger Jorn's Avant-Garde Archives," in McDonough, *Guy Debord and the Situationist International*.

20 Birtwhistle, *Living Art*, p. 93. While Ralph Rumney takes credit for introducing Debord to Huizinga, André Breton had also picked up on him as early as 1954. Huizinga becomes central to the understanding of the Situationists in Libero Andreotti, "Play-tactics of the Internationale Situationniste," *October*, Winter 2000.

21 Benedict de Spinoza, *Ethics*, Penguin, London, 1996, pp. 24–5, 33, S2.

22 Gilles Deleuze and Félix Guattari, *A Thousand Plateaus*, University of Minnesota Press, Minneapolis, 1987, p. 10.

23 Birtwhistle, *Living Art*, p. 92.

24 Ibid. Like Jorn, Huizinga was raised in an austere Christianity, and reacted with a certain willful aestheticism. See Robert Anchor, "History and Play: Johan Huizinga and His Critics," *History and Theory*, February 1978.

25 Alfred Jarry, *Exploits and Opinions of Dr Faustroll, Pataphysician*, Exact Change Press, Boston, 1996.

26 See Perry Anderson, *Considerations on Western Marxism*, New Left Books, London, 1977, the book which really consolidated the idea of Western Marxism. See also Perry Anderson, *In the Tracks of Historical Materialism*, Verso, London, 1985 for later reconsiderations.

27 *Organized movement*, Birtwhistle, *Living Art*, p. 100; *air currents*, ibid.; *Pyrric victory*, ibid., p. 35, *pact*, ibid., p. 103. Jorn's critique of Isou, "Originality and Magnitude," can be found in Asger Jorn, *Open Creation and Its Enemies*, Unpopular Books, London, 1994, originally published in *Internationale Situationniste*, No. 4, June 1960.

28 See Paul Klee, *The Diaries of Paul Klee, 1898–1918*, University of California Press, Berkeley, 1973; Viktor Shklovsky, *Mayakovsky and His Circle*, Pluto Press, London, 1974.

29 Birtwhistle, *Living Art*, p. 114. On the diagram, see Gilles Deleuze, *Foucault*, University of Minnesota Press, Minneapolis, 1988.

30 *Class society*, Birtwhistle, *Living Art*, p. 152; *nature's way*, ibid., p. 157.

31 Ibid., p. 161. Jorn's approach to prehistory is not unlike Vere Gordon Childe, *Man Makes Himself*, Mentor Books, New York, 1951.

32 Birtwhistle, *Living Art*, p. 161; compare to Engels on "primitive communism," *Origins of the Family, Private Property and the State*, Progress Publishers, Moscow, 1978.

33 *Art is cult*, Birtwhistle, *Living Art*, p. 166; *lost our paradise*, ibid., p. 173. One could see Bill and Jorn's disagreement as two readings of Kleist's famous essay on the marionettes. If paradise is locked, and yet there may be still be a way to enter around the back, is the key to be form or movement? Heinrich von Kleist, *Selected Prose*, Archipelago Books, Brooklyn NY, 2009, p. 264 ff.

34 See Guy Atkin, *Jorn in Scandinavia: 1930–1953*, Wittenborn, New York, 1968.

35 Jean-Paul Sartre, *Being and Nothingness*, Washington Square Press, New York, 1956, pp. 620–28. *Resisting world*, p. 621; *condemned to freedom*, p. 623; *empirical and practical concept*, p. 624; *curfew*, p. 625; *free upsurge*, p. 628.

36 Louis Althusser, *For Marx*, Verso, London, 2006; Louis Althusser and Etienne Balibar, *Reading Capital*, Verso, London, 2009. The English edition of the latter leaves out the contributions of Jacques Rancière and Roger Establet. A rare work which takes an interest in Jorn as radical theorist is Richard Gombin, *The Radical Tradition*, St. Martin's Press, New York, 1979, pp. 119–25.

5 A Provisional Micro-Society

1 A generous selection of Rumney's Cosio photographs are included in my *50 Years of Recuperation of the Situationist International*, Princeton Architectural Press, New York, 2008.

2 Debord to Jorn, September 1, 1957. Debord's *Correspondance* is published by Fayard. The first volume is also in English as: Guy Debord, *Correspondence: The Foundation of the Situationist International*, Semiotext(e), Los Angeles, 2009.

3 Ivan Chtcheglov, "Lettres de Loin," *Internationale Situationniste* No. 9, August 1964, p. 38.

4 Debord to Straram, October 3, 1958.

5 Debord to Constant, September 7, 1959.

6 Guy Debord, *Panegyric*, Verso, London, 1991, p. 59.

7 *Our official organ*, Debord to Korun, June 16, 1958; *never work*, Debord to Wyckaert, June 22, 1960; *Lumaline*, Debord to Jorn, July 16, 1960.

8 *Heavy hand*, Debord to Ovadia, March 30, 1960; *all material*, Debord to Straram, November 12, 1958.

9 *I reproach you*, Debord to Olmo, October 18, 1957; *any real work*, Debord to Rumney, March 13, 1958.

10 For Guggenheim's side of the story, see Mary V. Dearborn, *Mistress of Modernism: The Life of Peggy Guggenheim*, Houghton Mifflin Harcourt, Boston, 2004. She was not entirely wrong in seeing Rumney as an irresponsible alcoholic.

11 Ralph Rumney, "The Leaning Tower of Venice," in Simon Ford, *The Situationist International: A User's Guide*, Black Dog, London, 2005, and also *Vague*, No. 22, 1990, pp. 33–35. Rumney was involved with the ICA in London where Alloway was assistant curator from 1955–60, but Rumney's thinking took a very different direction to Alloway and the Independent Group, of which he was a prominent member. See Lawrence Alloway, *Imagining the Present*, Routledge, London, 2006. See also Alan Woods, *The Map Is Not the Territory*, Manchester University Press, Manchester, 2000, which contains Rumney's later elaboration on the distinction between game and play.

12 Debord to Constant, June 21, 1960.

13 *New Yorker*, June 9, 2008. On contemporary art as the art of the market, see Isabelle Graw, *High Price: Art between the Market and Celebrity Culture*, Sternberg Press, Berlin, 2010.

14 *Jorn the first partisan*, Debord to Constant, June 2, 1960; *I without the we*, Debord to Melanotte, February 10, 1959.

15 *Objective criteria*, Debord to Frankin, January 26, 1960; *good will*, Debord to Korun, June 16, 1958; *neither freedom nor intelligence*, Debord to Straram, August 25, 1960.

16 Or so Blanchot proposes. See Blanchot, *The Unavowable Community*.

17 *False disciples*, Debord to Gallizio, January 13, 1957; *perspectives*, Debord to Straram, November 12, 1958; *Situationism*, Debord to Simondo, August 22, 1957; *dogmas*, Debord to Gallizio, November 23, 1957. On Simondo: Cristiana Campanini, "Simondo Inedito," *Arte*, May 2004.

18 *Internal propaganda*, Debord to Constant, September 16, 1959; *artistically old men*, Debord to Constant, October 16, 1959.

19 *Most urgent problem*, Debord to Constant, March 3, 1959; *specialized collaborators*, Debord to Constant, February 28, 1959.

20 Cardinal de Retz, *Mémoires*, Société des Bibliophiles, Paris, 1903, p. 215.

21 Giorgina Bertolino et al. (eds), *Pinot Gallizio: Il laboratorio della scrittura*, Charta, Milan, 2005, p. 20. On Gallizio, see Nicola Pezolet, "The Cavern of Antimatter,"

Grey Room, Winter 2010, Frances Stracey, "Pinot Gallizio's Industrial Painting," *Oxford Art Journal*, No. 28, 2005.

22 Bertolino, *Pinot Gallizio*, p. 164. On the Alba conference, see Nathalie Aubert, "Cobra after Cobra and the Alba Congress," *Third Text*, March 2006.

23 Michèle Bernstein, "In Praise of Pinot Gallizio," in McDonough, *Guy Debord and the Situationist International*, p. 70 and Berréby (ed.), *Textes et documents*, pp. 64–68. See also Mirella Bandini, "An Enormous and Unknown Chemical Reaction," in Sussman, *On the Passage of a Few People*, p. 72. Gallizio's praxis beyond play and labor might be at the roots of what is now called in its recuperated form *playbor*, in which value is extracted from the very ambiguity of action's interests and motives. See Nick Dyer-Witheford and Greig de Peuter, *Games of Empire*, University of Minnesota Press, Minneapolis, 2009.

24 *Tumult*, Debord to Gallizio, January 30, 1958; *deficiency*, Debord to Constant, May 20, 1959; *sickening arrivisme*, Debord to Constant, June 2, 1960. *Fight their own glory*, Guy Debord, *Considerations on the Assassination of Gérard Lebovici*, Tam Tam Books, Los Angeles, 2001, p. 78.

25 Debord to Constant, November 26, 1959.

26 Constant & Debord, "Amsterdam Declaration," Andreotti & Costa, *Theory of the Dérive*, pp. 80–81; *Internationale Situationiste* No. 2, December 1958, pp. 31–32.

27 Alice Becker-Ho, *Princes of Jargon*, Edwin Mellen Press, Lewiston NY, 2004, p. 39. For Constant's account, see Andreotti and Costa, *Theory of the Dérive*, p. 154.

28 Constant, "On Our Means and Our Perspectives" (1958), in *The Decomposition of the Artist*, Drawing Center, New York, 1999, p. 7. See also Debord's letter to Constant, September 25, 1958.

29 Constant, "On Our Means and Our Perspectives," Andreotti & Costa, *Theory of the Dérive*, p. 77; *Internationale Situationniste*, No. 2, 1958. Constant was already familiar with Henri Lefebvre's 1947 edition of *Critique of Everyday Life*, which is also a significant influence.

30 *No painting*, Debord to Constant, September 25, 1958; *any spirit of the "pictorial,"* Debord to Constant, August 8, 1958.

31 *Really experimental faction*, Debord to Constant, August 8, 1958; *I don't have the right*, Debord to Constant, September 7, 1959.

32 Debord to Constant, April 4, 1959. See Frank Manuel, *The Prophets of Paris*, Harper, New York, 1965, on the utopians Debord accuses Constant of resurrecting.

33 Ibid. See Raoul Vanegeim, 'Comments against Urbanism', in *Internationale Situationiste*, No. 6, August 1961, also in McDonough, p119ff. An attack on Chombart, it also closes the book on utopia adventures in built form for the Situationists.

34 *Passion*, Debord to Constant, June 21, 1960; *indecision*, quoted in Debord to Jorn, July 6, 1960; *choose the terrain*, Debord to Constant, June 21, 1960.

35 Marcel Mauss, *The Gift*, Norton, New York, 2000; Georges Bataille, *The Accursed Share, Vol. 1*, Zone Books, New York, 1989. Claude Lefort, a key figure in the Socialism or Barbarism group, also took up the figure of the gift, but Debord had very little taste for Lefort and his interest in the group postdates Lefort's departure from it in 1958.

36 Jacques Derrida, *Given Time: 1. Counterfeit Money*, translated by Peggy Kamuf, University of Chicago Press, Chicago, 1991. *Nothing else*, p. 28; *presents itself*, p. 15; *subject and object*, p. 24. See also Douglas Smith, "Giving the Game Away: Play and Exchange in Situationism and Structuralism," *Modern & Contemporary France*, November 2005; Scott Cutler Shershow, *The Work and the Gift*, University of Chicago Press, Chicago, 2005, for a very helpful overview of the whole terrain of work and gift in twentieth-century social thought.

37 Claude Lévi-Strauss, *Tristes Tropiques*, New York, 1965, p. 62. Sartre is the proximate enemy here.
38 Debord to Constant, June 2, 1960.

6   Permanent Play

1   Charles Fourier, *The Theory of the Four Movements*, Cambridge University Press, Cambridge, 1996, p. 111. This chapter is interested in a classic Marxist approach to the relations between the genders, drawing on Fourier and centrally concerned with asking the property question. For the now more common approach, more concerned with representation, see Kelly Baum, "The Sex of the Situationist International," *October*, No. 126, Fall 2008. On the collapse of the critique of representation into consumer feminism, see Nina Power, *One Dimensional Woman*, Zero Books, Winchester, UK, 2009.
2   Kristin Ross, *Fast Cars, Clean Bodies*, MIT Press, Cambridge MA, 1995, p. 148. For the characters in Bernstein's novels, it is more like fast bodies, clean cars.
3   On de Scudéry's map and the spatial politics of its time, see Joan DeJean, "No Man's Land: The Novel's First Geography," *Yale French Studies*, No. 73, 1987. See also the introduction to Madeleine de Scudéry, *The Story of Sappho*, translated by Karen Newman, University of Chicago Press, Chicago, 2003. Anthony Vidler, "Terres Inconnues", *October* No. 115, Winter 2006, usefully connects the *Carte de Tendre* to psychogeography. For a far more contemporary version of the (anti-) novel of (Sapphic) desire, see Eileen Myles, *Inferno*, O/R Books, New York, 2010.
4   Debord to Straram, October 10, 1960. The possibilities of détourning novels as a transitional tactic are discussed in "Détournement: A User's Guide," in Knabb, *Situationist International Anthology*, p. 18.
5   Carol Hanisch, "The Personal is Political," in Shulamith Firestone and Anne Koedt (eds), *Notes from the Second Year*, Women's Liberation, New York, 1970. Debates rage over who actually coined the phrase.
6   Maurice Blanchot, *Friendship*, translated by Elizabeth Rottenberg, Stanford University Press, Stanford CA, 1997, p. 70. *Pure spectacle*, Henri Lefebvre, *Introduction to Modernity*, Verso, London, 1995, p. 337.
7   Debord to Frankin, July 15, 1959.
8   Xavier Canonne, *Surrealism in Belgium 1924–2000*, Mercatorfonds, Brussels, 2007, p. 142. Mochot was the stepdaughter of the brother of another Belgian surrealist, Paul Bourgoignie.
9   Michèle Bernstein, *La Nuit*, Buchet-Chastel, Paris, 1961, p. 40.
10 *They pass beside a column*, Bernstein, *La Nuit*, p. 18; *in a labyrinth*, ibid., p. 92.
11 Arthur Adamov, *Ping-Pong: A Play in Two Parts*, Grove Press, New York, 1959.
12 Asger Jorn, "La Création ouverte et ses ennemis," *Internationale Situationniste*, No. 5, p. 45; translated by Fabian Tompsett as *Open Creation and Its Enemies*, Unpopular Books, London, 1994, p. 39.
13 Debord and Wolman, "Détournement: A User's Guide."
14 On networks, distributed and otherwise, see Alex Galloway, *Protocol*, MIT Press, Cambridge MA, 2004.
15 Choderlos de Laclos, *Dangerous Liaisons*, Penguin, London, 2007; Michel Feher (ed.), *The Libertine Reader: Eroticism and Enlightenment in Eighteenth-Century France*, Zone Books, New York, 1997.
16 Debord to Straram, November 12, 1958.
17 Michèle Bernstein, *Tous les chevaux du roi*, Editions Allia, Paris, 2004, p. 116; *All*

The King's Horses, translated by John Kelsey, Semiotext(e), Los Angeles, 2008, p. 108.

18 Odile Passot, "Portrait of Guy Debord as a Young Libertine," *Substance*, No. 3, 1999, p. 77. Odile Passot is a pseudonym; this text was actually written by Jean-Marie Apostolidès. See his *Les Tombeaux de Guy Debord*, Flammarion, Paris, 2006.

19 See Marcel Carné, *The Devil's Envoys (Les Visiteurs du soir)*, 1942, with script by Jacques Prévert and Pierre Laroche.

20 Bernstein, *Tous les chevaux*, p. 36 ; *King's Horses*, p. 42.

21 Len Bracken, *Guy Debord Revolutionary*, Feral House, Venice CA, 1997, p. 245. Not the most reliable biography, but one with spirit.

22 Asger Jorn and Noël Arnaud, *La Langue verte et la cuite. Etude gastrophonique sur la marmythologie musiculinaire*, (Bibliothèque d'Alexandrie Vol. III), Jean-Jacques Pauvert Editeur, Paris, 1968. It received a surprisingly warm and astute review in *Man*, Vol. 4, No. 4, December 1969, p. 667.

23 Greil Marcus, *Lipstick Traces*, p. 423. Marcus offers a pioneering account of the Situationists, including insights into many of the figures of interest here (Wolman, Trocchi, Bernstein).

7   Tin Can Philosophy

1 Abdelhafid Khatib, "Attempt at a Psychogeographical Description of Les Halles," Andreotti & Costa, *Theory of the Dérive*, pp. 72–6 ; *Internationale Situationniste* No. 2, December 1958, p. 13ff. His Les Halles can be compared to that of Gérard de Nerval, "October Nights," in *Selected Writings*, Penguin, London, 1999, p. 204 ff.

2 See Martin Evans, *The Memory of Resistance*, Berg French Studies, New York, 1997; Todd Shepard, *Inventing Decolonization*, Cornell University Press, Ithaca NY, 2006.

3 Anselm Jappe, *Guy Debord*, University of California Press, Berkeley, 1999, is an excellent reading of the Hegelian-Marxist Debord. For the wider context, see Mark Poster, *Existential Marxism in Postwar France: From Sartre to Althusser*, Princeton University Press, Princeton NJ, 1975; see also V. I. Lenin, "Left-Wing Communism, an Infantile Disorder," *Collected Works*, Vol. 31, Progress Publishers, Moscow, 1964.

4 In "L'Internationale Situationniste, Socialisme ou Barbarie, and the Crisis of the Marxist Imaginary," *Substance* No. 90, 1999, Stephen Hastings-King offers a more subtle account of the various stages of Debord's relation with the Socialism or Barbarism group. When key members of the latter, particularly Castoriadis, turned away from Marxism towards a new kind of critique, Debord took his distance, and in Hastings-King's view, tried to supplant them as *the* revolutionary expression of the proletariat. However, Hastings-King does not quite see how *Society of the Spectacle* is a détournement of the contending texts influential on the left at the time. Lukács is subverted more than idolized in this famous text.

5 See Debord to Jorn, July 16, 1960.

6 Asger Jorn, *The Natural Order and Other Texts*, translated by Peter Shield, Ashgate, Farnham UK, 2002, p. 139. Jorn added new material to his 1960 "Critique" for the book *Value and Economics* (1962), which is included in this volume. References are to both the Shield translation of the later text, and to the original French text where the quote appears in both.

7 C. Wright Mills, *The Power Elite*, Oxford University Press, Oxford, 1957. On Mills:

Daniel Geary, *Radical Ambition: C. Wright Mills, the Left and American Social Thought*, University of California Press, Berkeley, 2009.

8   Jorn, *The Natural Order*, p. 135.

9   On Mauss and his critique of the Soviet economy, see David Graeber, *Toward an Anthropological Theory of Value*, Palgrave, London, 2001.

10   On Marx's love affair with capital, see Marshall Berman, *All That Is Solid Melts into Air*, Penguin, New York, 1988; Jean-François Lyotard, *Libidinal Economy*, Indiana University Press, Bloomington, 1993.

11   Asger Jorn, "Critique de la politique économique- Suivie de la lutte finale," *Internationale Situationniste*, May 1960, p. 25; *The Natural Order*, p. 132. Jorn anticipates another attempt to deepen the critique of political economy, see Jean Baudrillard, *The Mirror of Production*, Telos Press, St. Louis, 1975.

12   Jorn, *The Natural Order*, p. 126.

13   Jorn, *Critique*, p. 10; *The Natural Order*, p. 130.

14   Jorn, *Critique*, p. 11; *The Natural Order*, p. 139.

15   Jorn, *Critique*, p. 13; *The Natural Order*, p. 141.

16   Jorn, *Critique*, p. 28; *The Natural Order*, p. 135. A Jornian reading of Warhol immediately suggests itself, as an art of pure container value.

17   Jorn, *Critique*, p. 16; *The Natural Order*, p. 136. Compare to Georges Bataille, *The Accursed Share, Vol. 1*, Zone Books, New York, 1991. *Scarcity* would become a key term in Sartre's *Critique of Dialectical Reason*.

18   *State as container*, Jorn, *Critique*, p. 29 ; *The Natural Order*, p. 138. *Assault on the universe*, Henri Lefebvre, *Introduction à la modernité: Préludes*, Les Editions de minuit, Paris, 1962, pp. 37–8. See also Susan Buck-Morss, *Dreamworld and Catastrophe: The Passing of Mass Utopia in East and West*, MIT Press, Cambridge MA, 2002. The most remarkable writing on Stalin's assault on the universe is surely by Andrey Platonov: see *Soul and Other Stories*, NYRB Classics, New York, 2007 and *The Foundation Pit*, NYRB Classics, New York, 2009.

19   Debord to Jorn, July 6, 1960.

20   Jorn, *The Natural Order*, p. 142.

8   *The Thing of Things*

1   Lefebvre, *Introduction à la modernité: Préludes*, pp. 131–34 (hereafter *Modernité*); translated as Henri Lefebvre, *Introduction to Modernity*, Verso, London, 1995, pp. 128–30 (hereafter *Modernity*).

2   Henri Lefebvre, *Critique de la vie quotidienne II – Fondements d"une sociologie de la quotidienneté*, L'Arche Editeur, Paris, 1961, p. 51 (hereafter *Quotidienne II*). Translated as Henri Lefebvre, *Critique of Everyday Life, Volume 2*, Verso, London. 2008, p. 49 (hereafter *Everyday 2*).

3   Henri Lefebvre, *The Explosion*, Monthly Review Press, New York, 1969, p. 104. Andrew Merrifield, *Henri Lefebvre: A Critical Introduction*, Routledge, London, 2006. For Lefebvre's settling of accounts with his past, see *La Somme et le reste*, Economica, Paris, 2008.

4   Henri Lefebvre, *Key Writings*, Continuum, London, 2003, p. 167.

5   Kristin Ross, "Lefebvre on the Situationists: An Interview," in McDonough, *Guy Debord and the Situationists*, p. 268.

6   "Letters from Henri Lefebvre," *Norbert Guterman Papers*, Box 1/Folder 1953–1962; Rare Book and Manuscript Library, Columbia University Library, Paris 31-12-1958.

7 *To know the everyday, Quotidienne II*, p. 102, *Everyday 2*, p. 98; *transduction, Quotidienne II*, pp. 121–22, *Everyday 2*, p. 105. See Adrian Mackenzie, *Transductions: Bodies and Machines at Speed*, Continuum, London, 2006 for more on transduction, which Lefebvre borrows from Gilbert Simondon.

8 Like many of Lefebvre's concepts, it may be more of a collective production. In the case of the theory of needs, Lefebvre drew on the work of Dionys Mascolo, *Le Communisme: Révolution et communication*, Gallimard, Paris, 1953. Mascolo and Lefebvre joined forces with other non-party Marxists in 1956 in the journal *Arguments*. See Mark Poster, *Existential Marxism in Postwar France*. Poster puts Lefebvre's work after leaving the Communist Party in the context of the reception of Sartre's work and the development of *Arguments*, which is probably far more important than his brief association with Debord.

9 Henri Lefebvre, *Everyday Life in the Modern World*, Transaction Publishers, New Brunswick NJ, 2007, p. 13. Written in 1967, this was a summary of the projected third volume of *The Critique of Everyday Life*, which, when it eventually appeared, took on a quite different character. In it Lefebvre extends his analysis further into the great pleonasm of consumer culture, in which it is the consumers who come to suspect that they are what is consumed, and in which signs float free of their referents. "One might just as well say that all referentials have vanished and what remains is the memory and the demand for a system of reference." One can find here the kernel of the project of Lefebvre's most talented assistant. See Baudrillard, *The System of Objects*.

10 Eugene Thacker, *After Life*, University of Chicago Press, Chicago, 2010. *Every ontology*, p. x; *animating principle*, p. 12. Eugene points out to me that Raoul Vaneigem's *Movement of the Free Spirit*, Zone Books, New York, 1998 could be considered an attempt to radicalize the metaphysics of life as spirit.

11 See John Bellamy Foster, *Marx's Ecology: Materialism and Nature*, Monthly Review Press, New York, 2000. Where Thacker makes Aristotle the touchstone for his three metaphysics of life (time, form, spirit), perhaps one has to look, as Marx and Darwin did, to Lucretius and the Epicurians for materialist life.

12 Lefebvre, *Quotidienne II*, p. 17; *Everyday 2*, p. 11.

13 Lefebvre, *Modernité*, p. 100; *Modernity*, pp. 93–4.

14 Lefebvre, *Quotidienne II*, p. 79; *Everyday 2*, p. 75. Debord will develop cyclical and linear time further in the "Time and History" chapter of *Society of the Spectacle*.

15 Lefebvre, *Quotidienne II*, p. 84; *Everyday 2*, p. 81.

16 Lefebvre, *Quotidienne II*, p. 229; *Everyday 2*, p. 227. See Gayatri Spivak, *A Critique of Postcolonial Reason*, Harvard University Press, Cambridge MA, 1999. Lefebvre constructs a concept of modernity without reference to the colonial other.

17 Lefebvre, *Quotidienne II*, p. 138; *Everyday 2*, p. 134. Mention of *agôn* and *aléa* seems to suggest a familiarity with Roger Caillois, *May, Play and Games*, University of Illinois Press, Champaign IL, 2001. Lefebvre's comrade in the *Arguments* group Kostas Alexos developed the theme of play (and in a playful style) in *Vers la pensée planétaire*, Editions de Minuit, Paris, 1964; *Le Jeu du monde*, Editions de Minuit, Paris, 1969. On the everyday reduced to the tactical, see Michel de Certeau, *The Practice of Everyday Life*, University of California Press, Berkeley CA, 2002. De Certeau deals only with tactics, excluding the strategic dimension. De Certeau's study, so influential for cultural studies, was commissioned by the French state secretary of culture. See Derek Schilling, "Everyday Life and the Challenge to History in Postwar France," *Diacritics*, Spring 2003, p. 37, and also John Roberts, *Philosophizing the Everyday*, Pluto Press, London, 2006.

18 Lefebvre, *Modernité*, p. 125; *Modernity*, p. 121. On the development of game theory

and other cold war social sciences, see Philip Mirowski, *Machine Dreams: Economics Becomes a Cyborg Science*, Cambridge University Press, Cambridge 2002; Manuel de Landa, *War in the Age of Intelligent Machines*, Zone Books, New York, 1991; Paul Edwards, *The Closed World: Computers and the Politics of Discourse in Cold War America*, MIT Press, Cambridge MA, 1997; Lydia Lin, *The Freudian Robot*, University of Chicago Press, Chicago, 2011, addresses the (mis) translations between American and French Information theory.

19 Lefebvre, *Quotidienne II*, p. 196; *Everyday 2*, p. 193. Huizinga's was an essentially cultural but nevertheless entirely scathing critique of modernity, not least modern broadcasting and journalism. Debord and Lefebvre were probably not aware that he had preceded them in the critique of the spectacle. See R. L. Colie, "Johan Huizinga and the Task of Cultural History," *American Historical Review*, Vol. 69, No. 3, 1964. Peter Geyl, "Huizinga as Accuser of His Age," *History and Theory*, Vol. 2, No. 3, 1963, is a critical account by a contemporary.

20 Lefebvre, *Quotidienne II*, pp. 137–8; *Everyday 2*, p. 134. Fredric Jameson, in *Archaeologies of the Future*, Verso, London, 2006, p. 243, writes that only in Sartre, and in Laclau and Mouffe, is the problem of the group put back at the center of political thought. But perhaps another way opens up if one takes Lefebvre's rather less precise thinking about groups and the practice of the Situationists together.

21 Lefebvre, *Quotidienne II*, p. 205; *Everyday 2*, p. 203. On the latter-day consequences of the curious ontological status of games, see Jesper Juul, *Half Real: Video Games between Real Rules and Fictional Worlds*, MIT Press, Cambridge MA, 2005.

22 Lefebvre, *Quotidienne II*, p. 168; *Everyday 2*, p. 160. Lefebvre does not achieve the formal clarity of Derrida's famous essay, "Structure, Sign and Play," in *Writing and Difference*, Routledge, London, 2001. Instead there is a practical sense of the implications of play in Lefebvre.

23 *Discourse strives for totality*, Lefebvre, *Modernité*, p. 13, *Modernity*, p. 5; *every totalization*, *Quotidienne II*, p. 186, *Everyday 2*, p. 183 ; *insistence upon totality*, *Quotidienne II*, p. 184, *Everyday 2*, p. 181. A representative work of the so-called new philosophers would be André Glucksmann (b. 1937), *The Master Thinkers*, Harper Collins, 1980.

24 Lefebvre, *Quotidienne II*, p. 242 ; *Everyday 2*, p. 240. One branch of media and cultural studies has indeed tended towards an uncritical embrace of the popular, and a populism which upholds consumer choice against the centralizing tendencies of an older form of spectacle. See Henry Jenkins, *Fans, Bloggers, and Gamers: Media Consumers in a Digital Age*, NYU Press, New York, 2006.

25 Lefebvre, *Quotidienne II*, p. 264; *Everyday 2*, p. 262. A critique that could apply to Jean Baudrillard, for example. Lefebvre's reversible alienation seems curiously like territorialization and deterritorialization in Deleuze and Guattari.

26 Lefebvre, *Quotidienne II*, p. 343; *Everyday 2*, p. 343.

27 BBC News, August 10, 2005.

28 Lefebvre, *Quotidienne II*, p. 355; *Everyday 2*, p. 356.

29 Lefebvre, *Quotidienne II*, p. 356; *Everyday 2*, p. 357.

30 On *situation*, see Gerald Raunig, *Art and Revolution: Transversal Activism in the Long Twentieth Century*, Semiotext(e), Los Angeles, 2007. If, for Raunig, Hegel subsumes the situation too quickly into the dialectics of conflict, perhaps Raunig dissolves conflict too much into proliferating difference. See also Roberto Ohrt, *Phantom Avantgarde*, Galerie Van de Loo, Munich, 1990, p. 163 ff.

31 *The moment*, Lefebvre, *Quotidienne II*, p. 351, *Everyday 2*, p. 353; *the difficulty*, Debord to Franklin, February 22, 1960. This letter is the basis for a later article "Théorie des moments et construction des situations," *Internationale Situationniste*, No. 4, pp. 10–11; Andreotti & Costa, *Theory of the Dérive*, pp. 100–101.

32   Debord to Jorn, July 2, 1959.

33   Lefebvre, *Modernité*, p. 128; *Modernity*, p. 123. See also Henri Lefebvre, "The Everyday and Everydayness," *Yale French Studies*, No. 73, 1987 for a succinct statement of Lefebvre's more pessimistic approach to the everyday.

34   *Something worse*, Lefebvre, *Modernité*, p. 174, *Modernity*, p. 173; *ghost of revolution*, *Modernité*, p. 233, *Modernity*, p. 237. The hauntological quality of modernity, and Marxism's catalyzing role at the séance is the subject of Jacques Derrida, *Specters of Marx: The State of the Debt, The Work of Mourning & the New International*, Routledge, London, 2006.

35   Lefebvre, *Quotidienne II*, p. 81; *Everyday 2*, p. 77.

36   *Great Pleonasm*, Lefebvre, *Quotidienne II*, p. 165, *Everyday 2*, p. 164; *Thing of Things*, *Modernité*, p. 168, *Modernity*, p. 167; *faked orgasm*, *Modernité*, p. 255, *Modernity*, p. 259.

37   Lefebvre, *Modernité*, p. 277, *Modernity*, p. 283. This could be usefully compared to Roland Barthes, *Mythologies*, Noonday Press, New York, 1972. Barthes undoubtedly achieves closer and more illuminating readings, but at the price of losing Lefebvre's grasp of the totalizing tendencies of modernity.

38   Lefebvre, *Modernité*, p. 280; *Modernity*, p. 286.

39   Lefebvre, *Modernité*, p. 286; *Modernity*, p. 283. See also Michael Löwy: *Morning Star: Surrealism, Marxism, Anarchism, Situationism, Utopia*, University of Texas Press, Austin TX, 2009.

40   Constant attests to Debord's love of American comics in *HuO: Hans-Ulrich Obrist: Interviews*, Charta, Milan, 2003.

41   Lefebvre, *Modernité*, p. 294; *Modernity*, p. 302.

42   Lefebvre, *Quotidienne II*, p. 227; *Everyday 2*, p. 225.

43   Lefebvre, *Modernité*, pp. 236–37; *Modernity*, p. 364.

44   Lefebvre, *Modernité*, p. 298; *Modernity*, p. 306.

9   *Divided We Stand*

1   thinkproperty.com, September 8, 2008, accessed via Google Earth.

2   Charles Dickens, *The Mystery of Edwin Drood*, Everyman's Library, London, 2004.

3   Interview with Jacqueline de Jong, Algonquin Hotel, New York, October 17, 2009. All other quotes from de Jong not otherwise identified are from this interview. See also the contributions by de Jong and Karen Kurczynski to Mikkel Bolt Rasmussen and Jakob Jakobsen, *Expect Anything, Fear Nothing: The Situationist Movement in Scandanavia and Elsewhere*, Autonomedia, New York, forthcoming.

4   On the aborted Amsterdam show, see Sadler, *The Situationist City*, p. 115 ff. The show turned the museum into a labyrinth opening out towards the city, extended even further by a three-day dérive, coordinated by walkie-talkies. Part of the plan was published as "Die Welt Als Labyrinth," *Internationale Situationniste*, No. 4, June 1960, pp. 5–7.

5   Matta is quoted in Guy Atkins, *Asger Jorn, The Crucial Years 1954–1964*, Borgens Forlag, Copenhagen, 1977, p. 56. On Spur, I rely largely on the account of Diedrich Diederichsen, "Persecution and Self-Persecution: The Spur Group and Its Texts," *Grey Room*, Winter 2007.

6   Gruppe Spur, "Manifest," in Berréby (ed.), *Textes et Documents*, p. 90. On the role Adorno played in postwar German culture, see Stefan Müller-Doohm, *Adorno: A Biography*, Polity, Cambridge, 2009, and his surprise bestseller, Theodor Adorno, *Minima Moralia: Reflections on Damaged Life*, Verso, London, 2006. Unlike his

contemporary Lefebvre, he abandoned faith in the proletariat. Not surprising, given the divergent historical experiences of France and Germany in the 1930s.

7   Vincent Kaufmann, *Revolution in the Service of Poetry*, University of Minnesota Press, Minneapolis, 2006, p. 93. This excellent study might stand in for a host of others, some not quite so excellent, which effect the recuperation of *situationism* as either aesthetics or biography, or, in this case—both.

8   Vaneigem makes his presence felt in *Internationale Situationniste* from issue No. 6, but especially with a series of texts titled "Basic Banalities," starting in No. 7. See Knabb, *Anthology*, pp. 117–30, 154–72. He claims never to have met Constant. See Hans Ulrich Obrist, "In Conversation with Raoul Vanegeim," *e-flux journal*, No. 6, May 2009.

9   Atkins, *Asger Jorn, The Crucial Years*.

10 From a letter by Jorn to Debord, July 12, 1960, quoted as a postscript to a letter from Debord to Jorn, July 16, 1960.

11 Debord to Jorn, August 23, 1962. The Jorn quote is attributed to the pseudonym Jorn used, George Keller, in "La Cinquième Conférence de l'I. S. à Göteborg", from *Internationale Situationniste*, No. 7, April 1962, p. 30.

12 Debord to Vaneigem, February 15, 1962. See also letter to Tom Levin, November 1989. This is in Bill Brown's translation.

13 "Danger! Do Not Lean Out!", *Situationist Times*, No. 1.

14 "The Struggle for the Situcratic Society," signed by Nash, de Jong, et al., *Situationist Times* No. 2, 1962.

15 See Howard Slater, "Divided We Stand: An Outline of Scandinavian Situationism," *Infopool*, No. 4, 2001, p. 31. Slater makes a good case for the value of the Nashists, and I am indebted to it. See also Howard Slater, "The Spoiled Ideas of Lost Situations," *Infopool*, No. 2, 2000.

16 Jens Jørgen Thorsen, "The Communicative Phase in Art," in *Situationister 1957–1970*, Jørgen Nash et al. (eds), Bauhaus Situationist, 1966. Quoted in Slater, "Divided We Stand," p. 31. One could see Thorsen's communicative art as a precursor to the recuperated form of relational aesthetics. See Nicholas Bourriaud, *Relational Aesthetics*, Les Presses du réel, Paris, 1998, and for a critique: Claire Bishop, *Artificial Hells: Participatory Art and the Politics of Spectatorship*, Verso, London, 2011.

17 The head disappeared again in 1998: *New York Times*, March 21, 1998.

18 See Slater, "Divided We Stand," p. 32.

19 *Situationist idea*, interview in *Aspekt*, No. 3, Copenhagen, 1963, translated by Jakob Jakobsen for infopool.com; *chiliastic serenity*, T. J. Clark, *The Painting of Modern Life*, Princeton University Press, 1984, p. 10.

20 Jacqueline de Jong, "Critic on the Political Practice of Détournement," *Situationist Times*, No. 1, 1962.

21 Ibid.

22 Ibid.

23 Noël Arnaud, *Les Vies parallèles de Boris Vian*, 10/18, Paris, 1970. On the College of Pataphysics, see Alastair Brotchie (ed.), *A True History of the College of Pataphysics*, Atlas Press, London, 1995.

24 Benjamin Buchloh writes: "Dufrêne would orient himself toward a more disillusioned and skeptical acceptance of the social compartmentalization of transgressive activities … it led to a paradoxical position suspended between this pessimism concerning the revolutionary potential of the neo-avantgarde and an insistence upon radical gestures of opposition: to transform the internal structure of the aesthetic object; to emphasize the collaborative nature of the artistic project; and to demonstrate the relocation of artistic practice in the collective urban space of advanced

industrial consumer culture." Benjamin Buchloh, *Neo-Avantgarde and Culture Industry*, MIT Press, Cambridge MA, 2003.

25 See Emily Apter, *The Translation Zone: A New Comparative Literature*, Princeton University Press, Princeton, 2005, p. 226 ff. In "The Master of the Revolutionary Subject," *Substance* No. 90, 1999, Roberto Ohrt makes the point that, whatever their failings, the Situationists were much more international than many of the avantgarde groups of their time.

26 "Renseignements Situationnistes," *Internationale Situationniste*, No. 7, April 1962, pp. 49–54.

27 A theme taken up ably by Eduardo Rothe, "The Conquest of Space in the Time of Power," *Internationale Situationniste* No. 12, September 1969; Knabb, *Situationist International Anthology*, p. 371 ff. Rothe later worked for the Ministry of Communication in Venezuela.

28 On Jorn and topology see Wark, *50 Years of Recuperation*. After completing the manuscript for this book, I discovered Fabian Tompsett's translation and commentary: Jorn, *Open Creation and Its Enemies*, which had blazed the trail through Jorn's difficult texts, if only I had known it.

29 Jacqueline de Jong, "The Times of the Situationists," in Zweifel et al, *In Girum Imus Nocte et Consumimur Igni*, p. 239.

30 Atkins, *Asger Jorn, The Crucial Years*, p. 127. Atkins was a fascinating character in his own right. Comparing Atkins to Jorn's famous paintings, de Jong says that "his whole life was a Modification." Some of his early life story can be found in William Stevenson, *Spymistress: The Life of Vera Atkins*, Arcade, New York, 2006.

31 Asger Jorn et al., *Signes gravés sur les églises de l'Eure et du Calvados*, Borgen, Copenhagen, 1963, including an interesting essay by Jorn on the morphology of symbols and an elaborate working-out of his *triolectic* diagrams.

32 Two volumes that give a real sense of his intentions are: Asger Jorn et al., *Bird, Beast and Man in the Nordic Iron Age*, Walther König, Munich, 2005; Asger Jorn et al., *Men, Gods and Masks in the Nordic Iron Age*, Walther König, Cologne, 2008 (Jorn is quoted from p. 10).

33 *Polydimensional*, Jorn, "La création ouverte et ses ennemis," p. 327; *all my outpourings* and *Jorn's texts*, Shield, *Comparative Vandalism*, Borgen p. xxiii, Ashgate, p. 19. This is the standard work on Jorn's mature thought. As de Jong pointed out to me, Jorn did not think of his writing as art at all, but as something quite separate.

34 *Situationist Times*, No. 3, p. 30.

35 Slater, "Divided We Stand," p. 8.

36 *Dionysian dance*, Lefebvre, *Modernité*, p. 19; *most brilliant Situationists*, ibid., pp. 236–37.

37 Jorn, *Pour la forme*, p. 71; Terry Smith, "Spectacle Architecture Before and After the Aftermath," in Anthony Vidler (ed.), *Architecture Between Spectacle and Use*, Clark Studies in the Visual Arts, Williamstown MA, 2008.

10   An Athlete of Duration

1 Alexander Trocchi, *Invisible Insurrection of a Million Minds: A Trocchi Reader*, edited by Andrew Murray Scott, Polygon, Edinburgh, 1991, p. 196. Trocchi did not know that the right-wing Brazilian Integralist Action Party had used "sigma" as its emblem in the 1930s. *Accretions*, p. 181; *unpopular*, p. 177; *grids of expression*, p. 178; *ancestral bones*, p. 181. On the *modern* nature of the October revolution, see Leon Trotsky, *The History of the Russian Revolution*, Vol. 3, Ch. 43, "The

Insurrection." "The Invisible Insurrection" appeared as "Technique du coup du monde" in *Internationale Situationniste*, No. 8, January 1963, p. 48 ff.

2 Trocchi quotes Williams from an essay by kitchen sink dramatist Arnold Wesker (b. 1932), founder of the rival Center 42: "Secret Reins," *Encounter*, Vol. 18, No. 3, March 1962, p. 5. The Williams quote appears in *Internationale Situationniste*, No. 8, January 1963, p. 52. On Williams of this period, see Dai Smith, *Raymond Williams: A Warrior's Tale*, Parthian Books, London, 2009. Williams's argument for the public ownership (but not state control) of the means of cultural production are most forcefully made in *The Long Revolution*, Columbia University Press, New York, 1961, pp. 335–47, although the exact sentences Wesker and Trocchi quote are not to be found there.

3 Alexander Trocchi, *Invisible Insurrection*, p. 195. See Katherine Chaddock Reynolds, *Visions and Vanities: John Andrew Rice of Black Mountain College*, Louisiana State University Press, Baton Rouge, 1988, on the famous college.

4 Vladimir Lenin, "Dual Power," *Collected Works*, Progress Publishers, Moscow, 1964, pp. 38–41.

5 Hubertus Bigend makes an appearance in William Gibson's novels *Pattern Recognition* (2003), *Spook Country* (2007), and *Zero History* (2010) See *Spook Country*, pp. 74–75.

6 See Andrew Murray Scott's fantastically unreliable biography *Alexander Trocchi: The Making of the Monster*, Polygon, Edinburgh, 1991, and also Allan Campbell, *A Life in Pieces: Reflections on Alexander Trocchi*, Rebel Publishing, Edinburgh, 1997. On Girodias, see John de St. Jorre, *Venus Bound: The Erotic Voyage of the Olympia Press*, Random House, New York, 1996.

7 Alexander Trocchi, *Helen and Desire*, Rebel Inc, Edinburgh, 1997: *the sea*, p. 6; *alluvial sensations*, p. 33. Kathy Acker's détournement of it is in Amy Scholder (ed.), *Essential Acker: The Selected Writings of Kathy Acker*, Grove Press, New York, 2002.

8 Trocchi, *Helen and Desire*, p. 154. Compare to Deleuze and Guattari on becoming imperceptible in *A Thousand Plateaus*, University of Minnesota Press, Minneapolis, 1987.

9 Alexander Trocchi, "The Barbeque," from the *Moving Times* poster collected in Sigma Portfolio: A New Dimension in the Dissemination of Informations, privately duplicated, 1964.

10 Alexander Trocchi, *Cain's Book*, foreword by Greil Marcus, introduction by Richard Seaver, Grove Press, New York, 1992: *pinball*, p. 60; *chemistry*, p. 33. A rare appreciation of Trocchi as Situationist writer is: Michael Gardiner, *From Trocchi to Trainspotting: Scottish Critical Theory Since 1960*, Edinburgh University Press, Edinburgh, 2006. Malcolm Lowry was a favorite not only of Debord but of Lefebvre as well. See Malcolm Lowry, *Under the Volcano*, Penguin, London, 2000 and *The Voyage That Never Ends: Fictions, Poems, Fragments, Letters*, NYRB Classics, New York, 2007.

11 *New York Times*, April 3, 2007.

12 Trocchi, *Cain's Book*, p. 72.

13 James Campbell, *Syncopations: Beats, New Yorkers, and Writers in the Dark*, University of California Press, Berkeley CA, 2008, p. 204.

14 See Michael Duncan and Kristine McKenna, *Semina Culture: Wallace Berman and His Circle*, DAP, New York, 2005 and Wallace Berman, *Photographs*, Rose Gallery, Santa Monica CA, 2007.

15 *Under the eyelids*, "Potlatch: an interpersonal log," *Portfolio* No. 4; *new dimension*, "Subscription Form," *Portfolio* No. 12.

16 "Potlatch: an interpersonal log," *Portfolio* No. 4.

17 For critical responses to blog as media, see Geert Lovink, *Zero Comments*, Routledge, London, 2008; Jodi Dean, *Blog Theory*, Polity Press, 2010.
18 "Sigma Informations," *Portfolio* No. 5.
19 Based on the "Situationist Manifesto," originally published in *Internationale Situationniste*, No. 4, June 1960.
20 "Project: projects," *Portfolio* No. 22.
21 Martin Heidegger, *Parmenides*, Indiana University Press, Bloomington, 1992, p. 81.
22 Constant, "Discipline or Intervention?", in Mark Wigley, *Constant's New Babylon: The Hyper-Architecture of Desire*, Witte de With, Rotterdam, 1998, p. 142. I am greatly indebted to this almost priceless work. Almost priceless, in that at the time of writing secondhand copies change hands for over 1,000 euros.
23 Irving Rosenthal, *Sheeper*, Grove Press, New York, 1967, pp. 217–37.
24 Jeff Nuttall, *Bomb Culture*, Dell, New York, 1968, p.150. Dutch Beat sensation Simon Vinkenoog also assisted Trocchi on sigma for a time, and through his sigma Center connects it to Provo: Jaap van der Bent, "O fellow travellers I write you a poem in Amsterdam," *College Literature*, Vol. 27, No. 1, 2000.
25 Stewart Home, *Tainted Love*, Virgin Books, London, 2006, p. 162. The chapter from which this is taken also neatly describes the process of fabricating legends for the consumption of journalists.
26 Constant, "New Babylon: Outline of a Culture," in Wigley, *Constant's New Babylon*, p. 160. Hereafter cited as Wigley.

11 New Babylon

1 Interview with Constant by Linda Boersma and Sue Smit, *Bomb*, No. 91, Spring 2005. On the influence of wartime bombing and postwar reconstruction on Constant, see Tom McDonough, "Metastructure: Experimental Utopia and Traumatic Memory in Constant's New Babylon," *Grey Room*, Fall 2008. Constant's friend Armado also wrote about a German city and the memory of the war: *From Berlin*, Reaktion Books, London, 1997.
2 Constant had assistants for the New Babylon work, including Debord himself and Constant's son Victor. For Constant's reflections on his life shortly before his death, see Maarten Schmidt and Thomas Doebele, *Constant, avant le départ*, Icarus Films, 2006. See also Victor Nieuwenhuijs and Maartje Seyferth, *New Babylon de Constant*, Moskito Film, 2005.
3 Wigley, p. 132. Hilde Heynen in "The Antimonies of Utopia," *Assemblage*, April 1996, does consider it a utopia, with predictable results.
4 Asger Jorn, "On the Cult of the New in Our Century," translated by Alan Prohm, *Crayon*, 2008, p. 188.
5 Aldo van Eyck, *Writings: Collected Articles and Other Writings*, Sun, Amsterdam, 2008, p. 66. Of course there are other influences. Constant's thinking on the relation between art and architecture also stems from a negative reaction to a Mondrian show he saw in Amsterdam in 1946. See Adrian Lewis, "Constant and Hilton in Correspondence," *Burlington Magazine*, Vol. 140, No. 1145, August 1998.
6 *House-like city*, van Eyck, "Beyond Visibility," *Situationist Times*, No. 4, pp. 79–85; *awareness of duration*, van Eyck, *Writings*, p. 74. The contrast between objective clock time and intuited duration is perhaps a reference to Bergson. See Henri Bergson, *Key Writings*, Continuum, New York, 2005. Lukács drew on Bergson and Max Weber's iron cage to form a general theory of reification.
7 *Exteriorize man from time*, van Eyck, *Writings*, pp. 74–75; *at home nowhere*, ibid., p. 87.

The (anti)utopia of Superstudio, surely a critique of Constant among others, is an infrastructure for a global homelessness. See Peter Lang and William Menking, *Superstudio: Life without Objects*, Skira, Milan, 2003. And for a brilliant account of Italian utopian architecture and critical theory, Pier Vittorio Aureli, *The Project of Autonomy: Politics and Architecture within and against Capitalism*, Princeton Architectural Press, New York, 2008.

8 Le Corbusier, *The City of Tomorrow and Its Planning*, Dover, New York, 1987. Vertical separation of flows is just one of Corbusier's techniques for transforming the city so as to *preserve* its ruling order. Constant's détournement is a reversal, and as Debord and Wolman said, the direct reversal of the significance of an element is not always the most effective. Constant was not alone in borrowing the separation of flows. Van Eyck's Team 10 colleagues the Smithsons made particular use of it. See Sadler, *The Situationist City*.

9 See Larry Busbea, *Topologies: The Urban Utopia in France 1960–1970*, MIT Press, Cambridge MA, 2007; Jean Baudrillard, *Utopia Deferred: Writings from Utopie 1967–1978*, Semiotext(e), New York, 2006; Paul Virilio, *Bunker Archaeology*, Princeton Architectural Press, New York, 2008; Paul Virilio and Sylvère Lotringer, *Crepuscular Dawn*, Semiotext(e), New York, 2002. Manfredi Nicoletti, "The End of Utopia," *Perspecta*, Vol. 13, 1971, puts Constant in the context of twentieth-century utopian architecture as a whole.

10 Constant, "Lecture Given at the ICA, London" (1963), *The Decomposition of the Artist*, p. 12(a). Levittown, the original suburban tract development, a civilian application of techniques learned during the war for the mass production of airstrips, was a prime exhibit for the Situationists of spectacular architecture.

11 Friedrich Engels, *The Condition of the Working Class in England*, Oxford University Press, 2009; William Morris, *News from Nowhere and Other Writings*, Penguin, London, 1994; Edward Bellamy, *Looking Backward*, Oxford University Press, 2007. H. G. Wells, *The Time Machine*, Penguin, London, 2005, while clearly referencing the utopian literature, foregrounds the technological question, and interestingly plays on the spatial figure of above and below ground. Wells extrapolated the underground factory from aerial bombing, something which, as Paul Virilio points out, Albert Speer would render concrete in the dying days of the Nazi regime. Constant's underground factories thus have a rather more sinister genealogy than he allows. See Rosalind Williams, *Notes on the Underground: An Essay on Technology, Society and the Imagination*, MIT Press, Cambridge MA, 2008 to see just how deep the rabbit hole goes.

12 Norbert Wiener, *The Human Use of Human Beings*, second edition, Doubleday Anchor, Garden City, New York, 1954, p. 52. Wiener was somewhat more pessimistic than Constant: "In a very real sense we are the shipwrecked passengers on a doomed planet … we shall go down, but let it be in a manner to which we may look forward as worthy of our dignity" (p. 40).

13 Wigley, p. 234. On the transformation of capitalist relations of production by automation, see David F. Noble, *America by Design: Science, Technology and the Rise of Corporate Capitalism*, Oxford University Press, New York, 1979, and *Forces of Production: A Social History of Industrial Automation*, Oxford University Press, New York, 1986.

14 Wigley, p. 233. Automation was a controversial topic for the left in the postwar period. Constant shares the optimism of those like Serge Mallet that automation led to the development of a truly social production, which nevertheless did not lead to the ideological co-option of labor within capitalism, but on the contrary might give rise to a new form of working-class militancy. See Serge Mallet, *The New Working Class*, Spokesman Books, London, 1975.

15 *Bloomberg Businessweek*, November 24, 2010.

16 Wigley, p. 209. The motif of spatially separate networks for different kinds of travel has a long history. Sanford Kwinter credits Antonio Sant'Elia (1888–1916) with being the first to establish movement and circulation as the first principle of spatial design. Movement isn't something added after the fact to inert space, but rather that from which architecture is built. See Sanford Kwinter, *Architectures of Time*, MIT Press, Cambridge MA, 2002, p. 91. On experimental geography in the twenty-first century, see Trevor Paglen, "Experimental Geography," *Brooklyn Rail*, March 2009; Nato Thompson (ed.), *Experimental Geography*, Melville House, Hoboken NJ, 2009.

17 Wigley, p. 161. The most vivid image of the global alienation of space is a story by Lawrence Alloway's friend J. G. Ballard, "The Concentration City," in *The Best Stories of J. G. Ballard*, Picador, London, 2001. See *Re/Search*, No. 8/9, 1984, a special issue on Ballard.

18 Wigley, p.161. On wandering: Rebecca Solnit, *Wanderlust: A History of Walking*, Verso, London, 2006; Simon Pope and Claudia Schenk, *London Walking: A Handbook for Survival*, Ellipsis Arts, London, 2001; Francesco Careri, *Walkscapes*, Editorial Gustavo Gili, 2005.

19 Wigley, p. 162. On power and networks, see Alexander Galloway, *Protocol: How Control Exists after Decentralization*, MIT Press, Cambridge MA, 2006, and Wendy Hui Kyong Chun, *Control and Freedom: Power and Paranoia in the Age of Fiber Optics*, MIT Press, Cambridge MA, 2008.

20 Constant, "Lecture Given at the ICA, London" (1963), *The Decomposition of the Artist*, p. 13 (a). Antonio Negri, *Time for Revolution*, Continuum, London, 2003, contains two texts which are the antithesis of New Babylon, in their radical affirmation of *living labor.*

21 Here New Babylon reaches towards what would now be called the posthuman. See Dominic Pettman, *Human Error: Species-Being and Media Machines*, University of Minnesota Press, Minneapolis, 2011.

22 Johan Huizinga, *Homo Ludens*, Beacon Press, Boston, 1950; Jean-François Lyotard, *Just Gaming*, University of Minnesota Press, Minneapolis, 1985, offers a quite different revival of the figure of the game, via a détournement of Wittgenstein's *language game*. In neither Huizinga, Lefebvre, nor Constant is there a privileging of language, however. The revival of Schmitt owes a lot to Chantal Mouffe, *The Democratic Paradox*, Verso, London, 2000. See Gopal Balakrishnan, *The Enemy: An Intellectual Portrait of Carl Schmitt*, Verso, London, 2002.

23 Constant, "The Rise and Decline of the Avant Garde" (1964), *The Decomposition of the Artist*, p. 26 (a).

24 Wigley, p. 232. See Raoul Vaneigem and Attila Kotányi, "Basic Program of the Bureau of Unitary Urbanism, " in Knabb, *Situationist International Anthology*, p. 86 ff; *Internationale Situationniste*, No. 6, 1961, pp. 16–19, for the subsequent direction of the Situationist International after Constant's departure.

25 Wigley, p. 233. See Richard Kempton, *Provo: Amsterdam's Anarchist Revolt*, Autonomia, New York, 2007. For the Situationist take on the Provos, see Franklin Rosemont and Charles Radcliffe, *Dancin' in the Streets: Anarchists, IWWs, Surrealists, Situationists and Provos in the 1960s*, Charles H. Kerr, Chicago, 2005: "As it is the only reflection their poetry and taste for adventure has found in official theory is in Constant's New Babylon, where it appears as an abstract appendage to his plans for a fully modernized concentration camp, the world, he assures us, of homo ludens. Constant is about as 'ludic' as an ox" (p. 422).

26 Wigley, p. 232. The Situationists once described the Beats, and not without

justification, as "mystical cretins," but Allen Ginsburg's contemporaneous critique of "Moloch whose mind is pure machinery" is perhaps most relevant here.

27 Leslie T. Chang, *Factory Girls*, Speigel and Grau, New York, 2008, p. 6. This daughter of Chinese nationalists offers a politically dubious account, the strength of which is its attention to the everyday lives of factory workers.

28 *New York Times*, March 7, 2009. See Giovanni Arrighi, *Adam Smith in Beijing: Lineages of the 21ˢᵗ Century*, Verso, London, 2009.

29 Wigley, p. 60.

30 Constant, "Lecture Given at the ICA, London" (1963), *The Decomposition of the Artist*, p. 9 (a).

31 Wigley, p. 235.

32 Walter Benjamin, *The Work of Art in the Age of Mechanical Reproducibility and Other Writings on Media*, Harvard University Press, Cambridge MA, 2008. Benjamin clearly prefigures the concept of détournement in his writings on media, particularly the famous "Work of Art" essay. A topic for another time.

33 Among thinkers of technology Gilbert Simondon is undergoing something of a revival, even if the main undercurrent is a regrettable overdependence on Martin Heidegger. The former is too technocratic even for Constant, and for the latter, famously, only the Gods can save us. See Adrian MacKenzie, *Transductions: Bodies and Machines at Speed*, Continuum, London, 2006, for a useful introduction to Simondon, and Bernard Stiegler, *Technics and Time*, Stanford University Press, Stanford CA, 1998 for a striking synthesis.

12 The Beach Beneath the Street

1 "The Decline and Fall of the Spectacle-Commodity Economy," in Guy Debord, *Sick Planet*, Seagull Books, 2008, p. 5, also in Knabb, *Situationist International Anthology*, p. 195; *Internationale Situationniste*, No. 10, March, 1966, p. 3; Ronald Porambo, *No Cause for Indictment: An Autopsy of Newark*, Melville House, Hoboken NJ, 2007. Originally published in 1971.

2 Wigley, p. 162. See *The Memoirs of Lacenaire*, Staples Press, London, 1952. The poet-criminal Lacenaire was a celebrated figure, and everyone from Dickens to Stendhal wrote about him. He inspired the character of Raskolnikov. His legend spans the romantic, surrealist and Situationist movements. Interestingly, Foucault chose to publish *I, Pierre Rivière, Having Slaughtered My Mother, My Sister, and My Brother: A Case of Parricide in the 19th Century*, University of Nebraska Press, Lincoln, 1982, in part to counter the Lacenaire legend. Like Porambo, Lacenaire was a far better writer than he was a criminal.

3 Gerald Horne, *Fire This Time: The Watts Uprising and the 1960s*, Da Capo, New York, 1997, p. 129. Horne calls it a "potlatch of destruction among those denied the dream" (p. 15).

4 Janet Abu-Lughod, *Race, Space, and Riots*, Oxford University Press, New York, 2007, p. 293.

5 Guy Debord, *Society of the Spectacle*, Zone Books, New York, 1994, Ch. 1, section 17. It's an elegant paragraph, in which Debord connects Marx to Sartre with admirable economy.

6 Wigley, p. 236.

7 It was Georges Sorel (1847–1922), that unreliable fellow traveler of the syndicalist movement, who proposed the central role of the myth of the general strike: *From Georges Sorel: Essays in Socialism and Philosophy*, edited with an introduction by John

L. Stanley, translated by John and Charlotte Stanley, Oxford University Press, 1976.

8 Debord to Vaneigem, February 1966.

9 Viénet, *Enragés and Situationists*.

10 De Retz, *Mémoires*. One of the chapter epigrams of Viénet's *Enragés* is from de Retz, p. 25.

11 *The scene*, Viénet, *Enragés*, p. 21; *whiff of cordite*, Dominque Lecourt, *Mediocracy: French Philosophy since 1968*, Verso, London, 2001, p. 22. Lecourt juxtaposes the "brand image" of Althusserianism with Debord's "cult book" as setting the scene for May 1968 (pp. 17–22); *place of damnation*, Lefebvre, *The Explosion*, p. 104.

12 BBC News, March 27, 2002. On the living dead, see Evan Calder Williams, *Combined and Uneven Apocalypse*, Zero Books, Winchester, UK, 2011.

13 Bernard Stiegler, *Acting Out*, Stanford University Press, Stanford CA, 2008: *enormous suffering*, p. 41, *consumer's disgust*, p. 60. Far from being an individualistic society, the disintegrating spectacle produces the herd — Durn's "living dead." Like the Situationists, Stiegler conceives of desire as a kind of unlimited horizon. This infinite quality of desire is what pushes its frail vehicle, the body and its needs, on. This desire is fantastic, but it grounds the possibility of individuation. The spectacle subordinates the free time in which desire might find itself to the synchronic time of the contemplation of the world as a world of things. The spectacle disarms desire. Its goal for Stiegler is not to channel desire but rather to forestall *disgust*. It can only stave off "the coming slowdown of consumption, caused by the consumer's disgust." Would this impasse appear, however, were it not for the failed revolution of 1968? Perhaps it was doomed to fail. Perhaps it was always impossible, a desire out of joint with need. But without the very possibility of that impossible, look at what we are left with: the Nanterre of Richard Durn, rather than of the Enragés.

14 *Negation of the state*, Viénet, *Enragés*, p. 32. For his own account, see Daniel and Gabriel Cohn-Bendit, *Obsolete Communism: The Left-Wing Alternative*, AK Press, San Francisco, 2000. Danny the Red later became Danny the Green, as a member of the European Parliament.

15 René Reisel (b. 1950) was the son of the Communist militant, and a member of the Situationist International from 1968 until his exclusion in 1971. Later he became a sheep farmer and an activist in the Peasant Federation. See René Reisel and Jaime Semprún, *Catastrophisme, administration du désastre et soumission durable*, Editions de l'Encyclopédie des Nuisances, Paris, 2008. The Encyclopédie des Nuisances is a not unworthy continuation of the Situationist legacy.

16 *Self-respect*, Viénet, *Enragés*, p. 58. A note in Debord's handwriting giving the members of the Committee for the Maintenance of the Occupation is reproduced in Zweifel et al., *In Girum Imus Nocte et Consumimur Igni*, p. 62. One of Stiegler's concerns is the intergenerational, on which score alone the composition of this little group is interesting.

17 *Millions of people*, Viénet, *Enragés*, p. 76 ; *people strolled, dreamed*, ibid., p. 77.

18 Michael Hardt and Antonio Negri have attempted to displace Marx's Shakespearan figure of the old mole, with its implications of a surface behind which something is hidden, in favor of a more two dimensional metaphor. But there is no essence and appearance at work in the figure of the old mole. Rather, it's an apt image for materialism itself, in which necessity always reveals itself too late. As Hegel says somewhere: hell is truth seen too late. See Hardt and Negri, *Empire*, Harvard University Press, Cambridge MA, 2000, p. 52 ff.

19 *Despair*, ibid., p. 92; *isolated*, ibid., p. 59; *backwardness*, ibid., p. 86.

20 Hegel, Preface to *The Philosophy of Right*.

21 Alain Badiou offers the attractive notion of fidelity: of Lenin's to the Paris Commune, of Mao's to Lenin, and so forth, except that his very examples tend mostly to be betrayals. Détournement is the opposite of fidelity. Moreover, is there not something disturbing in how often Badiou, like his friend Slavoj Žižek, invokes the great leaders of the Third International rather than the movements they "led"?

22 For example, Buchloh, *Neo-Avantgarde and Culture Industry*. While acknowledging the diminishing returns of avant-garde gestures in the postwar context, Buchloh remains wedded to them, and, like them, to the institutions of the art world. This now seems even more of a dead end than Jorn's expressionism. For a Marxist reading of Debord, see Anselm Jappe's excellent *Guy Debord* and more recently Richard Gilman-Opalsky, *Spectacular Capitalism*, Autonomedia, New York, 2011.

23 Lefebvre, *Introduction à la modernité. Préludes*, pp 29–30; Henri Lefebvre, *The Sociology of Marx*, Random House, New York, 1968, p. 110. Quoting Karl Marx, *Theories of Surplus Value*, translated by Emile Burns, Foreign Language Publishing House, Moscow, 1969, p. 376. As Lefebvre remarks, this is clearly a Marxian reading of Balzac.

24 More or less from Shakespeare, *Henry IV Pt. I*, Act 5, Scene 2. Debord uses it for an epigram in *Society of the Spectacle*. *People* magazine (December 14, 2010) wonders about the limo ambush: "will the royal wedding be safe?"

25 Roberto Bolaño, *2666*, Farrar, Strauss, Giroux, New York, 2008, p. 105. Or to give another example: Thomas Pynchon, *Inherent Vice*, Penguin, New York, 2009, the epigram to which is "Sous les pavés, la plage!" (Beneath the pavement, the beach!)

26 Simon Critchley, *Infinitely Demanding: Ethics of Commitment, Politics of Resistance*, Verso, London, 2008, p. 1; Jacques Rancière, *Short Voyages to the Land of the People*, Stanford University Press, Stanford CA, 2003.

27 Writing to Franklin on August 8, 1958, Debord observes that the proletariat is the hidden God of the Socialism or Barbarism group. The reference is to the reading by Lucien Goldmann (1913–1970) of Pascal, *The Hidden God*, Routledge, London, 1964, but one might extend the critical move further. The unifying principle, or rather the alibi, that absolves us of the necessity to think and act for ourselves, yet which is nowhere actually present, might these days take the name of *power*.

28 René Viénet, "The Situationists and New Forms of Action Against Politics and Art," in Knabb, *Situationist International Anthology*, pp. 273–77. When it appeared in *Internationale Situationniste*, No. 11, 1967, pp. 32–36 it was illustrated by frames from André Bertrand's détourned comics, including the famous *Return of the Durruti Column*.

29 On which see Wark, *A Hacker Manifesto*, and David Berry and Giles Moss, *Libre Culture*, Pygmalion Books, Winnipeg, 2008.

30 On which see Wark, *Gamer Theory*, and Eugene Thacker and Alex Galloway, *The Exploit*, University of Minnesota Press, Minneapolis, 2007. Given the Situationist predilection for pinball, one might wonder what becomes of play in the age of the gamer. Both of these are, unlike most of *game studies*, critical accounts. See also Sven Lütticken, "Playtimes," *New Left Review*, No. 66, November 2010.

31 This is one of the great questions addressed in Trevor Paglen, *Invisible*, Aperture, New York, 2010. Work which also, incidentally, ups the ante as far as the détournement of Chombart's aerial surveillance goes.

32 On the "new international," see Derrida, *Specters of Marx*. Attractive as it sounds, it offers something less than the practice of the Situationist International, precisely on the question of the forms of free association that might yet bind those without status, without form, without party, without country, without nation, without citizenship, without common belonging to a class.

33 Jorn's insistence that there are two classes, respectively makers of form and content under commodity production, might be more helpful than the idea of an internal differentiation between material and immaterial labor, not least because there is no immaterial labor. The problem of communicating between different situations of struggle becomes clearer when one understands this as one of the qualitative differences. See Hardt and Negri, *Empire*, pp. 3–63. For those familiar with the opening gambits of the fabulous book, let's just say that this is why our owl and old mole have not become a snake or an eagle.

34 Manuel Castells, *The Urban Question*, MIT Press, Cambridge MA, 1979. Lefebvre responded to Castells's critique in *The Survival of Capitalism*, Schocken Books, New York, 1981. Biopower has since become a whole academic industry, the key text of which remains Giorgio Agamben, *Homo Sacer*, Stanford University Press, Stanford CA, 1998. Following Heidegger and late Foucault, the trouble once again is *metaphysics*, in this case within political theory, where sovereignty becomes power over life. When did those who went looking for an unassailable power within discourse fail to find it? A century after the death of God, one still awaits the death of its avatar, power, which has been *proven not to exist* time and time again. Take the 2011 events in Egypt and Tunisia, for example. Mehdi Belhaj Kacem: "January 2011 is a May '68 carried through all the way … it was the first Situationist revolution in history … that is, carried out by the people directly." (A Tunisian Renaissance: Interview with Mehdi Belhaj Kacem," by Alex Galloway, *Lacanian Ink*, January 31, 2011.

Index